MW01129598

Ballet Bad Boy

My Life Behind Barres

By George Latimer

With Sare van Orsdell

Ballet Bad Boy: My Life Behind Barres

Table of Contents

Part IV – Return to My Roots (1989 – Present)

George Latimer
Sara van Orsdell

Preface

In the spring of 1970, Kathy Bates, the great film and stage actress residing in Memphis, called me *L'enfant Terrible* (The terrible child). She had a great sense of humor. Bates, then an unknown in a career that would include the movies *Fried Green Tomatoes, Misery,* and *Titanic* knew we were both at the beginning of our careers. Mine would be a controversial one.

A few years later, when Kathy walked onstage with Jeremy Irons at the Oscars in Hollywood, those who had earlier doubted her talent nearly fainted. Kathy had left Memphis behind, but I had stayed on.

The first part of this book is about how I became that terrible child. The second and third parts document my impact on the arts and political scenes, and more than anything else, on the hope and encouragement I placed in the hearts of young performers in Memphis from 1967 to 1989. Lastly, in the fourth part and closing chapters of the book, I relate the events in my life that took place when I returned to my California roots.

Several people greatly influenced my career. Alis Goldate always told me I must be unafraid to "stand up and be counted." I think she wanted me to speak my mind instead of always expressing my beliefs through the non-verbal world of dance. Alis, too, had many struggles. Her great effort to produce *Memphis Night at the Kennedy Center* ended in real success. Yet, mixed with the audience's applause were the sour grapes of jealousy. How could a woman act with such independence? I never minded being counted, and as Alis urged me to become even more expressive and to write, I asked the question, What has more effect on a person's existence, nature or nurture?

Having won several essay contests sponsored by *The Oakland Tribune* as a child, I did have some early encouragement as writer. Carol O'Brien, my ballet coach, saved every letter I wrote her from Memphis, knowing that I'd want them someday.

If not for the expertise of Sare Van Orsdell, my co-author and living spiritual guide, this book might never have been written. There are many friends, teachers, and dancers who gave of their talents, dedication, and love over the course of my career. I want to express my appreciation to all the people I have worked with over the years, whether or not they are mentioned in this book.

When Ballet South had its reunion after I left Memphis, Peggy Howard, a spirited dancer, said, "You were an influence that rivaled my own parents in your lasting impact!" What a great tribute, I thought.

As I write the final words to introduce my journey I hear my friend Judy Rix saying, "It's too late to be shy now, George." Her help has been invaluable.

Lisa Carlson, owner of Wordstream West, made a major contribution as and editor of this book, and through her East Bay writing group. Wordstream West offers creative advice, editing, and promotion, and is particularly helpful to new authors.

Lastly, I want to thank Beth Hoge, dancer, instructor, and Director of Danspace, Oakland. Beth's help made it all happen in so many ways.

George Latimer
Oakland, California
Summer 2011

Part I

On Becoming *L'Enfant Terrible*
(1940 – 1966)

Chapter 1
Technicolor Lipstick

This true story is an intimate one, and it has taken me a lifetime to feel ready to share it — to reveal the truth about my life behind the scenes as well as the showbiz glitter that made some of my experiences seem larger than life. It is drawn from the drama, humor, and eccentricity of walking the line between obscurity and fame, two sides of a coin that have always balanced my emotional choices and led me into a constantly changing lifestyle. Many artists have influenced me and I, in turn, influenced a culture that was separate from that of my own birthplace.

Was there something in the drinking water?

Like me, the flamboyant 1920s dancer Isadora Duncan was born in Oakland, California, and she launched a revolution, not only in modern dance, but in ballet.

Jack London, the great adventure writer, was met every day by an elderly couple at the train arriving from San Francisco. Most of the time he was so drunk they had to lead him to his home in Oakland and deposit him on his front porch. Whether he fell asleep right there or eventually made it to his bed was a matter of chance.

Oakland was the birthplace of the Oakland Black Panthers and a revolution also started there that to this day continues in some form or other. Clint Eastwood, the great actor and film director, graduated from my high school about a decade or so before my own graduation.

In the 1940s, San Francisco was a safe distance from Montclair, my Oakland neighborhood across the San Francisco Bay. There was the train, of course, but I was too young for that mode of transportation to benefit me. But I remember hearing stories. One such tale was about the writer Ernest Hemingway who had his nightly drinks with another great writer, Gertrude Stein, at the infamous Black Cat Bar and Night Club in San Francisco's Barbary Coast now called North Beach.

When the Black Cat closed in the early 1950s, a Gray Line bus filled with reveling protestors stormed the establishment on closing night. The Gray Line logo had been altered to read the "Gay Line" with the "r" conveniently painted out.

A mock Cleopatra was carried to the door by 12 Nubian slaves whose make-up was beyond bad. They created quite a stir, but everyone got the idea. This parody became a final tribute to bygone days at the club.

On my side of the bay, a French windmill still stands today, tattered beyond recognition. Few realize that this sign was part of a marquee, a symbol of the old Moulin Rouge Theater.

In the late 1940s, Lily St. Cyr took her nightly milk baths on the stage, much to her admirers' delight. My ballet coach Carol O'Brien once remarked that Lily was beautiful, but a few ballet classes would have helped. The appearance of St. Cyr was followed later by Diane and her Monkey. This cleverly trained animal would remove Diane's clothes, and the audience loved it. The T & D Theater, right down the street from The Moulin Rouge, is now a commercial storefront.

I wish I had been there in the late 1940s to see the Marx Brothers' stage show based on their hit movie, *A Night in Casablanca* with Groucho, Chico, Zeppo, and Harpo. They were accompanied by a large cast of actors, singers, and dancers and a live onstage orchestra. I saw many of my favorite movies at the T & D Theater when I was older.

As my life progressed, I became an experimental and creative choreographer but never achieved the national fame I had dreamt of. The process of living, sometimes fearfully or recklessly, has led me to where I am today.

Growing up, I yearned to make an impact on society the same way many of my predecessors had, and I did succeed, but in a quieter way.

So this is my story. It all began in Oakland during World War II. To offset the terrible killing and suffering during the war, the public was treated to movies that created a time of national fantasy. I think of that time as one of "Technicolor Lipstick."

The need to escape the shadows of war was reflected on the silver screen and in the people around me. The war years were an era of pain and suffering and there was little chance to run away from that reality, except through the magic of the big screen and the music of the times. It was a strange and contradictory time to be born. A fantasy bigger than life or death became embedded in my subconscious as a four-year-old. During a period when people were losing their lives overseas in great numbers, this fantasy created dramatic and exciting expectations.

Most days during the summer of 1944 my mother would take my brother, my sister, and me to nearby Lake Temescal. How fortunate we were to live just two blocks from what was then a large rural pond surrounded by trees and a winding shady path. Only 20 miles from San Francisco, it was also home to a wide variety of bird and animal species.

Temescal had once been a sacred place, used for healing by the nearby Temescal Indians. The banks of red-orange clay produced healing mud baths and the Temescals used the pond's waters for sacred bathing. Later, Temescal Creek, which fed into the pond, was dammed up and Lake Temescal was created. A popular swimming area was located where the natural spring, huts, and red-orange cliffs had once been. A faster path around the lake replaced the old winding trail and many fishermen and servicemen could be seen trying their luck fishing along the banks while the melodious voices of the Andrews Sisters and other popular artists floated out from a radio at the swimming area.   We always brought our lunches, beach umbrellas, and a large car blanket on our daily mile walk to the beach. My mother was always at her best then. She loved the relaxed, fun-filled sunny days. We children felt life was warm and safe at our Lake Temescal where interesting things were always happening.

We arrived one day to see a young couple standing beneath the heavy waterfall. While their friends cheered and jeered them on, they clung, embarrassed and excited, to their swimsuits, which barely stayed in place under the torrent of falling water.

About 200 feet out in the water, we watched young men playing King of the Mountain as they climbed on and off a floating raft. On the beach, women and children splashed on suntan oil, coca butter or, hoping for a good, even tan, they rubbed baby oil mixed with iodine over their sun-drenched bodies.

We would wander around and find our own spot, then begin our usual ritual of wading and swimming all day long in the lake's inviting water. Later we'd dry off with our huge car blanket, which also served as a towel, and head home. We took home that day's treasures, minnows we had caught in jars, armloads of wild flowers, and weeping willow branches we had gathered.

My mother, Susan Capehart Latimer, was one of two daughters of deaf-mute parents. From 1908 to 1910 so-called normal children born to the "deaf and dumb" became quick candidates for adoption and my grandparents' doctor was anxious to accommodate couples looking to adopt. The two little girls, both redheads, had that unusual fair skin that comes with red hair. When my grandparents refused to release custody, the doctor expressed his regret, so the children were raised by their deaf mute parents. The seeds of an unusual lifestyle were forever cast for me.

My mother and her sister survived their different kind of childhood with some amount of trauma but still enjoyed many happy times with parents who showered them with love and affection. My grandfather made beautiful artistic furniture for a living and managed to keep a roof over their heads and food on the table. My grandmother helped by selling pencils on a downtown street corner in Oakland.

Thinking back, I barely remember my grandparents' smiling faces. Aaron Capehart and Leila Honeywell were both born in the 1800s, a few decades after the end of the Civil War, and were placed in the Colorado Home for the Deaf. They grew up together and fell in love and married. My mother inherited her father's creativity and, in turn, passed that talent down to me.

The only object crafted by my grandfather I still own is a unique tile table. As a child, I remember sitting at the table and drinking grape juice that Mother always diluted with water.

When we didn't go to the lake we would catch the bus, which stopped in front of our house, and my mother would take us to the big, beautiful Grand Lake Theater close to downtown Oakland.

Before I was 10 years old, I had seen all the classic films of the 30s and 40s. The musicals were my mother's favorites, and sometimes when we came home from the theater, she would turn on the radio with its large cloth-covered speakers, tune into the music, and dance all around the living room for us. She was 33 at the time. She inspired me and I sang the lyrics to myself and tried to dance. I already knew *Rainy Night in Rio, (What Do You Do When There Are No Starry Skies?)* and *Let's Face the Music and Dance!* I loved music and I loved to move with the rhythm. We would frequently stay until my father, George Laurence Latimer, Sr. came home for lunch. After eating, he would return to work and we would return to the lake.

We left our own town of Oakland so rarely that I was shocked to realize one day that San Francisco, one of the largest cities in America, was just over the horizon. I came to understand that this big exciting city represented the sum of all my fears, but it also awakened my imagination.

In Oakland, my existence seemed anything but harsh. San Francisco represented just the opposite. As I grew into a teenager, I shut out what I couldn't understand. Later, the flood of having an unprotected existence would hit me hard. Meanwhile, the world of musicals and films colored my every thought.

Having a music-filled childhood allowed the intensity of World War II to recede into the distance. But my child's view of the war was full of songs that seemed to end in exciting exclamation points, like *Oh, How I hate to get up in the Morning!, Praise The Lord and Pass the Ammunition!,* and *Spurs that Jingle, Jangle, Jingle!*

My mother would take me out to rest on a cot in the back yard and warn me to come indoors if I saw any large birds in the sky. She had read that chicken hawks had stolen children and she was unsure of what was up there. The hawk story failed to make me afraid because, by then, I had seen so many of the war films graphically showing the dramatic demise of German dive-bombers and Japanese suicide pilots.

We began to experience the blackouts in California that would send mother around the house lighting candles and pulling down the shades. So it wasn't birds that became my childhood problem, it was airplanes. I spent a lot of time cowering under the cot, trembling and crying at the sound of roaring propellers and their angry engines high in the sky.

During this time, I stole a duck out of the lake because, as I explained to my mother, I believed the bird was in danger. Showing great sympathetic naïveté, she let me keep the duck as a pet and even gave me a galvanized tub for him. The duck became my best friend. My older sister, Colleen, and my younger brother, Bill, short for William, shared my delight with this new family addition.

Once we took a vacation on the Russian River, about 80 miles up the coast and 30 miles inland. My sister, brother, and I were allowed to attend the campfire show in Guerneville. The event was part of a nightly retreat. A huge grill stood in front of the stage and several servicemen, partly dressed in uniforms but naked to the waist, were preparing the fire and soaking steaks in bourbon whiskey. The scent was intoxicating. In a matter of minutes, the wooden benches began to fill up with other families and many more servicemen.

The smiling soldiers approached my parents and asked politely, "Would you like to have some of the steak?" My mother and father were delighted. As smoke drifted into the Redwood trees and the sky changed from blue to black, a great feeling of camaraderie and good will developed between the families and the soldiers, as many of our neighbors were in the military or had children who served.

The year we ate those steaks was 1944. The campfire stage curtains were jerked back to reveal a band playing the music I had been hearing almost daily. Saxophones and clarinets sang out sweetly and we found ourselves listening to the *sound of swing.* Several couples began dancing in the open space near the benches. My mother asked us if we recognized the man leading the band. It was Harry James, movie star Betty Grable's husband!

Grable was a big 1940s screen icon whose movies we had seen many Saturday nights at the theaters, and my mother, a Grable fan, was thrilled to see her husband in person.

If not for radio and films, we would have had little contact with the outside world. As we watched and listened to Harry James, I found myself mesmerized by someone I had seen on my neighborhood silver screen and realized for the first time that this star was a real person.

The sounds of the band, the aroma of the Redwood trees, soldiers pulling the girls close and letting them swing away again, created a vivid and lasting impression. That lost expression on some of the soldier's faces who were not so lucky at finding companionship or even the temporary satisfaction of partnering a girl at the dance, was something that I would remember with great understanding as I grew older.

Chapter 2
Home Spooning and Other Family Lessons

Everyone liked my Dad. After he died too young, a crowd turned out at the funeral chapel. During the eulogy, the pastor revealed that my father had lent everyone money. Many, knowing my Dad's good nature, had simply forgotten to pay him back. Dad, loved by all, motivated my own generosity.

My father's real parents died when he was only four, so he was raised by his great grandmother Amelia Hunter Latimer, a regal-looking Victorian era lady, and a Mormon, the daughter of a founder of the Mormon church. I still have charcoal sketches of her in the attic. Her eyes were large and dreamy, a physical trait that my sister inherited.

As children, we would anxiously await our father's return from work each day. In the evening, we would all climb onto his lap and rest our heads against his T-shirt covered chest, our little ears tuned toward the large radio where Fred Allen and Eddie Cantor's voices filled our living room with laughter. We'd see a film during the day at the theater and a few weeks later, we'd hear the same movie dramatized on *Lux Radio Theater* with the original stars. These were the sorts of evenings during my childhood that made me feel warm and safe.

A smoking fire crackled in the fireplace as the sounds of my mother cooking drifted in from the nearby kitchen. Since meat was rationed during the war, we ate lots of fresh vegetables straight from my mother's garden. Milk with thick cream on top was delivered daily in glass quart bottles. Homogenized milk would be an invention of the future. I still remember how we loved and respected our milkman. Dan, the ice man was a weekly visitor. Dan delivered 50 pounds of ice for our ice box, which kept our food fresh. These routines went on through the war years, until I was about six years old.

One day a startling event occurred. My mother walked into the kitchen and began screaming. Two large yellow eyes looked out at us through the iron grill in front of the stove. In search of warmth, an owl had flown down the chimney and into the stove. A month later a new electric stove and our first refrigerator arrived, and daily living became easier, but we missed the friendly visits of our milkman and ice man.

I vividly remember my first days at grammar school. I was six years old. One day we stopped all activities to listen to a *Standard Oil School Broadcast*. We were each given a large sheet of paper, which we stretched across our desks. We were told to interpret the music we would hear with a huge glob of finger paint. Every broadcast was different. I enjoyed this even more when we received large amounts of red and orange paint and were told to draw what we mentally saw while the sweeping and exciting music of Grofe's *Grand Canyon Suite* was played for us. As much paint dripped onto the floor as ended up on the paper, but my teacher, Barbara Head, didn't seem to mind at all.

Pearl Harbor was bombed around this time and my mother pulled the shades and began lighting candles. Her voice became quiet after we listened to the radio reports. Later, we saw newsreels at the theater and fear swallowed us up. Because we were so frightened, our parents decided to take the three of us to bed with them.

I remember my dad behind me and my mother in front of me, lying close, in what is now called spooning. My brother Bill was in front of my mother and my sister was behind my dad. About a year or so later, they decided we were too old to cuddle all in the same bed and we were banished back to our own room.

Later, I realized that children are subconsciously sensual, and it had probably taken my mother by surprise. Shortly after that, she stopped bathing my sister, brother, and me together and we were ordered not to touch my mother's breasts. It seemed that suddenly we were too old for this comforting closeness. The fact that my parents could see the physical evidence when little boys got aroused was, I'm sure, part of the motivation for us suddenly being treated like little adults. This was a difficult time for me. The warmth and safety of parental closeness retreated into the past, leaving me with a strong and scary perception of myself in the world. I was, indeed, alone.

After the first grade, my parents let us walk to school. Montclair School was about a mile from our house. The walk was either through a particularly developed residential area with huge forest-like trees, many of them Redwoods, or along paths through a wooded area. One side of the land was owned by the Western Pacific Railroad. My mother warned us not to talk with tramps we saw going through on the railroad cars. She said bad things could happen to children who weren't careful. I wondered if "these things" were anything like when the "white slavers" put hypodermic needles into children's legs, which I had heard could happen. These children were never heard from again and were usually depicted as ending up in harems in faraway places like Persia, Arabia, or Baghdad. I had also heard my mother's friends talking about these things. The idea sounded scary, but fascinating, and more than a little glamorous to me.

Love tests us all and to tell you what I mean, we have to go back to 1944. That was the day four-year-old Deanne told me that if I loved her, I would let her blindfold me and have her way. I reluctantly agreed and as soon as she did, I found myself shoved back into a big patch of prickly blackberry bushes! As I snatched the blindfold off, squirming in pain, and fighting my way out of the stickers, she just stood there looking at me with a Mona Lisa smile. It was very confusing at first. But, after all, I was unusually sophisticated for a kid and figured it all out later. Deanne had truly tested my love.

Years before, carrying me in her arms, my mother took me to the 1939 World's Fair on Treasure Island in San Francisco Bay. On this man-made oasis, Little Egypt, the daring veiled dancer of years past, performed along with other stars such as Johnny Weismuller. He was taking a break from being Tarzan for MGM movie studios, and was now paired with the young Esther Williams who swam in exotic pools. Later, when I looked at slides from that innovative 1939 art celebration, I was awed by the creativity that went into designing the magnificent *Arabian Nights* sets.

Mother would take all of us to a special show at the Oakland Orpheum. Eight vaudeville acts would be featured, followed by the latest MGM film. There was a free dish giveaway at each night's performance. Yes, in 1943, vaudeville was still alive. I actually remember the magic acts and our blue and white patterned Chinese dish collection, which grew larger with every visit.

My parents once took me to Catalina, the Island of Romance, where they danced to the big swing bands at the Avalon Pavilion. On those days, we all stretched out on beach blankets and played in the shallow water afterwards, with the sounds of Glen Miller's music still echoing in our parents' heads as we swam. Mother later described the dance setting and showed us pictures of the event.

Back home in Montclair, my siblings and I began socializing with neighborhood children. There was Phyllis, my sister's friend, who totally scared us by performing homemade magic acts. One memorable day, she stood with a basket on her head and draped a sheet over herself. The basket grew to an alarming six feet in height, creating a monstrous effect. My mother scolded Phyllis and my sister for scaring the daylights out of us.

When Phyllis moved away, we felt lonely and saddened by the loss, but then Ted moved in. He was around 12 years old and close to my sister's age. Ted was full of energy, spunk, and spit. The sight of him tossing 12-inch, 78 rpm records across the creek established him at once in our eyes as spoiled and wasteful. His mother, Lillian, truly a beautiful woman, watched this behavior and laughed despite her better judgment. She was largely responsible for Ted's uncontrollable energy and erratic disposition.

"Oh, Ted! No!" She would giggle while her son calmly reassured her, "Mom, I'm just playing flying saucers." Since science fiction films were relatively new, Ted's explanation to his demure-as-Deborah Kerr mother seemed pretty funny to us.

My father was rarely home except at night, and now, with Ted always around, he had new competition as my role model. I couldn't understand Ted's disregard for the value of material things. My own dad worked night and day for what we owned. Ted's dad, a tall disheveled sort of man, owned a huge successful shipping company, and this allowed the family to move two years later to one of the few real mansions in our area, just a block from our modest house. Ted became my hero and maybe my anti-hero, too. He was an adventurous sort who knew no boundaries. He may have been only five feet two, but to me, he was a leader and seemed at least six foot five.

My mother gave Ted's family permission to take us on numerous trips. I particularly liked going to Isleton. It was near a slough of water that fell off from the Sacramento River where we laughed and played, went swimming and barbecued the fish we caught.

One day we went to the horse races in Pleasanton where we saw the tall, exotically beautiful Ava Gardner standing with her new husband, little Mickey Rooney. He made up for his diminutive size with his energy and magnetic laughter. The sun glasses they both wore did not conceal their features and I realized as I watched them that the people we saw weekly on the silver screen had another identity off screen.

Ted's mother, Lillian, loved my sister Colleen. But when Colleen talked about her, my mother's temper would flare up in a nervous and erratic way. Lillian had decided that she wanted to adopt Colleen as her own daughter. This could be the reason for my mother's temper, I reasoned. I was a little afraid of my mother at times because of her unpredictable nature, but the idea of Lillian adopting my sister seemed peculiar to me. Lillian and her husband would go off to work, leaving Ted alone in a 20-room Spanish-Moorish style mansion to play and fend for himself. I know Ted felt desperate at these times, especially when I learned about his parents' increasing alcoholism. His father seemed craggy and old compared to the lady-like Lillian.

My relationship with Ted had gotten a little strange, but I'll explain this later. I would have done anything to please our fearless leader, Ted. He and Keith, who was my sister's age, were also friends. At times, I felt quite left out because it seemed that all three of them were aware of an adult world that I didn't know existed or how to deal with.

One day, we all took a trip back to Isleton, where Ted's family owned a small yacht. We anchored the boat close to shore and swam in the small waves made by passing boats. Without warning, a wave crashed over the top of Lillian's two-piece bathing suit, taking the top off as it moved away. Totally unaware of what had happened, she kept asking us why we were laughing. We laughed even harder.

That night we cooked outdoors, listening to Ted's 45 rpm record player (45 records were new then). We heard the latest big hits by Desi Arnaz, *Cuban Pete* and *The Peanut Vendor*. The music provided a jarring contrast to the Victorian music box disc player at Ted's parents' mansion where Strauss and Bach were the usual sounds echoing down those hallways, so the new records were exciting.

Ted was quite ingenious. I didn't know for some time that he had arranged the mirror on his parents' bedroom door so that it would reflect onto his own bedroom mirror. If he left the door slightly ajar, when his parents came home intoxicated they would be completely unaware that their intense sex life was on view for Ted almost nightly.

Ted grew up quickly, therefore, I did too.

One family activity I looked forward to was driving to Santa Rosa and out to the farm of Ruth and Frances Willford. They had many farm animals and I truly loved to pet them. I don't know how my father afforded as many vacations as we had, but I imagine it was due to very careful planning. We just never felt poor.

My imaginative mother explained how we didn't need toys when we could make things out of clay which was readily found near our house. We would get our masterpieces fired and finished at the kiln down the street. Seeing the finished products of our imaginations was always exciting. She also encouraged us to write stories, and brought us pads of paper and pencils in addition to the clay.

I also looked forward to our visits to Frances and Ruth's farm. They were close friends of my parents. The grownups would visit all day while the Willford's son, Albert, took us to visit the farm animals. Fortunately, I never made the connection between the chickens in the coup and the chicken dinners we usually ate at a picnic table out in the yard.

I particularly loved Oliver, the lamb who stood patiently by while we took turns petting him. On one of our many visits, I kept asking, "Where is Oliver?"

Albert, who my parents thought of as a suitor for my sister, became silent. Finally, as we were eating dinner, my question about

Oliver became so insistent that Frances began to laugh. I didn't understand what the joke was until Albert broke the news that we were, in fact, eating Oliver. Of course, I became hysterical. No one could console me. Frances was a kindly man, but he continued to smile along with the others. The complexity of existing, of survival, and what was necessary, became an unanswered question for me until many years later.

My parents showed physical affection in a truly innocent way. There was nothing inappropriate about their hugs and kisses. If there was only a hint of anything sexual about some of their veiled references, the words went over our heads completely. The only mention of sex came one day from my mother as she talked with our next-door neighbors, Alice and Marshall. She explained that other neighbors had expressed concern about the couple. Alice was very sophisticated in her dark and beautiful way, and she spoke to us children in a gentle tone. Marshall was dark and handsome in his white admiral's uniform and had actually survived the war without being injured.

With a sly glint in her eye Alice would smile. She frequently wore his Navy Admiral's hat. My mother feigned disinterest in Alice and Marshall's affairs. But the neighbors' concern grew as Alice and Marshall continued to sunbathe in the nude on the other side of our hedge. We were all curious, but despite some of the neighbors' complaints, my parents let the idea slip away unnoticed and never mentioned it again. Neither my father nor my mother liked to criticize the actions or motives of others, even if they didn't fully understand them.

In the meantime, I was becoming more aware of the opposite sex, mostly from exposure to the films being made. My parents took us to see everything except Jane Russell in *The Outlaw* in 1946 and Ingrid Bergman in *Stromboli*. Looking back today at these films, they seem relatively innocent.

My fourth-grade girlfriend was Alice Tarail, a beautiful girl who later reminded me of a young Anne Bancroft. She said, "I can't let you be my boyfriend because you are a gentile, but it's okay for us to be friends." I stared at her dumbfounded, with no idea what she was talking about. Later, I had to ask my dad.

"Jewish people have different customs than we do," he said. I still didn't understand. All I knew was that Alice was interesting and mature beyond her years. I was a constant visitor in their home, which had a great playhouse, pathways, and citrus trees. Their house took up a whole city block and had a view of the entire San Francisco Bay. One day Alice and I were caught playing doctor. We were curious about what made her a girl and me a boy. Her parents gave us a friendly warning to respect each other's boundaries and we took this advice very seriously. We remained friends for years. Yet, as a child, I never completely understood why our actions caused such alarm in the adults; except that there must have been social rules I didn't know about that we were supposed to follow.

About the age of 10, I secretly took the bus to the Telenews Theater in downtown Oakland. They usually featured films like *They Wear but the Wind*, and later *Reefer Madness*, or *Mom and Dad* and *Glen or Glenda*, all for adults only. That week they were more high toned, and the theater featured *The Red Shoes*, the great 1948 dance fantasy drama. I was so inspired!

Around this time, a new ballet school opened beneath the meat market right down the street from our house. I was a frequent visitor to the drugstore next to the school, and I could hear *Swan Lake* through the store walls. Having been drawn by the music to the studio door, I gathered up my courage and knocked. A frail-looking woman in a washed-out ballet costume answered the door. Her features were faded as her tutu and *pointe* shoes. Looking down at me with an expression of irritation and disgust, she said, "We don't teach men!" My first attempt to study ballet was one that filled me with guilt and shame.

Aunt Pat and Aunt Wanda would come to visit sometimes. These two cheerful ladies were somehow related to my mother. I finally realized that Pat was Virginia Capehart, my mother's sister, and her nickname stuck until the day she died.

Considered to be the artistic child of the family, my creative efforts were quite known in our neighborhood. One day I was singled out by my aunts for a trip to the San Francisco Opera House to see Lucia Albanese in Puccini's *Madame Butterfly* and Rodgers and Hammerstein's *Oklahoma!* which I had seen before on one of their national tours.

My eyes were opened even wider when my aunts taught me formal table manners at the Sheraton Palace dining room, a historic place to experience elite dining for "society more than polite."

Despite the wonderful things that were happening to me, when guests came to our house, people would always say, "Your sister is so beautiful." She was. Or, "Your brother is so handsome." He was. Then they would add, "And, George, you have the nicest smile!" This was a crushing blow to me, because we all competed with strong enthusiasm for the attention of others.

My dad had "men's night out" which my mother accepted as a necessary event. In his own sweet innocent way he enjoyed his trips to the Moulin Rouge. Once a month or so, my father joined Eddie, Carl, and several other friends and went to see Tempest Storm, Lady St. Cyr, and Candy Barr, stars of the touring burlesque shows at the Moulin Rouge or the El Rey theater in Emeryville, or *The President's Follies* playing in San Francisco. This was the closest my father ever came to being unfaithful to his wife. His friends truly enjoyed the great acts performed by these famous burlesque stars.

I always wondered what happened to these stars until 10 years ago, when I saw an aged Tempest Storm on HBO's *This was Burlesque!* It was hard to believe, and you couldn't tell she was then 80 years old. Tempest Storm married Herb Jeffries whose hit 1950's record was *Flamingo (Flying over the Islands.)* Their marriage was the most controversial interracial marriage since Lena Horne and Lennie Hayton.

Once, the twosome came into the Capwell Store in Oakland where my sister operated the elevator after school. Their presence almost caused a small riot. Herb Jeffries, black and handsome, and Tempest Storm, with her long hair dyed red, made an electrifying couple. Tempest Storm was an amazing dancer in her time. At 80 she still had the body of a young woman. She had remarkable talent for gyrations and wearing tassels, which suggested more than one could imagine happening with a piece of curtain.

When I was about 12, my father's friend, Eddie, joined the staff of *Variety,* the Los Angeles-based showbiz magazine. Our whole family wore 3-D glasses to see Eddie in one of many small film roles in *Second Chance* with Linda Darnell, Cornell Wilde, and young Jack Palance. Then, we heard that Carl, Dad's other friend, was arrested, caught having sex in a men's room. My dad was very upset. Something as sordid as this would never have occurred to him. He brooded for days.

My social life picked up a bit as my brother became one of the most popular athletes at school and a line of eligible young men began forming to date my sister. Among the suitors was a nervous John Brodie, the great football player of the 1960s. He was one of my sister's first boyfriends and there were many more. Shyness may have been their game, but it certainly wasn't mine.

At 12, I attended every public dance a kid could go to. I had seen Ralph Edwards, whose relative owned the house up the street, dancing with a frying pan on his head, so I figured if I couldn't win them with good looks, I would go for silly. So silly I was, that is, until I fell through a plate glass door, seriously cutting my arm. I was on the mend for a month or so. It was about 1951 when I realized that social skills, humor, and Vaseline-coated hair could produce something cute even though not handsome, and that I would become more popular than my competitors, after all. It was with this newfound understanding, and with gleeful anticipation, that I watched the dawning of the great era of rock and roll.

***

There was a huge moment of excitement when my Aunts Pat and Wanda asked my brother and me to take the train to Los Angeles with them. At last, I might see Hollywood! There were other relatives to see including my mother's cousin Berniece, her husband Paul, a retired jeweler, and their twin Scotties.

I was impressed with these dogs. Their intelligence and energy were unbelievable, shown in the way they responded to those around them. Berniece had named them Chuffy and Duffy, and they rushed to the door to greet us when we arrived. My brother and I had bought sunglasses and loud Hawaiian shirts from Woolworth's in Oakland so we would fit in, or so we thought.

Berniece was a tall, stately woman with a deep aggressive voice, in sharp contrast to Paul's passive, observant demeanor. Berniece was a dead ringer for Tallulah Bankhead and the Norma Desmond character in *Sunset Boulevard.* Or the Baby Jane Hudson character in *What Ever Happened to Baby Jane? M*y cousin's commanding presence made us shy, but I liked her immediately. Their house was a huge stately Hollywood home, not quite a mansion. We constantly questioned her to tell us all about what we called the Tales of Hollywood. We wanted to hear all the gossip we could!

She spoke of a new starlet, Mitzi Gaynor, who, according to Berniece was a member of the wild and loose Hollywood party crowd. I had already seen Gaynor in several musicals and I liked her, so couldn't bring myself to make any harsh judgments about her behavior.

My dad's friend, Eddie, made the *Los Angeles Times* headlines for dating Rita Johnson, an MGM star who had just played opposite Clark Gable.

The trip turned out to be wonderful and Pat and Wanda were so kind to my brother and me. One day we lathered on lots of suntan oil and my aunts took us to Grauman's Chinese Theater where we saw *The Bird of Paradise.*

After that movie, I was in a state of shock. I asked myself over and over how could the islanders portrayed in the film allow the heroine to dive into the brilliant Technicolor volcano and sacrifice herself to save her people from the volcanic eruption. The story haunted me for a long time, as did the scene with Hedy Lamar being crushed by stone columns when Samson destroyed the Temple of the Philistines in *Samson and Delilah.* The fascination with these heroines and their terrifying emotional plights was only a symptom of my awakening sensuality. A year or so later, I would cringe in agony as I watched Jennifer Jones shoot Gregory Peck and then climb toward his seemingly helpless body, only to be shot by Peck. I was in an emotional state as I watched their stumbling progress over the hot desert rocks until they reached each other and died together in a sweaty, torrid embrace. Hollywood was squeezing these intense scenes out right and left in hot shades of reds and orange emotion for the moviegoer. My life was never the same after seeing those films. From then on, the actions I took and the decisions I made would always be accompanied by inner dramatic musical scores.

One day our "aunts" and Berniece took my brother and me to Marion Davies' former beach home, which had now been converted into a restaurant we called the Beach Home Restaurant.

Famous for her film roles, she was mostly known for being William Randolph Hearst's mistress. Rumor had it that when he died, Davies had not even been invited to her lover's funeral.

Bill and I were so "in" that we insisted on wearing our sunglasses indoors. The view was astonishingly bright and sunny because the windows reflected the closeness of sun and nearby rocks and small crashing waves.

At the time, I didn't have any idea who Marion Davies was, but we recognized Ann Sothern, at that time a major movie star. She managed to look beautiful and poised as she ate, despite our stares. My brother and I had seen most of her MGM comedies including *Maisie.* Pat and Wanda seemed amused at our reactions but were never critical.

The image of Ann Sothern remains with me still. She quietly ate her lunch with a studied nonchalance. Few people seemed to glow as she did and her eyes never left her luncheon date. Nonetheless, I felt she was aware we were staring at her. She was a true beauty whose warmth on the screen came alive in person and permeated the room and all in it. Her smile put her gentleman friend at ease, even as we watched. She radiated an unusual energy and I knew I was in the presence of someone pretty special. She had been studying us just as we had been studying her.

On our return to Oakland, I felt that I had developed a worldly knowledge known only to grownups even though I was just 10 years old.

Then life took another turn. Most people would condemn a child molester. But how can one judge a 14-year-old who lived in an eccentric home like my friend Ted?

Actually, I was a willing victim because I wanted to please Ted who was the neighborhood hero, and I wasn't mature enough physically to have an adult response to his behavior toward me. My relationship with Ted started when he and his friend Keith wanted me to do some things that bordered on bizarre behavior.

One day Ted told me I should let him hang me by my feet from the top of the deserted mansion where he lived. No adults were ever home during the day, so Ted was basically left alone by his parents most of the time. Ted had a brilliant, perhaps eccentric mind. I guess hanging me upside down from the roof was very entertaining for him. I trusted Ted so completely that it never occurred to me that my life was literally in his hands.

For about two years, a great deal of touching and feeling began between Ted and me. Actually, I never minded. The touching part of my relationship with my mother had ended, and Ted had become a part-time parent. We were both caught up in a sensuality that we hardly understood, and we felt okay about it until one day I had my first orgasm. This sent Ted into a tidal wave of guilt, horror, and self hatred. How he knew society's sense of right and wrong when his parents were so outrageous and unconventional still puzzles me. Later as a teenager, my friendship with Ted remained strained, and when he married in his 20's, he could never look me straight in the eye.

Had my parents suspected something out of the ordinary they never let me know. You would think that my tears when Ted ended our friendship would be a dead giveaway. But, my parents were true innocents. When Ted, sobbing, threw his baseball glove and toys onto our front lawn, the act only brought out a mild questioning comment from my mother, and my father wasn't home much during the day, so he wasn't even aware of Ted's actions.

After I had recovered from my episode with Ted, I found that the girls at school seemed to like me more than ever. Even at 12 we were already having dances and I was popular. Not shy like most of the other boys, I could dance really well. I had also developed the art of mature conversation. It seems that at 12 I had already become a minor star.

Chapter 3
As the Twig is Bent...

The next few years didn't seem terribly significant to me. I remember how nervous my mother became after my parents discovered that my father had a heart problem. Perhaps it was due to this new situation that we were sent to bed earlier than I thought normal for other children in 1952. Sleep was impossible and my sister took up reading. She feverishly read *Forever Amber* followed by *Gone with the Wind*. Her reading light was a flashlight tucked under the covers of her bed.

My sister and I had twin beds next to each other and many times we'd fall asleep holding hands. My brother's bed was across the room from ours. Looking back, I felt that his distance from us became a symbol of his independent spirit. But, each night we would all chatter back and forth until we fell asleep. I didn't realize that middle-class families usually did not have all the children sleep in one room. My sister slept in the bed next to me until the day she ran off and got married. I have fond memories of those shared evenings that brought the three of us so much closer.

In the summer of 1952 I got the opportunity to attend Oakland Technical High School's summer program. My mother and father wanted the best for me as I yearned to develop my talent in many different ways and they never said no if the opportunity was appropriate to developing that talent. And so it was that I began my first dance class, my very first exposure to a creative writing program, and a music class, all which I attended daily along with students who were much older than I.

I remember discussing Arthur Miller's *Death of a Salesman* in the writing class. Detailed discussions were a daily event. One day the teacher told us he was co-authoring a book about the accidental discovery of the lost city of Sheba.

He told us he had been flying in a small plane with a friend when they discovered what looked like the upper part of a spire sticking up in the middle of the desert. This amazing discovery led to an expedition sent in to do an extensive excavation of the site. The discovery was significant because there had been no known evidence that the place had ever existed except through Biblical records. In fact, the site had been a thriving desert city at one time.

Sheba was one of two cities mentioned Biblically and later historically as being on an ancient trade route and was ruled by the Queen of Sheba, a learned astronomer and astrologer and later the wife to King Solomon, who shared her interest in the movement of the heavenly bodies.

Our class moved on with interest to the unveiling of this adventure story that although factual, reminded me of the discovery of Shangri-La in the film *Lost Horizon.* My imagination took off, and I began to develop a great admiration for my coolly reserved creative writing teacher, Kenneth Brown. I remember Mr. Brown's photos of his life which was one of daring, independence, and courage.

The music class was a great challenge because, once again, most of the students were older and more sophisticated. I learned to play Beethoven's *Fifth Symphony* on the clarinet my father had bought me second hand from his friend Carl. Although I could hardly handle the notes, I was excited by the challenge. I loved classical music, was inspired by it, and found the dreamlike *Bolero* by Ravel intoxicating. I could barely keep up with the older students.

The dance classes I took were rigorous. At 13 I was the only male in the class. By the end of the summer we were all asked to choose a piece of music to accompany our dance routines, which we would perform in front of our fellow students. I loved music from the beginning but I must admit that as a child I was frightened by the monstrous sounds that came from the old wind-up phonograph we owned.

I still remember Greig's *In the Hall of the Mountain King* and the terrible sounds the old phonograph made as its springs lost their tension. Later, my Aunt Pat brought us an electric one.

For my performance, I carefully chose a record of *Gayne* by Khachaturian. I liked the *Sabre Dance* that was played on the radio almost as much as *Rock Around the Clock.* I chose a rollicking sing-song sort of piece from that same ballet.

I thought I had danced it rather well. After the students applauded in a mandatory way, my teacher, a young college girl, asked what music I had chosen. I handed her the 33 rpm record which was relatively new on the market. She studied the label and read the small print aloud. The title rang out: *The Dance of the Rose Maidens.* Everyone laughed, and I quickly learned a life-long lesson that day: always read the small print.

Three days went by before my face changed from fiery red back to its normal sun- tanned adolescent shade.

In the early 1950s, television was still in its youth, so weekly trips to the movies were at the top of the entertainment list for my teenage friends and me. They became emotional experiences for us on more than one level. The Chimes Theater on College Avenue in Oakland was known as the passion pit. We could watch a movie and then in those dark seats, do everything except actually have sex. Nice girls didn't go that far back then. We sat huddled in our seats and gasped in disbelief as Gene Tierney murdered her brother in a revival of *Leave Her to Heaven*, and we wept as James Dean tearfully reconnected with his dying father in *East of Eden.* These intense and moving film dramas colored our own experiences and made them seem bigger than life during those formative adolescent years.

"As the twig is bent, so grows the tree." It's a truly disturbing saying. I'd like to think we all have a fighting chance to change fate, even if our genes betray us from time to time.

Psychiatrists seemed to miraculously solve people's problems on the screen in no time at all. Remember *The Seventh Veil* with James Mason and Ann Todd? Todd plays a concert pianist and Mason, her psychiatrist. He manages to unravel her defenses, as though they are Salome's seven veils. This allows her to finally flourish as a mature artist, to accept her past, and to fall in love. An underlying theme is that strong will and sexuality are formed when we are young children.

But still, psychiatrists were only people in the most refined melodramas. *Lady in the Dark* was actually from the 1940s, but most teenagers never got a chance to see this Kurt Weill musical psycho-drama until the days of early television. Remember Ginger Rogers singing *Jenny Made Her Mind up When She Was Three?* The drama was later cleaned up for the movie version. The theory of altering genes was only a dim possibility back then so, unable to foresee our unbelievable future, we went on our merry or not so merry way, unsuspectingly in the dark about what the future could bring.

I had numerous puzzling incidents that projected the fantasy of the screen out into real life. For example, there was this strange group of foreigners coming out of the Chimes Theater one rainy Saturday afternoon. I was fascinated with the subtle difference in the way that they were walking in front of me. They were most gleeful and laughing at everything. They must have been at least in their mid 20s. As they walked along in front of me, a ceramic penis fell onto the sidewalk. A gale of giggles erupted from the foreigners as well as quick shock from other passersby. Seeing the flying ceramic penis coming their way, people quickly pushed and shoved to get past the strange group of laughing young men. A cobra could have dropped out of the sky and onto the busy sidewalk for the response around me. I honestly didn't know what the object was until I walked up and looked at it more closely. At that point, one of the fellows who later revealed his home was in Persia (now Iran), grabbed the ceramic piece off the sidewalk and hid it under his coat. I was startled and couldn't imagine such a thing happening, especially since I had just stepped out from a matinee screening of *The Song of Bernadette*! The sound of heavenly choirs of disembodied angels at Twentieth Century Fox still resounded in my head as I puzzled over the ceramic penis.

Why were those strangers so tickled about the clay penis? What were they doing with it and why did they have it with them? My innocence was already being shattered by the movies.

I was so moved by Bernadette that I decided never to miss another Jennifer Jones movie. Later, when I saw *Ruby Gentry* which was more frank than *Duel in the Sun,* I happily realized my education was soaring in new directions.

Every Friday we had a dance school at Claremont Junior High School which was a few blocks from the theater. The custom was to give your school jacket to the girl of your dreams. My dreams changed frequently, so a different girl would wear my jacket every three months during that three-year period.

We danced the swing to *Opus One*, played by Tommy Dorsey who was still popular in the 1950s, and to *Pine-top Boogie Woogie.* We slow danced to the Ames Brothers' *Garden in the Rain* and did the Samba to Percy Faith's *Delicado.* The most red- hot dances, considered modern and revolutionary, were *Rock Around The Clock* and *Pachuco Hop.* I used up four Wildroot Cream Oil tubes, Bryl Cream, and Vaseline Hair Tonic in one semester. My father, admonishing me, warned not to use what he called "coal oil" as he had done at that age. He said, "It will make your hair thin out or maybe even fall out."

My world grew rapidly into a wonderful, glamorous fantasy place. I skipped the French fries and cherry Coca-Cola the other kids had for lunch and bought 12-cent 78 rpm records. They were used records from juke boxes that were bought by fans of popular music. I came home every day and listened for hours until it was time to go to the next dance.

And then I had a stroke of luck. My English teacher, Patricia Canfield, who was usually amused by my dramatic class antics, let me produce the school play. I wrote and directed *Dead and Unaware*, in which a woman returns from the dead to inflict comic violence on the living during a horrendous thunder and lightening storm. Nice title, I thought. The play was very funny and silly. To this day I'm grateful to Patricia Canfield for the opportunity she gave me.

Ms. Canfield had golden yellow hair, almost crayon yellow. Behind her back, the boys called her "Mrs. Can Feel." Her sparkling eyes betrayed her love of laughter, especially when she looked at me. I realized she would hide behind her teacher's manual so the class could not see her constant amusement. I was fortunate that she liked me so well. At the time, I thought of her as an older woman, but now I realize she was probably only about 30 then.

To this day, I have remained friends with Irene Adams, who was the lead in my play. She later went on to act in regional theater, graduated from medical school, and is now a much honored head of an AIDS and Cancer clinic in Belahorizonte, Brazil. She personally supervised saving the lives of thousands of Brazil's street children.

A year or so went by and I was coming out of the Twelve Cent Record Store when I noticed the same foreigners I had seen the year before looking out of an upstairs window.

This meeting with these young men would launch one of many unconventional odysseys that have enriched my life and set me apart from more traditional lifestyles. In taking this path, I have met some of the most interesting and sometimes famous people in the world.

I found later that all six of these young men lived in an apartment over the shop. This information startled me. At that moment, one of the many California spring rains began, leaving me stranded under the record shop awning. The most handsome of the young men saw that I was trapped and called down to me, "Need to get out of the rain?"

I was more than a little shy as I stood there, attempting to hide my teenage acne. I wasn't sure what to think of these guys.

The man called down to me again, "The stairs are to your right. Come on up."

My curiosity won out. I went upstairs, and found the door at the top of the stairs open. I walked into the apartment and four smiling, dark-haired people with flashing white teeth greeted me. "We see you buying the records every day, what do you do with them?" asked one man with a middle-eastern accent.

I explained that I studied dance and wanted to be in the movies. I wanted to learn as much as I could about acting. After a Coca-Cola and much conversation, I learned that the men were from Iran. All I knew about what was then called Persia was that movie star Yvonne De Carlo danced ballet in Harem pants and passed her talents off as authentic, exotic Persian dancing in films. I wasn't sure her technique was Persian but it was definitely exotic!

The men asked if I would dance for them. I replied, "One day I will when I've had more lessons."

The subject soon changed to information about my sexual choices. "Do you like girls or boys?" one of them asked me with great curiosity. I answered "girls" because it was true. I was feeling a little nervous as I guessed what they truly wanted to know.

After a few awkward moments for me, Majid, the handsome one said, "I know someone that would like you a lot. She will help you. Her name is Helen. Next time you buy records, come upstairs, and I will make arrangements for you to meet her." I began to think of them as prurient Persians.

If I had not so loved music, theater, and later ballet, I'm not sure where I would have ended up, but I do think there has always been something stable and down-to-earth about me. My mother's influence and her support of my interests in the arts anchored me, and my dad's kindness was always there, too.

One Christmas visit my great-aunt Mary Jackson (Aunt Mary) took my hand and said, "Never forget you are a direct descendant of Stonewall Jackson." For years I confused my relative with Andrew Jackson until I realized this Confederate general bordered on insanity. But he was a connection to the South, where I eventually lived.

Chapter 4
Always Read the Fine Print

At 14, life started anew. I grew bolder about taking the train into San Francisco and was rewarded in many ways. I saw the original production of *Kismet* with Alfred Drake, Dolores Gray, and Dorretta Morrow. Jack Cole's choreography was original and, for the times, extremely sensual. I yearned to get involved in the glamour of the ballet and realized I was going to have to earn enough money to pay for dancing, acting, and singing classes.

Despite my age, I got a job as a busboy in the Ukrainian Bakery at First and Mission Streets. I believe I was hired because I smiled a lot and was the only employee who could speak fluent English.

My bosses were Anton, Tibor, a man named Joe, a woman called Petruska, and Jack, the chef. I had heard of the ballet *Petruska* and never realized it could be a lady's name. This group was comprised of old friends from Hungary and they had been through the horrors of World War II. Anton, who never smiled, told me he had seen his whole family executed.

I was treated coldly at first, but eventually they began to trust me. One day Anton asked, "On Sunday, do you go to a church or synagogue?"

I explained that I went to neither, but I had a very open mind about religion. I wanted them to like me, but what I said was the truth. Much to my surprise, after the customers went back to work following the lunch break, Petruska swept the uneaten mashed potatoes off the half empty plates into a bowl to be warmed up for the dinner crowd. Why this place was called Ukrainian Bakery was beyond me because no one was Ukrainian – they were Hungarian.

Joe and Petruska intrigued me. Joe was always chasing her around the steam table and she giggled like a teenager even though she was 60. She grew to like me and would reward me with a bag of apple strudel. To my disappointment, the stale strudel looked all right on the outside but most of the pieces were full of mold. They paid the busboys three dollars per hour and gave us lunch or dinner. The food actually tasted good until one day I was eating one of Jack's stuffed bell peppers and almost took a bite of a giant cockroach that had been cooked into the pepper.

Jack became friendly, too, and then I realized he was also being overly friendly to my current girlfriend. She soon learned not to come and visit me at work.

Jack had once been married to Ann Corio who was in several of the 1940s films, including a western starring Randolph Scott. Her real claim to fame was that she was a famous stripper in the era when burlesque was grand and glamorous. Jack told me that together they had trained a monkey to pull her clothes off during her act. Her most novel act, he said, was one in which a snapping crocodile was coached to pull off her clothes. Jack confessed that he was afraid of the crocodile. They kept it under a steam heater in their hotel rooms on a bed of wct blankets. Jack would wake up in the morning with the reptile loudly snapping its jaws, demanding to be fed. No wonder they divorced after 15 years.

Dino, the Greek waiter, soon presented another problem. He was sort of head busboy and took to asking me to go down and get things out of the walk-in refrigerator in the basement. After I had gone down several times and stood among the corned beef, roast beef, and the turkeys, I'd hear another set of footsteps coming down the stairs. Dino would come in and shut the refrigerator door behind me, quietly yanking down my pants and trying to get me to have sex with him. I explained each time that I liked him but wasn't interested in his sexual advances.

"But you have such a sexy body!" He would exclaim. Evidently he had learned many words in English but not the one I wanted him to understand which was "No!"

Fortunately, Anton saved the day by suddenly entering the refrigerator.

My dad didn't like my commuting every day to San Francisco since I was still a minor. The San Francisco Ballet was there, and I was determined to get some kind of work with them. I had not yet had a formal ballet class, but it was on my agenda. I had decided that my voice was too weak to make it just on acting. To please my dad and to make money nearer home, I went to work part time for his company, Duchess Catering Service. They owned all of the food concessions around Lake Merritt in Oakland. On July 4, 1954, I accidentally burned up 144 dozen hamburger buns. I was only supposed to warm them up. On July 4, 1955, I accidentally served 400 Coca-Colas that were half Clorox to customers at the Duck Pond where I sold drinks in the bird sanctuary. You see, bottles of Coca-Cola syrup and Clorox were stored in very similar containers. Actually, no one noticed until several people complained near the end of the day.

A few weeks later on a very hot day, I spilled five gallons of Popex liquid margarine onto the floor of the concession stand. We used this kind of oil in the giant popcorn machines. As the oil spread, waitresses began to slip and slide across the floor and I learned some very colorful curses concerning my birth. But I never got fired. Well, I was a very hard worker, and the employees all loved my kind and generous dad.

In the summer of 1955, Irene Adams, our friend Al Perez, and I auditioned for *By the Beautiful Sea*. This nostalgic musical had enjoyed a moderately successful run on Broadway because of its wonderful star, Shirley Booth. We all joyfully rehearsed, feeling very grown up as most of the other cast members were mature adults. Since we were the only theater to produce *By the Beautiful Sea* outside New York, we hoped the rumor was true that Shirley Booth herself was planning to come see the show.

Ted Smalley was the director and the George Felker the choreographer. Their warmth encouraged us as young performers. All seemed to go well during the first few weeks. Al took off one week to visit the set of Paddy Chayefsky's *The Catered Affair*. Debbie Reynolds starred in this comedy drama and Al, being president of the Debbie Reynolds Fan Club, interviewed her.

When Al arrived in L.A. a letter from Debbie Reynold's mother was waiting for him at the hotel.

"Please come tomorrow instead of today. Debbie's big scene is shooting tomorrow. Maybe Bette Davis won't be on the set. She hates strangers on the set and her glares can be lethal," she wrote.

When Debbie's mother met Al at the MGM gate, she said, "Take a good look around," in a cryptic voice. Al was confused about what she was referring to – the demise of the artistic films that MGM had been famous for producing. "Al, it's all over but the funeral," she continued.

Debbie, who was extremely friendly and casual, conducted her interview with him from behind a partially closed bathroom door while seated on the toilet.

Al returned exhilarated from his experience with tales of Bette Davis arriving on the set and everyone jumping out of her way because she was the undisputed "queen of the movies." He told us about Debbie's big chance to do a serious acting scene. Her tearful rendition received a huge round of applause from the technicians on the set and Debbie, looking beautiful and radiant, turned and humbly bowed to them.

By the third weekend of *By the Beautiful Sea*, we had learned to sing rather well, we thought, and all of us had become more confident about our dancing.

Our theater was The Jack London Sqaure Theater which, along with other Jack London Square establishments, was on a pier extending out into the estuary of San Francisco Bay. One night as we danced and sang, the sounds of sirens came from far away and grew louder. Within minutes, our voices could barely be heard by our audience. It seemed that the Show Boat, one of the two tourist restaurants, a little further down the pier, had begun to sink. Unknown to us, the entire end of the boat was sinking. As we struggled to carry on, the Show Boat began to give off giant glug-glug-glug sounds, followed by rising noises of rushing water reminiscent of a huge bathtub emptying water down a giant drain. But we continued to sing and dance. By this time our audience appeared to be aware that something was amiss and some began to hurry out of the theater.

Outside, everyone ogled the disappearing Show Boat restaurant, watching red and white checkered tablecloths floating by along with soggy candles, and uneaten loaves of French bread, leaving a rippling wake of more debris behind while the wailing siren become louder by the minute.

Ted, our director, hoping to keep the show going, began shouting at us, "Enunciate!" His lips exaggerated the E and N, hoping we would sing louder. Then Dorothy Blais, the female lead, and quite a talent, began laughing and cried, "We have new dialogue!" in response to the louder noises of the gurgling water. Needless to say, *By the Beautiful Sea* ended rather abruptly. Later, my friend, Al, in a moment of true mourning, sighed and said with all seriousness, "I guess Shirley Booth will never see us now." (Dorothy was recently honored in Stockton, CA for her work as mentor to others.)

Ticket money was, of course, refunded.

As you will soon see, disasters followed me wherever I went. But life was never dull!

I wanted to start classes at the San Francisco Ballet but had this fear of traveling the two-hour train trip into San Francisco that included a bus ride to 18th and Geary where the school had been located since 1933.

One day, Linda, then my girlfriend, came to meet me at my latest job site, another job provided by Dad, at Fairyland in Oakland's Lake Merritt Park. I always looked a lot younger than my real age, which wasn't necessarily an advantage. This time I was selling Coca-Colas, popcorn, and hot dogs. A rough-looking Latin man shouted at me, "I guess you've found where you really belong!"

I was deeply hurt and didn't understand this insult until Linda said, "He's only kidding, George. Didn't you notice you're working at Fairyland and that makes you the butt of lots of jokes?" I stared at her in astonishment, and then we both began to laugh at the double meaning the park's name implied.

Chapter 5
Freedom's Gate

Another year went by before I would meet the infamous Helen as I was avoiding the prurient Persians like the plague. At 15, I had only a trace of guilt feelings about sex. I wasn't brought up to be religious. I had seen numerous religious films with amazing special effects and choirs of heavenly voices. I took everything in but was not particularly drawn toward any of the dogma.

I didn't know I was named after a famous Mormon icon, the Reverend Lawrence Hunter. My father was a descendent of Mormon families and I'm still not sure what the Mormons believe. I just know they're spiritual in many ways and we're related.

At times we were terribly afraid of my mother whose high-strung nervous system would take her over the edge when my father came home late from work. Dad's developing heart condition was caused partly by genetics and partly from the stress of having three jobs. We would pretend to be asleep when my mother checked our room to see if we were awake. We thought of her as the Gestapo. She knew our trick of talking in whispers. My sister had a lifelong fear of my mother and I always felt sympathy for her because I, too, was afraid of my mother's suddenly changing moods.

On an unusually warm night for northern California, my brother and I were trying to sleep despite the fact that we were uncomfortable. Along with the usual night sounds, we thought we heard some violent quacking and in the morning we discovered that all of our pet birds and my ducks had been eaten by weasels. If I was ever insane, this was the time. I went into shock. In a daze, I stormed into the bathroom and began pulling at the plaster on the walls with the toilet plunger. My mother, instead of being angry, gently took the plunger from my hands. After that sad event, there seemed to be no end to my tears.

Later, my mother and father explained to me that they weren't going to let me have any more pets because I got "too upset." Even I thought I had slipped into psychosis. Fifty years later, I would explain to my therapist that I had felt so lucky because my parents didn't get angry at me. She agreed, but felt my parents had not been all that helpful when they had encouraged me to think there was something abnormal about my tears and grief over the dead pets.

A lot has been written about girls discovering the first sign of blood and the beginning of menstruation. Those who had not been prepared for this event by their mother would find themselves startled and fearful. For example, remember the shower scene in the film *Carrie*? In that scene, Sissy Spacek's character, Carrie, is truly traumatized.

I don't think much has been said about 11- and 12-year-old boys who were unprepared for waking up in the middle of the night. Their heart would be pounding and they would be out of breath with a feeling somewhere between pleasure and pain, the emphasis on pleasure, as they realized that the sheets had become mysteriously wet. This was as startling and frightening to them as the first blood of menstruation was for uninformed girls.

My parents never got around to giving me a sex education or even talking to me about the subject until I was 16. There was no mention of sexuality in our public schools either. For me, by 16, it was already too late, and I wondered why I wasn't blind or mentally ill, which could have happened, according to my mother's books. My turbulent sleep was crowded with fantasies about my Claremont Junior High School girlfriends, my beautiful sister, and her new boyfriend, a Native American.

My sister was the picture of femininity. Later, people would compare her personality and looks to those of Lee Remick. Her boyfriend, Joe Houck, was tall, dark skinned, with a body made for rock climbing and outdoor adventure. He began every sentence with a crookedly wicked smile and always exuded an earthy charm. I had thought my sister was in love. She was no longer reading romances in bed under the sheets by flashlight. Romance for her was suddenly real. But the unpredictable has always been in my life, and a few months later when my sister began college, we received a phone call from her telling us that she had eloped, not with Joe, whom we all loved, but with someone else named Douglas Carter.

No longer would my sister ask me to hold her hand while she bathed or had difficulty falling asleep. I was 15 and my sister was 19 and I immediately expressed the trauma and loss by crying a lot. My younger brother, Bill, who was 13, seemed oblivious to this news from my sister.

My dad had cherished my sister, too, and the sense of betrayal permeated the air. My mother had become the authority figure in our house and communication between my sister and my mother, despite familial love, had broken down. In 1953 my parents could never approve of a man seven years older than my sister, who had already been married, and was relatively sophisticated. He talked badly to my parents, too, using heavy sarcasm when they expressed their concern.

"After all," he would say, 'Colleen is old enough to decide what she wants. She's 18."

If my sister loved this man, I thought, then they would take him into our family. My mother stewed and steamed as she worked in her garden and my father disappeared into our basement, a dark and dreary place, where he cried for weeks.

At one point my mother and my dad sat down in the living room without my brother and told me, "We were too strict with your sister. We're not going to make the same mistake with you."

Suddenly, at 15, I had all the freedom of an adult. When I came home at one o'clock in the morning, my parents would never scold, they would only ask where I had been. But I never abused the privilege. If I came home late, it was because I was rehearsing a show or ballet. I conducted my secret life during daytime hours so I never had to lie.

Chapter 6
Under New Influences

My new friend Tucki was Swedish and a dancer. I admired her sophistication and mature beauty. She seemed older than the rest of us and was, in my opinion, more mature than most of the Tech High School students. She was in my drama class, and everyone noticed that her figure was fuller, her hair blonder than blonde. Her hair hung down, veiling part of her face. When she smiled through this bright cascade of blonde hair she reminded me of Veronica Lake, the sultry blonde movie star of the previous era who had starred with Alan Ladd in *This Gun For Hire* and Fredrick March in *I Married a Witch*.

I remember that Tucki was the only one who giggled when she called me Georgie, and I liked that. One day she introduced me to her mother, Gladys Knutson, who was the pillar of a local theater group. Mrs. Knutson was always formal and distant but when she laughed, her entire personality changed. She would become half grand lady and half Elsa Lancaster. Gladys Knutson was starring in a startling new production of *The Picture of Dorian Gray* by Oscar Wilde. Another actor, Aldo Bozzine, starred in many Century Playhouse productions, too, and rumor had it that Century's productions were dominated by his performances. Bozzine was trained in Shakespearean theater as well as modern drama, and he was gay.

Several of John Carradine's children were part of this local theater whirl, and people loved to gossip about their sexual orientations. I had seen Carradine's creepy portrayal of Bluebeard and Dracula a few years back and hoped to meet the movie star in person one day. I was excited when Gladys told me, "You can usher at the theater almost any night and see the show free, George."

Carol and Edward O'Brien were the founding directors of Century Playhouse and rarely had to "paper the house," a showbiz term for giveaway tickets. The actors' group had been forced to move out of the old Paris Theater in Oakland due to demands made by the stage hands' union. These demands could have bankrupted the theater and left no money to pay actors their paltry salaries.

The next new home of the playhouse would become the Rivoli Theater, a mile from the University of California Berkeley campus. It will always be remembered as a marvelous but crumbling example of the true grandeur of the 1930s movie palaces. At one time marquee lights at the Rivoli gave it a jewel-like grandeur, luring in the audience with the magic of actors' names in lights.

When I arrived to do my ushering, a woman with huge, flirtatious brown eyes met me at the ticket booth. She turned out to be the mother of the director's wife and a former Ziegfeld Follies showgirl named Ruth Ann Martin. She led me into the crowded lobby with its giant chandelier. Across the crowd, I heard someone attempting to make popcorn and, unable to speak English, trying in another language to coax the machine to behave. Her voice and language blended with the theater's surreal atmosphere. The woman with the big brown eyes came by and told me to wait for the other ushers before disappearing into the crowded lobby. Then eight large doors swung open.

When the show was over, the audience spilled out into the big lobby that smelled of mold, lavender, and hot popcorn. After a while the crowd left, and I could hear Ravel's *Daphnis and Chloe* coming from somewhere inside the theater. It was from my favorite ballet of the time and I especially loved the opening strains of *Daybreak*. I crept toward one of the large doors, opened it and let it swing shut behind me. The entire theater was thick with blackness except for one pool of white stage light. I stared, transfixed at the elegant figure of a woman dancing alone in the spotlight, unaware of anyone's presence. Her dark hair hung loosely down about her neck, and as the music increased in intensity and volume, it rippled out around her in an aura of shining light.

As the voices in *Daybreak* grew louder, not a recognizable word floated above the melody, just soft "ahoooo" sounds. The singing soothed and softened the smooth string music as I sighed in delight, imagining enchanting images of a dancer gliding over a warm lake in a grotto. A strong emotional connection to the mysterious female dancer arose in me – it was love at first sight. I was about to meet Carol O'Brien, who would eventually become my closest lifelong friend.

Tucki auditioned for the lead role in *Seven Year Itch* by George Axelrod. Even though *The Girl Upstairs*, as she is called, is supposed to be 25 years old, Tucki was perfect. The show became a huge success, paying the bills for months to come. Later, Marilyn Monroe played *The Girl Upstairs* in the film version and gained national acclaim. When the theater closed a year later, the Century Playhouse director, Edward O'Brien, was forced by Actors Equity to change his name to Richard O'Brien. His name was similar to the already well known actor Edmund O'Brien who starred in many movies, including *D.O.A.*

Richard O'Brien went on to play opposite Jocelyn Brando, Marlon Brando's sister, in the *Immoralist* by André Gide in a long run in San Francisco. He also played the headmaster in *Tea and Sympathy* in its San Francisco premiere. In the films, he appeared with Diane Keaton as the priest in *Looking for Mr. Goodbar*, and the president of the United States in *The Andromeda Strain*. He was in over 250 roles during his acting career and he became my surrogate father in theater. I can see him now in my mind's eye taking Burt Lancaster back to San Francisco in *Birdman of Alcatraz*.

After enrolling in Carol's ballet classes I showed up to my first class dressed in a T-shirt and a red bathing suit. While all the other students giggled Carol calmly welcomed me into the class and introduced me to Raoul, who would eventually marry Tucki. He told me what I should wear to the next class. I remember being very embarrassed at the time for being such a greenhorn.

Raoul was probably 30 years old and I was very intimidated by his glow of masculine aggression and self confidence. He showed me how to put on a pair of tights and wear a dance belt and assured me, laughing, "No, you're really not naked although it does feel that way."

Tucki was at my first formal ballet class, smiling sweetly, ready to support me along with Raoul, Gladys, and six or so other actors who were rehearsing *Mr. Roberts* and *Stalag 19*. There, among these students, I felt thrilled and inspired, and I knew without a doubt that I had discovered what I would do for the rest of my life.

I actively began to develop muscles. I changed the way I ate. I got down to a svelte 135 pounds. I overcame the feeling that I was naked when I danced. I began lifting weights. My brother thought I had gone crazy.

I deeply admired Carol's expertise in ballet. This excellent teacher would have a tremendous affect on my ballet career.

Born January 7, 1919 in Glendale, California to George Handel Martin and Ruth Minnot Martin, Carol was an energetic and imaginative child who began to dance almost before she could walk. Her grandfather was a famous Christian minister in China during the 1800s. He became a hero to the Chinese in San Francisco's Chinatown because his mission had rescued girls forced into prostitution after immigrating to the United States. His letters to the United States government presented a vivid picture of China during that time in history and have been published.

Carol's mother, Ruth, began to realize that love alone couldn't hold two incompatible people together. George was conservative and intellectual, and she was a former Gibson girl who had made the theater her life. The neighbors began secretly to take Carol with their own children to dance classes. Imagine conventional peoples' shock at Carol's mother, returning to her career as a Ziegfeld Follies showgirl, and leaving her husband alone to raise their two daughters, Carol and Muriel.

This event hit the girls hard. Carol's sister seemed to be living subliminally as she was integrated into Carol's performance with the Meglan Kiddies, a group of dancing cuties who would entertain before and after feature film screenings and talent shows in L.A. beginning in the late 1920s.. That's how Shirley Temple and Judy Garland first got their start. Carol and Muriel's father, George tried his best to cope with the situation and finally turned to Carol's grandmother, a true Victorian lady who attempted to fill the empty role of mother for the two girls.

Despite the fact that Shirley Temple and Judy Garland were both Meglan Kiddies performing in one Hollywood event after another, the grandmother never approved of Carol's dancing. To her, the stage was a wicked place, and no lady would be a dancer. But Carol persevered in her dancing and never gave up hope that her mother would one day return home for good.

Carol's father went to work for Western Electric, the company that produced most of the sound for movies from the 1930s to the 1950s. Although he was highly educated, he was unsophisticated in the ways of the world. He had a job at MGM and was checking the intercom between Greta Garbo's dressing cottage and the main sound stage. Not realizing that George was working in her dressing area, Garbo walked into the room totally nude.

"Damn!" she shouted in her famous husky accented voice. George had never heard a lady swear so angrily and the situation shattered his Victorian concept of feminine behavior.

Carol's father remarried, but Carol barely survived her father's marriage to her new social-climbing stepmother. Bertha made it clear that she would not tolerate children. She had set her sights on George, a man who came from what she thought of as true society. For her, marrying him and becoming part of the Martin family were a big step.

Bertha, the incarnation of calculation and manipulation, had married a passive man who was at a loss at how to deal with her. Carol, 16 and Muriel, 15 were put on a one-way train ride to New York, where they were met by their loving mother, who could barely support them on a Zigfield Follies girl's salary. They survived the giant hurricane in 1937. When all turned to disaster, their mother reluctantly put them back on the train to L.A.

A year later they ended up on the streets of Los Angeles. Carol had bravely decided to save herself and her sister. Even after Muriel became seriously ill, their father refused to help them. So Carol got a job in a candy story to pay for a room in a respectable part of town. She studied ballet daily with Ernest Belcher, Marge Champion's father. She stood at the barre with Marge and Maria, and Majorie Tallchief. Marge later teamed with Gower Champion and became well-known in the movies. The other two would later become accomplished dancers as well. Both achieved start status.

Remember the famous radio program of the 1950s *Queen for a Day*? Bertha, always the grand manipulator, managed to convince the audience of the show that she loved little children and was a true humanitarian. She was able to garner the audience vote and won. When she heard this, Carol angrily called the show and told them that Bertha was definitely not the person she claimed to be and that instead, her stepmother fit the description of the wicked stepmother or the Wicked Witch of the West.

As Carol progressed into her late teens, she began to make an impression at Fox West Coast Theaters. In a year she became one of their main bookkeepers, managing receipts for the Los Angeles area theaters. Part of her job was to escort the biggest stars like Hedy

Lamar, Lana Turner, and Linda Darnell to the secret powder room at Grauman's Chinese Theater where they could add final make-up touches before World Premiere movie showings. One night as she was carrying out her duties, she met Edward O'Brien, a struggling young actor who had been Max Reinhart's protégé. Reinhart, a great movie director of the silent era, loved Edward like a son, but hopes for Edward's young stardom were cut short when Max abruptly died of heart disease. Before he died, he produced Shakespeare's *Midsummer Night's Dream* at the Hollywood Bowl with Mickey Rooney. Afterwards, Warner Brothers made it into a film.

Edward looked very much like the imagined young hero of an Irish drama, brown curly hair and dark green eyes. Later, Jerry Wald at Twentieth Century Fox talked to him about appearing in James Joyce's *Ulysses*. Carol and Edward spent a lot of time together and began to fall in love. Then Carol became the protégé of a Russian Ballet teacher, Madame Shirmatova, who dreamed of taking Carol back to Russia. She also shared two- hour private classes with Vera Ellen, who later became an MGM star, dancing with Gene Kelly and Fred Astaire in *On the Town* and *The Belle of New York*.

Telling Madame Shirmatova that she could not go to Russia with her led to a tearful farewell and Carol decided to change course. She made a cerebral decision and convinced Edward that education was more important than Hollywood glamour. They moved to Berkeley and both received degrees from University of California, Berkeley. Edward started his own theater before embarking on a huge TV and movie career. This is where I also met Carol's mother, Ruth Ann.

Ballet was far removed from football but it was just as physically demanding. My mother seemed disturbed when I asked for new ballet shoes for my 16th birthday, but stoically, she gave me the money. My dad just smiled. My sister smiled, too, when I told her about my new friends.

All summer long, I went to Lake Temescal. I was told that swimming was the only approved exercise for dancers and there I met many of my old high-school friends. None of us had heard of too much sun in those days and we all longed to be beautiful tanned Adonises.

About 200 feet out there was a float crowded with sunbathing swimmers, many of them men who enjoyed parading around in their swimwear. I secretly wished I could look like them. Their suits were wet and looked completely transparent as they strutted about on the float, and I knew all of them were aware of this. All I had the confidence to wear were my Polynesian Paradise cut-off trunks. I thought they looked the same as the ones worn by Tab Hunter when he starred opposite Linda Darnell in *Island of Desire*. Somehow, movies of the 1950s and transparent swimwear were in opposition. The 1950s fads and lifestyle had a carefree naïveté while all the transparent swimwear screamed another message. The styles were definitely out of sync.

It was on a day like this that I met Dale. He was sitting on the raft, pretending not to notice me, but I was immediately drawn to him because of his Australian accent. His hair was reddish blonde and his skin was similar to my mother's (she was also freckled but not particularly fair). I envied the kind of compact muscular body he had. I never gave the appearance of having an athletic build until after I matured, which happened later in my mid 20s.

Dale made some attempt at conversation and I asked him if he missed England. He laughed, explaining that even though he was from Australia he was a major in the United States Army. He asked if I needed a ride home. This was puzzling, and I wondered about the conflicting information he was giving me. Army majors aren't homosexual are they? Secretly I had always been afraid of being homosexual because I had been exposed to some terrible role models when I was younger. This man didn't fit any stereotype and definitely seemed manly to me. I instantly warmed to his friendship which seemed innocent enough. I had to admit that if he was homosexual, he was carrying it off with masculine self-confidence.

It's difficult to write about my early attraction to Dale. He told me how attracted he was to me and I had to wonder why. What was it that drew him to me?

The whole event gave me a strange, indescribable feeling. I was a stranger to myself most of the time and didn't have a good sense of self. I had a very confused picture of how I looked and about just who I was. Why would anyone like Dale be attracted to me?

No one is warned about or prepared for that first intensity of close physical contact. I felt that Dale must have thought of me as something to devour, as I imagined him pouncing on me like a hungry tiger. What I wasn't ready for was the definite masculine approach to sex – the sweat mixed with a trace of whiskey, the intimate body smells, the saliva, the weight of another man's body on my own. Dale's intensity was a shock to me and I drew inward, emotionally untouched but absorbing all the sensations as Dale and I interacted. I floated, feeling distant and uninvolved. I became the watcher in this unfolding sexual drama, separating myself from being there, not quite believing it was happening to me. My emotional detachment pulled me away, but the sensuality drew me in. I was enjoying this physical attention and glad I didn't have to assert myself. Perhaps if I had tried, though, I might have experienced some sort of earthly cosmic energy. I kept trying to convince myself that this wasn't the real me.

Dale's green and yellow car pulled up about three times a week, just as I was leaving school. He would drive me home, but I continued to ask to be let off at least two blocks from my house. I still couldn't believe Dale was homosexual. In fact, I thought no one else would believe it either. He looked so straight!

But then, what had been my image of a homosexual?

How was he *supposed* to look?

I began to stare at myself in the mirror. The push and pull of fear and seduction became overwhelming. I was repulsed and excited at the same time.

Dale begged me to live with him and this request pleased me immensely yet horrified me at the same time, as my parents would never have approved and our relationship had to remain secret. After a year with Dale, I slowly began to drift away from the relationship and there was nothing legal he could do about it. What I couldn't understand was the unexpected detachment I felt about the whole experience. After all, I was a minor. I had gone beyond my depth and now turned back toward familiar landmarks.

I began walking Melba home. She was a truly beautiful African American girl who was in my English and music classes. She was quite shy and that enhanced her appeal. When I asked to carry her books she would turn her Bambi-like eyes away.

Not truly understanding racial tension, I didn't realize why she looked around as though afraid, not of me, but of some unknown other. As time went on, Melba accepted our friendship, and we enjoyed our walks home together each day. We became close friends. The relationship was an easy one, not demanding or emotional and with it came a sense of relief. Maybe I wasn't gay after all.

Chapter 7
My Turning Points

As I approached my sixteenth birthday, I made an exciting discovery that has always remained an inspiration for me. This new awareness began when I first heard the music of modern Hungarian composer Béla Bartók, whose music was played by the San Francisco Little Symphony. I had never heard such exciting and innovative modern music played live before. I was haunted by the echoes of *Music for Strings, Percussion and Celesta.* Hearing these talented musicians in person making such other-worldly sounds was one of the most inspiring and thrilling experiences of my young life.

Of course, there was still sex. I wondered what it was all about. A special program aired on KRON-TV that caused me a great deal of anxiety. My whole family was glued to the TV set as they watched while the subject of homosexuality was explored. Most disturbing was the final outcome of the program – it was determined by medical standards to be a mental illness. The general opinion of most medical investigators was that this illness could be cured by psychotherapy. Experts treated this as an accepted fact during the mid 1950s.

I was scared and appalled. Was I one of *those* people? Was my sensuality that unusual? Certainly not, I thought. I am no freak. Except for my childhood attachment to Ted and later Dale as I entered my teenage years, I'd always dated and had been extremely popular with girls. And I so liked their company.

I couldn't bring myself to discuss this subject with my family, so with unanswered questions continuing to bombard my thoughts, I remembered my Persian acquaintances and let myself drift back toward them. Maybe they would be the ones to give me the answers I craved.

Majid was glad to see me. I always thought he was unusually handsome, and this reaffirmed my observation that some men's bodies, just like women's bodies, were in many ways appealing.

I let Majid know that I wanted some real answers about sex. "What are women really like?" I asked him earnestly, meaning sex with women.

"You mean you don't know?" he said.

"Yes. I really don't know," I replied honestly.

Majid became thoughtful and then smiled. "I told you before. I have a friend you must meet. How old are you now?"

I told him I was 16.

"I think that's old enough. Come, we go eat dinner and I will introduce you to Helen!"

And so began what I later thought of as my "Paint by Numbers, Sex by Numbers" affair with Helen.

Helen, if I had to give her a movie image, looked like a young Claire Trevor, who co-starred with Humphrey Bogart in *Key Largo*. She waited on our table and I thought her energy had a forced kind of warmth that was mixed with a real worldly toughness.

During the meal, Majid smiled up at Helen and said, 'George doesn't know who he is, Helen."

They laughed together, and then she gave me the once over. "He looks healthy enough to me, so maybe we'll find out."

"My shift is over at nine and I need some help moving my coffee table, George. Would you come over and give me a hand?"

I was not totally sure what was going on but was having definite suspicions and a longing to become more knowledgeable, so I replied, "Sure!"

Later, at Helen's apartment, without Majid who had managed to politely excuse himself, one thing led to another. Helen was least twice my age, although she looked much younger and seemed very experienced when it came to sex.

But sex with Helen was not the least bit romantic. It was, well, sex by numbers. By sex by numbers I meant it was like a painting by numbers. Each lacked the ingredient I loved: sensuality. At the time, I didn't realize sensuality was what turned black and white movies into living Technicolor, opening the senses to the rich, joyous awareness of being alive in the human body. A good example is a movie made several years ago called *City of Angels* with Nicholas Cage and Meg Ryan. That movie explains everything, how Cage, an angel, so desired to feel the physical world of sensation, that he gave up his life as an angel.

As a 16-year-old, I appreciated the new knowledge of sexual intercourse, but the mechanical coldness was scary. I remember some of my conversations with Helen after we had sex.

She would ask me, "What part of a woman's body do you like the most?"

"I don't know," I honestly replied.

She persisted, "Do you like her breasts? Her legs? Her behind?"

I just couldn't answer that question. I wasn't aware of any of it.

Helen sighed and stood up. "I know. Why don't you take a bath while I wash the dishes and sweep the floor?"

After cleanup time, we had sex again, and Helen went through her repertoire which, according to the Kinsey sex research I had read on the sly, was rather limited. She kept asking me what felt good, but I thought only that I was being given experiences and then quizzed to see if I understood them. The sensory part of the experience was lost in the academics of her questioning.

I learned that Helen wanted a relationship and not just a casual one-night stand. If I wanted, she told me all the things she would do for me, including giving me a hair perm. That request just seemed odd to me, so I refused. We became dinner companions for about a week usually followed by sex. I realized I was about to be owned, and I fled Helen forever.

Linda, who had been my non-sexual, but romantic girlfriend for several years, went skating with me at the Berkeley Ice Rink. She was as strong and healthy as I was without even trying. I had to work to stay strong. She was born with strength. Her hair was the color of honey and it fell carelessly across her forehead. She had to clip it back. She smiled a lot, something that almost concealed her inquisitive mind. Her pronounced overbite might have put some guys off, but I didn't care. She was pretty in that 1950s sort of way. When she wore my jacket at the ice rink and the movies she made me feel important.

I told her about my experiences with Helen and the advances of the Greek busboy in San Francisco, and I revealed my confusion. Linda listened, smiled softly, and replied wisely, "Maybe you can't judge your deeper needs by how well you function physically. I would say you have a choice, George."

"Can you help me?" I dared to ask.

She gave me a shy look, then glanced away and answered with great
honesty and caring, "I'm sorry, George, I'm just not ready for sex yet."

Later, alone with my brother whom I rarely saw, I tried to talk with him but he only joked, saying, "You should try sea otters. I hear they're rather sensual. After all, George," he added sarcastically, "you're good at everything, aren't you?"

I never discussed the subject of sex with my sister. She lived in San Francisco's married couples' housing by then, and she was always so sweet and seemingly ethereal that I could only hint at the truth. Talking to her about sex seemed totally out of place.

Virginia Kibbe was a friend from high school whose father owned a huge plate glass company in Berkeley. She was a very nice person, but painfully shy. At her parents' suggestion, she began inviting male friends along with her female friends to a home high in the Berkeley Hills owned by the Quitzows called the Temple of Wings. It was a Grecian Palace. The Quitzows were of Armenian descent and related to Isadora Duncan. They had two sons who performed with José Limon, one of the greatest modern dancers of that time. I was extremely curious. Everyone said that the Quitzows ate nothing but fruits and nuts, and astrology guided their every movement. I had never heard the word "vegetarian" at the time and evidently neither had my friends. I did know, however, about Isadora's unconventional behavior. Her style of dance was legendary. To my surprise, I found that she was from Oakland, too.

The Quitzows had dance concerts in the Duncan style and it was rumored that they wore nothing but scarves and veils between themselves and the universe. I had heard of Isadora's terrible death. Her long trailing scarf was caught in the wheel spokes of a convertible, causing her strangulation. What I didn't know was that she had influenced the development of Russian ballet with her free style of expression. In fact, Fokine, the great Russian choreographer, had given Isadora Duncan credit for the innovative use of arms and torso in some of his greatest work. His *Swan Lake* was restaged after the original Ivanov choreography, making it more expressive than the original. He claimed that his breaking away from more traditional steps was inspired by her free and dramatic movement.

To enter the Quitzow's home was truly an experience. I was 17 years old, naïve, and slightly afraid, when I stepped into what seemed to be Ancient Greece. It was startling. The walls were covered with pictures of women in what seemed to me to be the most bizarre poses. The men wore as much make-up as the women and the pictures were more dramatic than pretty. They were apparently inspired by Greek tragedies such as *Oedipus Rex, Medea,* and *Electra.*

We danced on cold stone floors with long Grecian pillars just outside the windows. Virginia was very open to everything we did or maybe she was so shy that she couldn't express what she honestly felt. Glen Miller played on the record player as we danced and held our partners with great care. There were about 10 couples participating. We learned the waltz, the foxtrot, and a weird rumba.

Mrs. Quitzow, our instructor, was probably the oldest person present and she wore a Grecian style robe-like dress. She called out our instructions in a shrill, high voice. Actually, she was very kind and gently led us down the V-shaped stairs which were divided into two equal stairways true to traditional Greek style. The stairs opened up into a cave-like room where cookies and punch were served.

After we went through the American dancing, we joined hands and performed the traditional Greek dance of the serpent. The steps were basically the old vine step with occasional mysterious glances and hissing sounds.

About three months later, the José Limon Company gave a dance performance at Wheeler Hall in Berkeley. When Mr. and Mrs. Quitzow came in the entire audience applauded. When I saw their son Val dance, I understood why. At the time, to bring up a son to dance as beautifully as he did was daring and unconventional.

The José Limon Company performed a very moving creation about Jesus and his disciples; even now it is considered a landmark in modern dance. José Limon had a beautifully sculpted face and body, and noticeably graceful hands. He used his entire body to relate complex emotions to his audience. Seeing him, I realized right then that I was falling in love with modern dance.

Virginia told me about a young dancer from the San Francisco Ballet School I had heard of but never met, Suki Schorer. Her father was a famous, outspoken professor at the University of California at Berkeley. Her parents were becoming concerned because the life of a dancer left no room for normal social activities, like dating. They knew I was polite and gentle, so they arranged for us to go to a dance at the Claremont Country Club in Oakland. Suki was a tiny, demure blonde. Rumor had it that she was her instructor, Harold Christiansen's, favorite, even though she was only 15 years old. I questioned her in a subtle way about her classes. I knew she left school every day around lunch time and was taken to the San Francisco Ballet School where I was studying after school and following my work every day, too. This schedule meant that I didn't get home until late evening. Talking to her, I realized what a cloistered life she led. Although she was familiar with the great composers Tchaikovsky and Chopin, she was unaware of the exciting Hungarian composer, Béla Bartók, whom I had become so familiar with a year or two earlier. It seemed she didn't even know about Stravinsky, Debussy, or other great composers I admired.

I realized that where music and drama were my passion, the athletic side of the dance was more familiar to her. So, I became a good reference guide for her.

Suki's shyness was an obstacle. We danced, had dinner, and at about 10 that night Suki's parents drove me home and we went our separate ways.

I followed Suki's career, first in the *San Francisco Chronicle* and later in *The New York Times*. She became one of the principal dancers with the New York City Ballet, originating many roles. I saw her dance in New York in George Balanchine's *The Unanswered Question* and later in many other ballets.

I saw Suki again in 2000. She had gracefully made the transition from dancer to the head of the School of American Ballet. When she spoke in San Francisco during a pre-curtain talk for the San Francisco Ballet, I stood in line to speak to her. She barely remembered our date, but I had vivid memories of that evening.

In a demanding tone of voice, she quickly changed the subject, "Did you buy a copy of my new book?" She asked. I acknowledged that I had. Suki's transformation from a delicate ballet student to one of Balanchine's assistants to becoming the head of one of the world's largest and most successful ballet schools had definitely changed her into someone who emanated success. Her polite harshness was not what I had anticipated. Life had taken a 360-degree turn for her and I was reminded of the toll on innocence that a successful career sometimes brings.

Today Suki is appears regularly on television, promoting a new drug to help people with osteoporosis. In the commercial she touts the drug in a soft voice as she teaches a ballet class.

Chapter 8
Too Much Love?

Dancers always find themselves embattled between strength and flexibility. While most sports tighten the muscles, which results in a person becoming muscle bound, male dancers are encouraged to do some weight lifting as part of the body strengthening process.

Nightly, I would soak in the tub, sometimes for hours, afterward doing deep stretches. I'd place the television outside the bathroom door because of my fear of electrocution. Several times I had escaped serious injury from that possibility. Once a vacuum cleaner in a restaurant wasn't grounded and shorted out in my hand. Another time, I was thrown across the room by an electric toaster, not realizing that my feet were in water. But I survived and later was told by an astrologer that the close vicinity of my natal Uranus to my Sun caused these electrical encounters. She said that Uranus energy was frequently displayed as electricity and the unusual electromagnetic field around my body attracted these encounters. I apparently have a natural tendency to create "electrifying" experiences in my life and could become the catalyst for others. Looking back over my eventful career, I am certain that has been the case.

The Bay Area has more than its share of eccentric people. For instance, almost daily, on my commute to and from San Francisco, I would speak to Alan Ginsberg, the famous 1960s beat poet. He seemed to be an interesting person, but once I thought I heard him laughing about a party where children were sex objects. I could have misunderstood, so I tried my best not to be judgmental. It was hard to reconstruct what was truth and what emerged from my own imagination.

On my graduation night I learned not to drink any more than a glass of wine or one half of a mixed drink at a time. But before then, I had another incredibly bad experience which finally sealed this bargain for me.

The *San Francisco Chronicle* dance critic, Albert Johnson, had invited the cast of *Taming of the Shrew* to his elaborate San Francisco Victorian home for a cast party. I was a replacement member of the cast, playing the part of Sly, the clown-like character, and had quickly learned one can't ad lib Shakespeare. On opening night, I goofed up the last line in the show, delaying the curtain call, the lights going out, and the applause. I was very upset over my lack of professionalism.

Albert Johnson was a striking, brilliant African American. He and his blond male lover would make dramatic appearances at most theatrical productions and I always looked forward to his reviews in The *San Francisco Chronicle*. Upset with myself about my muffed line, and hoping to dull my pain, I become extremely intoxicated. While on the third floor of his beautiful antiques-decorated house, I began to demonstrate some of the ballet steps from *Sleeping Beauty* we were about to perform in San Francisco. I bumped into a huge ornate grandfather clock and sent it crashing down the steep stairs to the second floor. I immediately retired from the landing to another room doing my best to act innocent and unaware of what had happened. I don't believe he even realized who the guilty culprit was, and I admit I was afraid of getting bad reviews when I entered Eternity. Due to that fear, I never revealed my horrible mistake and now am very careful with alcohol.

Looking back at my high-school years, one of my favorite memories was of my drama instructor, Mrs. Lynch. Like me, she was a little on the unconventional side. I realized it when she gave me a copy of *A Streetcar Named Desire* and later *Cat on a Hot Tin Roof.*

She thrust the first play into my hands and knowingly confided, "Tennessee Williams is the playwright to read. These plays are not for everyone, George," she added enthusiastically.

When I read the plays, I understood the "why" of it. They spoke of forbidden subjects that were not yet on people's lips. I was fascinated. She encouraged me to volunteer at the new television station, Channel 9 in San Francisco. When I followed her advice, she made me president of the school's newest club, The Non-Commercial Television Association (NCTA). Channel 9 was a member of the Association and was one of the first ongoing PBS stations in the United States. I remember that I could hardly wait to experience this responsibility. My weekly assignment was to pull cable for a new television personality and that was when I had the pleasure of meeting Julia Child, television's answer to cooking.

My job was to keep the cables away from the cameras so that they could move freely in the studios. Julia was very funny. At times she would burn an entire pan of food and then say, as she looked happily into the camera, "I'm glad you saw that. You certainly wouldn't want this to happen to you!"

I volunteered every week for almost a year, never dreaming Julia would eventually achieve major fame. After all, she didn't seem that extraordinary to me, in the culinary sense. Despite her mishaps, she always kept her sense of dignity and humor.

Time was flying and I realized I was going to graduate from high school in just a few months. Suddenly I began to feel older.

By now I was working hard at ballet, along with that part-time job pulling cables. In the final throes of graduating from high school I was also being exposed to some of my mother's most eccentric moments.

There was the day that I came home from school and found two dozen Chinese lanterns hanging from the living-room ceiling.

They were illuminated with Christmas tree lights. I loved the colors, I remember thinking, and it was then that I began to notice that the house, which my mother had always kept clean, now seemed to have an increasing amount of colorful clutter.

The lanterns lasted about a month then were transferred to the back patio where my friends and I played records and danced the swing and the bop.

The birdbath was the clincher. One day, the backyard birdbath miraculously appeared in the living room. How my mother found the strength to move something that weighed at least 80 pounds staggered my imagination. When I came home the next day, I found that the birdbath had been filled with water and transparent glass Christmas tree ornaments were floating in the water.

I knew that my mother had always been somewhat eccentric, but I thought she was just getting more creative with her eccentricity. I was only 17 at the time, so I attributed all these changes to her unusual temperament. This was further confirmed when I got on the Oakland bus to go to school one morning.

The bus was filled with high-school students who were giggling and pointing toward the back of the bus at what they said was "a crazy lady sitting back there with a large flowering tree in her lap." I joined in the laughter until I took a good look at the woman. The object of their attention was my mother.

The tree stood higher than my mother and was complete with flowery pink blossoms that clashed with her bright red hair. I made a note to talk my mother's behavior over with my Aunts Pat and Wanda. At 18, full of myself, I was primed to take that big step into the wonderful new world that awaited me out there. So I never got around to talking to my aunts.

I continued at Channel 9 in San Francisco and my two most current friends were my school dancing partners, Alice and Susan Callahan. The twin girls were good dancers and always flirting with me, telling me I had bedroom eyes. Their comments were funny and I enjoyed their company and replied with my own cheerful, obnoxious banter. They would go with me to Channel 9 and afterward we would drive over to see my sister who was living behind a giant deserted mansion in a little cottage on San Francisco's Potrero Hill. The mansion was a little creepy because the windows were shuttered and boarded up, but the cottage and the ancient garden were still intact.

My sister and her husband had moved there to have more room after the birth of their daughter, Amanda, their first child. Later, the mansion became the Shaeffer School of Design. As for Alice and Susan, they eventually inherited the controlling stock of J. C. Penney!

The three of us practiced all the latest dances, including the bop, which was brand new, the cha-cha, and a new version of the tango. Elvis Presley was a new artist and *Blue Swede Shoes, Blue Tango, Ebb Tide,* and *String of Pearls* - revived from the 1940s - were hits.

I never had a planned ride home when school dances were over, but my antics attracted a lot of attention, which I felt was unfair. But I did usually have someone offer me a ride home. And I was always looking for a ride home after ballet classes, too. One night three of my friends told me that they would give me a ride. Somewhere along the route, they decided to divert from the route and head out to the Grand Lake Theater. They kept looking at their watches, laughing the whole time and after a while, to my surprise, they grabbed me and pulled off my shiny chartreuse shirt, dark green tie, and black pants and shoes.

Three Coins in the Fountain was playing in Technicolor cinemascope and stereophonic sound and had become a huge success. At 10:20 p.m., exactly as the picture let out, my friends threw me out of the car in front of dozens of people. I was wearing nothing but my jockey shorts. This act was payback time for my usual attention-grabbing behavior. Their quirky revenge was well rewarded by my embarrassment and humiliation as the theater crowd milled around me, laughing at my partly naked body.

Graduation came just after my 18th birthday. I thought I was a man then, even if I was afraid of what the future would hold. Because there were 1,000 people in my class graduation was held on two separate nights. An empty feeling crept up inside me as I realized that the world out there was a big place. Where did I fit in?

That graduation night altered my drinking habits forever. After the ceremony, and as usual, looking for a ride home, I got in a car with a total stranger, following his invitation which went like this: "I'm going to San Francisco to a party. You wanna go?" This sounded good to me. After all, it was graduation night!

We went to the party and drank our way through the night. I must have had a dozen beers. We left the party and probably visited four different bars, a totally new experience for me. During the early morning hours, we rented a hotel room in a real dive and fell into deep drunken sleep. The next morning, we woke up, naked and still drunk. To our dismay, we couldn't find the car or remember where we had parked it. My friend of the night decided to pay a cab driver to search the area, but he came up with no results. We never found that car, and that was when I realized I needed help.

My Aunt Pat and Aunt Wanda talked my father into sending me to a therapist. My Dad apologetically explained that six months was all that he could afford, and it would have to do. Carol, my ballet coach, knew of a psychologist named Byron Nestor. She taught his children and had found him to be an admirable person.

I stepped into Nestor's Berkeley office and the first thing I realized was that his specialty was disturbed children. Nestor turned out to be a handsome, dark-haired man, about 40. He gently asked about my family life and what I thought was wrong. I remember talking quite a bit. The last thing he said to me as I walked out the door startled me. "Do you think there can be too much love?" he said.

I mulled over his statement for weeks.

I learned that Pat and Wanda seemed shaken that I was angry and unsettled about my sexual orientation, and now I was seeing their relationship in a different light. I began to question the longtime close relationship that existed between the two women. My mother's emotional response to all of this told me that she was startled because what had long been a family secret was no longer hidden.

Dr. Nestor thought I should pursue my natural feelings. Since I was not sure what they were, my confusion was complete, but I no longer dated Linda and there was no love interest in my life at that point. How could I be so worried at 18 when everything was ahead of me?

Irene moved ahead with her acting career and landed the lead role in *The Member of the Wedding*, a Carson McCullers play which had been on Broadway with Julie Harris as the lead. It was going to be presented at the Theater on the Wharf. The role was originated by Ethel Waters and later played by Mary Ellen Pollar, who then became the folk singer Odetta's manager. It ran all summer long.

The lines were so moving in this Carson McCullers play that I agreed to play Greek God Barney, a minor role, just to hear the lines night after night.

A decade later when Carson McCullers died, *Time Magazine* remarked that the death of one of America's greatest writers had almost gone unnoticed. Her funeral in Mississippi was sparsely attended despite the fact that so many critically acclaimed films had been made of her novels: *Member of the Wedding, Reflections in a Golden Eye*, and *The Heart Is a Lonely Hunter*.

Irene's innocent teenager role was matched by Mary Ann's performance as the wise old African American nanny. The audiences were deeply touched each night for months as, shrouded in fog, the show played at the Theater on the Pier. The *San Francisco Chronicle* called the play a Bay Area treasure.

I was related to Aunt Pat but not actually related to "Aunt" Wanda, yet I had grown up loving both of them. Now that I knew the truth about their relationship, I thought how sad that their 40-year partnership went unacknowledged by society and was surrounded by mystery and the fear of exposure. They had been good parents to me in addition to my real ones. Also, I began to realize that, for me, therapy was going to be a bottomless pit, but the process would probably help me for the rest of my life.

The first day I attended the San Francisco Ballet School, I withdrew into total shyness. I noticed a large sign on the bulletin board as I entered the men's dressing room.

"You, too, can be Cyd Charrise!" The sign apparently was meant to have a double meaning, but the words themselves excited me because I always loved Cyd Charrise!

The room was crowded that day. Most of the dancers were participating in loud talk which, at times, included rough, sexual jokes. Even though there were a few who stayed to themselves, the loud ones were scary for me to watch because they were so open and flamboyant in their talk. I realized later that I was afraid I might become like them, so I chose to remain separate and apart. Fighting for some kind of orientation for myself, I realized that I had been silently repeating, "I'm a guy – I'll always be a guy."

I knew that the San Francisco ballet had received a large grant from the Ford Foundation and wondered if I could become a Ford Foundation dancer. I liked the idea and decided that would be my goal.

My first year at the San Francisco Ballet found me working very hard. Lew and Harold Christiansen were world-famous task masters. The location at the corner of 18 and Geary was established in 1956, but the school had already existed back in the 1930s.

I had heard that the teachers could be sadistic in class, yet I didn't find that to be true. I had an insight. The male dancers' open acceptance of their sexuality which repelled me was also displayed by the constantly joking conversation in the dressing rooms.

Looking back now, if I had only known myself better, I probably would have made friends there.

The school produced some nationally acclaimed dancers, including Terry Orr, Michel Smuin (of the San Francisco Ballet), Thatcher Clark, David Anderson, and of course, Roderick Drew, all of whom impressed me with their dignity.

I liked both Lew and Harold Christiansen and Lew said that if I ever needed any help to let him know as he could invite me to attend rehearsals at any time. I was flattered and encouraged by this gesture. He must have recognized my talent in some way to make me that offer. Sometimes I'd see Michael Smuin being coached in "Theater Studio." This room doubled as a classroom and theater. Lew apparently considered Michael to be like a son, the one who would follow in his footsteps at the San Francisco Ballet.

In the meantime I took classes at the San Francisco Ballet School. Even as a teenager, Cynthia Gregory's remarkable talent was evident. Her future success was no surprise to me when she became the star of New York's American Ballet Theater. Michael would later not only direct his own successful ballet company, but would choreograph such films as *The Cotton Club* and *The Fantasticks* as well.

When I was asked to take class with the ballet company, Jocelyn Vollmar and Sally Bailey, two unforgettable ballerinas of the day, were also dancing beside me.

I was inspired to take private lessons from Bene Arnold, the company's stern ballet mistress. The huge sum of 50 dollars for 45 minutes of private instruction took everything I could scrape up. She was a lovely person and very encouraging.

As I left class one day, I noticed Roderick Drew, one of the most handsome men I had ever seen, leaving the building. He looked at me as though he was harboring a mysterious secret. This young man would become one of the most dazzling ballet stars in San Francisco and New York.

***

At 18 I had gotten my first apartment at Leavenworth and Hyde and was living on my own. San Francisco was all that it had seemed to be in the past but had also taken on a new decadence. Sex acts seemed to be happening everywhere – not only in the shadowy parts of every neighborhood, but even on the main streets.

Doorways and alleyways were used as outdoor bedrooms and I was more than tempted to look - or do more. It was exciting, exhilarating, but also frightening. My sweet parents had certainly not prepared me for this! Meanwhile, one night my landlady insisted that someone was pursuing her in the hallway walls and seemed to express a morbid fear, so she invited herself into my room. As her face peered out from under her blonde tresses, I didn't find her acting very convincing at all.

Around that time I was offered a well paying job as a waiter in Sally Stanford's restaurant on Pine Street, a former brothel where Sally had been madam from 1940 until getting busted in a raid led by Edmund G. Brown, Sr., then the attorney general of California. Youthful innocence, I was told, was the ticket to outrageously high tips. Later, at 72, Sally would become mayor of Sausalito across the Bay, despite – or because of – her reputation. (Dyan Cannon later portrayed her in the made-for-TV movie *Lady of the House*.) I was actually afraid to work at the restaurant on Pine, but now I realize how stupid that was. What was I protecting?

In those days, whenever I would be asked to dinner, I was the expected desert, and I got used to it. Once I was asked to have breakfast on the ground floor of my apartment building. I guess I must have been the guest of honor. As my eyes slowly adjusted to the morning light in the room, I realized the comic nature of my situation. There were about eight nude men splayed on couches, all acting as though they were the epitome of exquisite male brawn and handsomeness. Strawberries and whipped cream decorated their erections. "Come in," the host almost sang in an operatic voice. (What would Julia Child have thought?) Luckily I couldn't stay long because my rehearsals began in about an hour.

The overly available sex and the gay scene were both getting to me. I panicked. Soon I arranged to meet my then girlfriend, and together we rushed into signing a lease on a small apartment in Oakland. To this day I can't look at the corner of Leavenworth and Hyde Streets without thinking back to those crazy days.

Chapter 9
Going Modern

Despite Lew's encouragement, I left the San Francisco Ballet after only two years. The reason was partly because I grew interested in ballets that involved as much acting as dancing and partly because of my greatest fear – my homophobia. I was simultaneously drawn to the other male dancers and at the same time feared that I would soon become one of them.

Sage advice from my fellow dancer, Sharon Miller, is what encouraged me to leave. She said, "Being a star of ballets you don't really like is akin to a dead end." This sentiment made sense to me.

I loved the classic older story ballets that were momentarily out of fashion at the San Francisco Ballet. Then there was even the bigger problem that dancers barely made enough money to live on. Sharon once joked with me while I waited for the train back to Oakland. "At least you don't have to do what I do to survive," she said. I grinned, thinking about Sharon dancing topless *en pointe* to classical music in a local night club. She continued, "I don't think Lew or Harold have any idea that I do this. *Eschapé, eschapé, bourée,* shimmy. Repeat. Can you imagine that I dance *Swan Lake* topless? But, really, George, at least I'm not broke!" Both of us could appreciate that moment of truth.

Just then, Roderick Drew walked by, looking like a combination of Prince Siegfried, Hamlet, and Marlon Brando rolled into one. I wondered if I could ever be anything like him. He looked back, his eye catching mine and he smiled as though he knew something I didn't. He had done this before. Did he know? Was there some kind of non-verbal communication between gay people? Was he aware of my unresolved sexual orientation?

During my two years at the San Francisco Ballet School, I began taking another kind of dance instruction: modern dance.

I screwed up my courage and went to my first serious modern dance class all by myself. My friend Sharon said, "It's not for me, but you should go."

I worried about Sharon because the Christiansens, unlike Robert Joffrey in New York, preferred tall statuesque dancers.

The modern dance school wasn't far off Van Ness Avenue in a quaint building with rows of trees framing an orange doorway. The school director was Welland Lathrop who accompanied the class with a drum he carried while dancing. I recognized several dancers from the San Francisco Ballet. One was Dennis, a tall ballet dancer whom I admired. It would seem that he would be limited by his tremendous height. Actually, I misjudged him, because he soon appeared in smaller roles. I was envious of Dennis, but his joking friendliness made me like him.

"Modern dance isn't that different from ballet," he said. I didn't agree. Ballet made me feel like a regal prince and in modern dance the use of the upper body collapsing then lifting, and the hips moving in a rotating fashion accompanied by Welland's provocative drum beats was an earthier, more primitive experience.

One day, my eye landed on a strikingly beautiful woman who came in late for the class.

"That's Ingrid Bergman's daughter, Pia Lindstrom," Dennis pointed out. 'She's here every day."

I know I must have looked the fool with my awkward staring. She was so fascinating to me that at times I even forgot to dance. I had seen her on early television working as a reporter for NBC. She had a remarkable resemblance to her mother. She had short sand colored hair and a tall athletic body. I kept thinking of her mother, Ingrid, in her most expensive failure, Cecil B. DeMille's *Joan of Arc*.

Pia seemed to wear little make-up, yet was luminous, glowing from within, like her mother. This was the look that the make-up artists at Paramount had attempted to duplicate, but it was Ingrid's inner quality that transcended make-up.

Pia did not show up every day. She was actually a good dancer. I realized that my staring had become extremely embarrassing, but I couldn't seem to get enough of that "Ingrid" look. Welland was a good teacher, but I resented him saying that ballet dancers were like nobility.

"All they can do is dance about pussycats and birdies. We dance about gutsy human emotions," he said. I later learned that he was married to a psychoanalyst.

On weekends, I would venture with my friends down the coast to Big Sur. The years of free love and rock and roll of the 1960s had yet to begin and Haight-Ashbury dwellers were still called beatniks.

Sharon had a new boyfriend in Point Reyes. I had never been there before. At the famous Point Reyes lighthouse, I was overwhelmed by the long stretches of desolate beaches that went on as far as the eye could see. We bought boxed lunches in the little town not too far from the lighthouse. While Sharon went to see her boyfriend, I made my way down a winding trail to the white sand dunes which looked more like a scene from a desert epic created by some Hollywood set designers. I was unnerved by the lack of people and the vastness of the ocean. Hardly a rock interrupted the sand. How could this be here, so close to crowded San Francisco, yet so desolate? I ventured out to the wet surface of the jagged rocks. I heard something stir. Fear was a common emotion for me and one that I embraced as natural. The beauty around me was inspiring, but gave me an empty feeling because I felt truly alone.

I didn't know whether the man saw me or not. I couldn't move. The figure more white than white, moved below me on the beach. He was stark naked. My first thought was that he was concerned about who saw him. But then I realized that except for some darting sea birds, nothing living and moving could be seen. After a few minutes, I realized it was Roderick Drew! A true loner, he seemed unaware that I was standing only 10 feet away. Every muscle of his body was incredibly defined, but the ghastly whiteness of his skin seemed out of sync with nature. He jumped over the waves, laughing to himself, splashing when he hit the surf. I had never seen a man who had no extra weight on his body, only muscles. His straight brown hair whirled about him in the wind when he hit the cold hard beach. I found myself wondering at the discovery that men's bodies could be every bit as beautiful as women's. I thought about this intriguing new knowledge as I watched him from my hidden seat up in the dunes.

There was no doubt that I had always wanted to be Roderick Drew. He was only about 28 years old at the time. I still had a decade before I'd be that age. He suddenly stopped moving and I realized that in some strange way he knew that I was watching him. Turning around slowly, totally lacking any sort of pretense or modesty, he walked toward me. By the time he stood some 20 feet from me, I found that I was speechless with shock.

He called out, "Do you want to swim?"

I couldn't seem to find my voice, but realized that I was nodding. He gestured for me to follow him. When I disrobed and we both were in the surf up to our waists, he turned and looked me straight in the eyes. His voice was suddenly hoarse. He said, "Well, then." And that was all he said.

He pulled me toward him in a playful way. Even in the cold water he was fully aroused.

He spoke again, "This is what you wanted, isn't it?"

I never answered as we came together there in the rushing waters.

Later, Sharon came to pick me up, sighing one minute and laughing the next while she talked about the new love of her life. I listened to her, but remained silent, lost in my own thoughts. I knew I would remain quiet. I could not talk about what had just happened to me. The experience I had just taken part in was so intense that the event itself would remain sealed in my mind and for me alone.

I couldn't believe the life I was leading was actually happening to me. I had heard there was an audition to replace Larry Massey, the dance lead in a musical *The Boy Friend*. The show originated in London with an unknown star, Julie Andrews. Its success led to a New York run and it eventually played in San Francisco with a local theater group. The show was such a huge success, running for three years, that the San Francisco version made it possible for the theater group to leave its East Bay origins and move to the new San Francisco theater, The Bella Pacific. This theater was located on Pacific Avenue in the heart of San Francisco's historic Barbary Coast area. What had once been a thriving house of prostitution was now a theater.

Our dressing rooms were formerly the "working girls'" cubicles. Our stage was The Company of the Golden Hind, its namesake the legendary clipper ship. The actors secretly called us The Brass Ass.

Chapter 10
In a Forbidden City

With the great success of our performances, and the dollars pouring in, I think Larry Massey wished he had never quit the show which continued to run for three years. I was lucky. One of my partners had danced with the Royal Ballet, and my most unforgettable partner was Lois de Banzie. I had admired her aunt, the English actress Brenda de Banzie, who had appeared in Hitchcock's *The Man That Knew Too Much*. I had just seen this film and thought she was an amazing multi-layered villain to the all-American hero and heroine roles played by Doris Day and James Stewart.

Real talent ran in that family. Years after the show closed, I was walking down the street and happened to look up at a marquee. There was my old partner, Lois de Banzie's name. Teresa Wright was starring in *Mornings at Seven* by John Osborne and was featuring Lois de Banzie. Later on, I had to watch the movie *Annie* twice before I realized the woman playing Eleanor Roosevelt with tons of make-up was Lois.

One day at practice, Lois very nicely said to me in her heavy British accent, "George, it's great to perform with you, but you have to remember there are other people on the stage." Much later I realized she was talking to me about controlling my exuberance and glee at having a lead dance part in the show! All went well for those three years as I moved from 18 to 21 years of age. After each show, as I walked up Pacific Avenue, I didn't realize that this would become such an important period for free speech among entertainers in the United States.

This fact came home to me when I realized that nightly, the police were arresting the cast of *Jean Harlow Meets Billy the Kid* in San Francisco's Fisherman's Wharf area. I saw the new comedian Lenny Bruce continually arrested outside The Purple Onion where he performed for years. Phyllis Diller was less controversial, but she pushed the limits at the Hungry Eye.

As my 21st birthday approached, I began joking with the cast about how I would celebrate the occasion. They asked what I wanted to do. I flipped off a casual but risqué answer, "I want to drink champagne out of a stripper's shoe!"

I guess I said this because as you'll read later, I have a history with strippers. After the show, two cast members took me out to The Forbidden City, a world-famous club with an elaborate all-Asian stage show. All at once the music stopped. An announcement came through the microphone. "We of the Forbidden City would like to wish George Latimer a happy 21st birthday!"

I looked up, startled, and saw one of the featured dancers, a diminutive Chinese woman with an extremely pretty face, coming down the runway toward me. She was billed as the city's most exotic *erotic* midget dancer. Much to my embarrassment, she slithered toward me and stood slightly over me on the runway as she removed her clothes in time to an Asian version of *Night Train*. She ended up wearing only a g-string and pasties with wonderfully sexy high-heeled stiletto shoes. She smiled down at me as she removed her shoe while the waiter uncorked a bottle of champagne. Then I was handed the shoe which barely contained some of the champagne.

"Drink!" she purred as the audience began to sing "Happy Birthday!"

Carol O'Brien said to me at our next class, "I wish I could be with you on some of your adventures." She grinned, "Just maybe in one of your pockets!"

Carol's husband, Eddie had landed the role of the headmaster in *Tea and Sympathy*. This play was considered truly shocking then and also featured scenes of great tenderness and sympathy.

It was about a young boy, who doubting his own manhood and fearing that he may be homosexual, is protected by Laura, the heroine. Her husband is the headmaster of a small New England college and scorns the boy. In the play's climactic and daring (for its day) final scene, Laura takes sympathy to an emotionally moving extreme, offering herself to the young man. As she unbuttons her blouse, she utters, "Years from now, when you think of this, and you will - be kind." At this point, the audience is stunned by the honestly of her words. The original Laura was played by Deborah Kerr, an actress that I have always loved.

***

After a particularly athletic class, Eddie stopped by the studio. He turned to me, taking on the tone of his repressed homophobic character, and said, "Do you want to go hiking, young man? We have an extra sleeping bag."

Carol giggled but kept a serious expression on her face. She said, "Eddie, leave him alone." I got embarrassed, as usual, when it came to any hint about my sexual preferences, and blushed many shades redder than red.

We performed a request show for Mayor Alioto at the Mark Hopkins Hotel. By then, I could perform *The Boy Friend* in my sleep. The featured dance number in the show was the tango and the dance was performed with 1920s deadpan sensuousness.

A week later, Jay Pilares, who usually danced the male part, became ill. I was asked if I could fit into his costume and perform the energetic tango, and I agreed. I was a little nervous on my way to the theater and forgot my dance belt. A dance belt is part of a padded jock strap that, because of its color, blends under the tights or costume and creates a smooth appearance. I only weighed 135 pounds, but Jay was smaller than I. Not thinking ahead, I also wore my white jockey shorts.

The first notes of the *Tempo di Tango* began. My partner, a dark-haired beauty named Rosalind, held a scarlet rose clenched between her teeth. We quickly lunged toward each other; I turned and took the rose from her mouth, now holding it between my teeth. I heard a ripping sound. Despite this distraction, we both managed to stay in character. The show must go on at all costs, or so we believed. She wore black lace; I was in a black styled matador costume. Everything was great except I suddenly began to feel a breeze. I twisted my head and looked down. My white jockey shorts were protruding out of my black matador pants. The audience howled. But we just kept dancing, not breaking character. The more we danced the more the white was revealed. The audience laughed so hard some people were actually collapsing into the aisles. When at last the dance ended, we received a standing ovation. But I had learned a lesson. The director, Rachmael Ben Avram, only scolded me slightly.

Ben Avram had put the theater in the black for three years. When we closed, the cast members were tearful and our musicians kept missing notes. Crying and playing musical instruments hardly go together. Rosalind MacLennon and I have been friends ever since then. She became a newspaper drama and dance critic, first in Pittsburgh and then in the suburbs of Washington, D.C.

There was probably no place as much fun as San Francisco in the 1960s. I was happy to be there, but I suffered continually with my own worries, not so much about my career, but about how I was developing as a person. My sexuality, my desire to understand, my continuous analyzing of my actions, thoughts, and deeds filled my mind, but I kept busy and pushed ahead.

We rehearsed *Sleeping Beauty* each afternoon and I found that the Brits who ran the new ballet company were warm, yet reserved. They seemed fascinated by my outgoing personality which they realized gave me a great range of emotions. Their obvious reserve caused one of them to tell me with an apologetic smile, "We never wear our hearts on our sleeves."

During the day, I went to my new job at The Orange Tree which was located at First and Mission streets. I had heard that my boss, John Ryckman, loved artists, especially dancers.

John had a quick wit and said funny little things like "You have to be loony tunes to work here." Or, "The mentally ill make my best employees."

John had been a close friend of Pierre Salinger's family at one time, and I'll always remember his smile which seemed to say that he loved every moment of his life. His friend of many years, Stephen, had previously worked as an executive for Shasta Cola and now ran a second Orange Tree in the heart of the business district.

On my first day, I learned how to make sandwiches with cream cheese, orange juice, and ground pecans. This favorite delicacy was served on a piece of health bread.

"This will put bees on your knees!" John grinned as I mastered my first sandwich.

We were told that we could set our own hours at The Orange Tree as long as the work got done and the health counter was always manned. To my surprise, people lined up around the block to get into the store, and we served up to 400 customers a day.

John was continuously joking and would say such things as, "Lady, would you please keep your tits out of the fruit salad?" The recipient, always a regular customer, would respond with a laugh.

John's joking inspired the employees to make some of their own wisecracks. Tova and Lisa, two beauties from Denmark, responded with their own jokes and could be found viciously slicing bananas into the huge plexiglass fruit bowl, saying wickedly to their boss, "This is you, John !"

One day, Alma, our newest employee, had gone to see Bette Davis in *Of Human Bondage* at the Fine Arts Theater. She came in the front door, violently wiping her face. She looked at John and said with a poker face, "Every time I kiss you, I want to wipe my mouth!"

"Do it again, Alma!" John laughed because she had sounded just like Bette Davis.

Sandy and Ruth were jovial, too. They were in therapy, so our food preparing conversations could be deep and thoughtful.

Juana, an East Indian brought up in the Philippines, had her own jokes. One Sunday when I asked her a question, she replied with great seriousness, "George, on Sundays, we speak nothing but Spanish. Tomorrow we speak nothing but English." She looked at me slyly as I stared at her in disbelief, then she burst out laughing, "You want to learn, don't you? Well, I do too!"

At that moment, a scream came from the back room. We rushed toward the sound and found Tova standing up on a table, stamping her feet.

"A tarantula just came out of the bananas!" she cried.

We all panicked. John came in and said, "Calm down, calm down! You're all nutsy coo-coo."

"But John," screamed Tova, "It might be deadly!"

Under our watchful eyes, the spider ran across the room and disappeared into a hole in the wall and was never seen again. The next day John called an exterminator to come in and spray. I had an allergic reaction to the insecticide which caused my face to blow up just like Leo G. Carroll in the Universal Pictures movie *Tarantula!* Needles to say, I left work early that day.

Classical music always filled the air at The Orange Tree. One summer day I met June Wilkerson who was currently singing the part of Cho Cho San in *Madame Butterfly* then playing at the San Francisco Opera. She became my singing coach. Later I was blown away by her great performance as the star of Menotti's *The Medium*.

I can't say enough good things about her. June was so versatile. She was even asked to join the Gilbert and Sullivan

Company in London. They had seen June, all 350 pounds of her, playing Lady Jane in *Patience* where she sang and accompanied herself on a cello.

I had gone to see June play Katasha in *The Mikado*. While singing on a Japanese bridge built for the production, the bridge began to split apart, causing June to totter, then stagger, and finally fall with a big splash into the pond below which was part of the set. The audience gasped and stood up in horror. Seconds later, June popped up in the water, barely missing a note of her contralto solo. She received a standing ovation.

John and I had the radio on one morning at the restaurant. The news was in progress and we heard the commentator say things like, "Homosexuality is a disease just like cancer." He attributed this statement to the findings of a major psychiatrist. John looked at me and said candidly, "Well, I'd rather have this than cancer."

Several months later the American Psychiatric Association announced that homosexuality was no longer considered a mental illness.

"Thank God!" John sighed when we heard the announcement and I wondered if my therapists were wrong about me.

A few years before these events, KRON television produced a documentary called *Gays in San Francisco* which I had watched with my entire family. I kept quiet and began to wonder if I was becoming more neurotic. I wanted no part of the mental illness that seemed to be sweeping San Francisco according to the latest mental health group. But then, I pondered, since I always had girlfriends, maybe this applied to only a part of me.

Funny things were always going on at The Orange Tree. Jimmy, who started out as a busboy there, was always experimenting like a mad scientist as he poured special liquids and powders into the giant blender. He said, "This stuff is full of nutrients!" as he added brewer's yeast, wheat germ, gelatin, and some other mysterious looking powder to his fruit salad before he turned the power on high. The blender whined into action, and to our astonishment, immediately exploded, throwing everything up against the wall. We stared in fascination as the contents oozed down to the floor.

Later, after the mess was cleaned up and the restaurant was full of people, the stereo poured out the soothing strains of a Strauss Waltz, *Voices of Spring*.

Jimmy blurted out, "George, can you dance ballet to this?" I didn't answer as I still felt embarrassed about being a ballet dancer.

Sandy, another employee, laughed, "It's a little late to be humiliated now, George. You should be proud instead of ashamed." She was backed up by my co-worker, Ruth, who nodded in agreement. Another customer, overhearing, tried to make me laugh by saying, "Your behind looks like the twin peaks of the iceberg that sent the Titanic down!"

"It's all that ballet dancing," laughed Ruth, who was a great modern dancer herself.

We had heard the news on the radio that President Kennedy had been shot, but it did little to prepare John for the announcement, years later, that the Mayor of San Francisco, George Moscone and supervisor Harvey Milk had also been shot to death. John burst into tears, crying, "Let's all go home!" and he closed the restaurant for the day. John also worked in politics. He worked first with Pierre Salinger who did public relations for Kennedy and later with Harvey Milk. The entire country was shocked that the defense for Dan White who claimed a mental breakdown, worked. White claimed that certain chemicals in junk food that he ate made him psychotic. This was become known as the Twinkie defense in this famous San Francisco murder trial.

Earlier, John sued the Golden Gateway, a new apartment mega complex for not letting two men live together in their new building. And he won the case!

Three years later I left The Orange Tree with a tearful good-bye and moved to Memphis to become Assistant Artistic Director of the Memphis Ballet. While I was gone, Stephen, John's partner for many years, suddenly died of cancer. John gave up The Orange Tree and went to work at the bonds department of Crocker Anglo Bank. There he met Mary, a nice woman who had just lost her husband. They fell in love and are still happily married today, living in the Sunset District of San Francisco.

The last Halloween I worked at The Orange Tree everyone danced through most of the afternoon and into the evening. Russell, one of my fellow dancers, wanted to get into costume and go over the Golden Gate Bridge to Sausalito. He invited me to go with him and we had a plan. I covered my body with Polynesian Nature skin dye and also dyed my hair coal black. John gave me an authentic Tahitian wrap but I didn't know what to wear underneath, so I put on my dance belt.

Russell and I went to The Kettle, a popular night spot and restaurant in Sausalito and went into our act. We danced on the tables, doing a sort of Hawaiian war chant, and immediately caught customers' attention. I had an unquenchable thirst for attention, as you know by now, and soon would get my fill. Around midnight, I felt a sharp pain between my legs and I could hardly move. A stranger took me to Marin Memorial Hospital where a doctor laid me on a gurney in a busy hallway in the emergency area.

"You have boils on your testicles," he informed me as he left me uncovered, exposed to all the hospital traffic while he went off to get medicine. I wondered if it was the skin dye or the recommendation by a women friend that suggested I bathe in a hot tub with a dissolved bar of soap to keep my skin looking youthful.

At least an hour passed before he came back. Meanwhile, nurses joked and patients laughed as my nakedness. The Tahitian wrap had vanished and I lay there with brown legs, brown chest and face but a white crotch. I didn't know what to do and I found that the pain was so bad that I couldn't get up off the gurney.

"Maybe you should sue the hospital," my friend Sandy later advised. Friends finally came to pick me up and to my disbelief gave me a tattered bathrobe to wear home. I changed my bathing habits, believe me. But to this day I never use soap on my face. I learned to use a scrub or an oil wash.

Later, I not only danced in *Sleeping Beauty* in San Francisco but was hired up and down California for regional productions. How many performers can claim to be the premier dancer of Stockton, California? I had developed a very prince-like appearance by this time. I weighed in at 140 pounds and was filled with energy and exhilaration.

The female director of the Stockton Ballet became my role model. She was still performing at age 80 and was only forced to retire when she broke a bone while swinging across the stage on a rope as she played a gnome!

Joey and his wife Ingrid became my new friends. They were a beautiful and unusual couple. Ingrid was stark white, a blue-eyed blonde, demure and 24 years old. Joey was of mixed racial background, 25 years old, with coffee-colored skin and huge green eyes. Pretty Ingrid stayed with their new baby while Joey toured as a dancer whenever he could. Ingrid tolerated Joey's amazing high energy, remarkable for his age. Joey probably needed and found an outlet for all that energy with his occasional promiscuous behavior. We didn't know about AIDS then and Ingrid accepted Joey just as he was.

In a friendly sort of way, Joey and I toured together and eventually ended up at the Sheraton Motel. I discovered that Joey's sexual interests not only were for his wife, but for me, too, but only when we were on tour.

Joey said to me, "I love my wife and I am happily married, but after all I could never bring you home to meet my parents, now could I? It all would be too obvious."

I didn't think I was obvious at all. In fact, sometimes I was obviously heterosexual!

Racial tensions didn't seem to be part of Joey's life except when introducing someone other than his wife to his Berkeley parents. This is how Joey explained the situation: "My race isn't a factor, but my parents might think that the only bond possible between us would have to be sexual."

Joey's conscience sometimes worked overtime, I thought.

Pupils at Colorado Mute and Blind Institute, about 1887-1888

My grandparents were educated in an institution.

My father was a gymnast.

Ballet Bad Boy: My Life Behind Barres

Part II

Trying to Be Rudolph Nureyev

"I do not try to dance better than anyone else.
I only try to dance better than myself."

- Mikhail Baryshnikov

Chapter 11
Trying to be Rudolf Nureyev

No wonder I was obsessed with dance. It had been deeply imprinted in my psyche since my earliest years when I overheard my mother talking about going to the ballroom at Avalon on Catalina Island. I would have been a year old then. I also remember my parents patronizing the Coconut Grove Ballroom in Santa Cruz, still popular after World War II, featuring big bands like Benny Goodman and Artie Shaw. Even in the early 50s lively brassy sounds filled the cavernous space. I still remember that old building with a sense of awe. Much later, I would take my mother dancing at the Ali Baba ballroom in Oakland. The place reminded me of a huge movie set for *Ali Baba and the Forty Thieves* with Jon Hall. Too bad the ballroom got torn down.

In the early 50s, while my parents were collecting their favorite recordings, I was buying film music albums by Alfred Newman, Max Steiner, and Dimitri Tiomkin. I felt a little guilty that I enjoyed film music as much as Beethoven's Fifth. It seemed that part of me was becoming a dedicated artist and the other part was growing eccentric, even out of control.

By the time I was 18 I loved the arts more than anything else, but I also felt the constant pull of more primitive urges. My subconscious mind would lead me. The need to be touched clouded my judgment. I began taking risks and putting myself in potential danger. It was my subconscious that powered decisions I would never have made had I had more control and been more consciously aware. Frankly, I didn't care much of the time. The force of emotions that led me was as strong as a tornado and the price I paid for satisfying my feelings was guilt and shame.

Was I mentally ill? I wondered. My new therapist, Dr. Lloyd Patterson, laughed at my comical and dramatic sensibilities and descriptions. This Freudian psychoanalyst surely needed a break from all the seriousness and suffering he was constantly exposed to by his other patients.

As part of a University of California project, my high school received vocational, aptitude, and psychological testing. I was convinced I had done a great job of hiding my conflicts, answering every question with sweetness and light.

Q. Did your parents love you?

A. Yes.

Q. Are you happy?

A. Yes…

Even so, my friends the twins, Alice and Susan, and Doris Richards, and I were all singled out for further counseling.

"Is there anything you want to talk about?" they asked.

"No," I replied, all the while wondering what they saw in me that I was so unable to find in myself. It made me nervous.

Alice and Susan seemed fine to me, too.

Looking back, I remember thinking that Doris appeared to be the epitome of mental health: she was always cheerful. Her boyfriend, Louis, was the most handsome boy in school. He and Doris were both athletes, and he had a body I envied, especially after three years of taking showers with him at the gym.

A decade later, while watching *20/20* with Geraldo Rivera on ABC Television, Mr. Bruce Dain was introduced as one of the first females to make a gender change. There was something awfully familiar about him despite his beard, curly hair, and handsome looks. Imagine my surprise when Geraldo revealed to the audience that Bruce's former name was Doris Richards of Oakland, California!

Later, Doris sued the El Cerrito School Board for attempting to fire Bruce (Doris) from his position as gym teacher. She won the case! The whole thing was unreal, like science fiction unfolding from the past. I admired Doris's spunk.

By 1961, after three years of psychotherapy, my therapist encouraged me to stop thinking of therapy as a prison term and to simply come in for a weekly talk. He urged me to try to seduce the women I knew. So I did. My girlfriend at the time, Mimi, labeled me "the perpetual hard on" in honor of my overly ardent efforts.

Mimi was also a dancer and totally feminine. Several inches shorter than I, with gigantic blue eyes, she also had a boyish Shirley MacLaine cropped haircut and muscles almost as strong as any man's. A year younger than I, she exuded a worldly quality. Her ample energy filled the room. Her voice was husky in a sort of June Allyson way. We took a class together, went to the ballet, and traveled from San Francisco to Oakland on the bus for intimate and affectionate moments in my small apartment.

Mimi and I talked about the draft, and I felt I should not serve. She laughed and replied, "Maybe they will need a ballet teacher on the front lines. Maybe we could go as a couple!"

Dr. Patterson understood my worry. He praised me for making love to Mimi but frowned at my idea of serving my country. He gave me a sealed letter to present to the Berkeley draft board. I had no idea what he had written.

"This should help," he said as he handed me the letter. I only knew one other person who was registering at the draft board and we nervously went through the lines where we had to strip, were weighed, and checked for hernias, and given various tests. Right before the psychological interview, I was handed my clipboard. I couldn't believe Dr. Patterson's letter was right at the top. What he had written sent a jolt through my entire body.

"Mr. Latimer is desperately seeking parental figures of either sex in a psychopathic fashion. His registering for the Armed Forces would present a danger to himself and to his fellow servicemen," it said. I got nauseated reading it.

It was the word "psychopathic" that frightened me. Seeing such a weighty label like that applied to my problems made me feel guilty and ashamed. So I hid my fear once more behind an outgoing appearance of self-confidence.

Dr. Patterson was shocked and angry that the letter had been on display for all to see, especially me. He thought the episode was extremely damaging. He asked how the psychologist in charge could be so stupid. He explained that the word "psychopath" was used to describe my lack of conscious awareness during my pursuit of emotional satisfaction or security. Suffice it to say that by then the army didn't want George Latimer.

In 1960 I auditioned for the Elizabeth Harris Modern Dance Company and was accepted. The position gave me the largest weekly paycheck I had ever received for dancing.

Elizabeth had danced with the José Limon Modern dance Troupe in New York. In her early 40s, she was still a beautiful dancer with long honey-blonde hair that reminded me of the actress Gena Rowlands. She hired Roberta MacDougle from the San Francisco Ballet to give the company ballet classes each day. A former Balanchine dancer, Roberta was an excellent teacher who made us work hard. Every command was infused with her own brand of humor. Another bonus for me: Ruth Bossieux and Shela Xoregos were in the company and Ruth eventually became a lifelong friend. I had always admired Shela's unusual spirit and vitality, and in the future she would get the chance to choreograph one of Los Angeles' special events.

Yma Sumac was to perform at the Hollywood Bowl. I could imagine the intense atmosphere, the colored incense smoke, and the exotic veil-like costumes, accompanied by her incredibly exotic singing voice. I owned the recordings, *The Legend of the Virgin of the Sun God* and *Voice of the Itaboy*, first on 78 and then on 10-inch 33 rpms. I would have loved nothing more than to have seen the show in L.A., but money dictated everything, and my financial priorities were to eat healthy food, take ballet classes, and pay for my psychotherapy.

The Elizabeth Harris Company would be an artistic and experimental venture. Pauline Oliveros was Elizabeth's friend, and together we danced to *Concerto for See Saw, Mynah Bird, and Steaming Tea Kettles*. Modern dance class always followed ballet classes. Elizabeth, always ahead of her time, paid us to train in modern dance ballet for three hours a day. Then we had five or six hours of rehearsal. It was a total immersion for me into the music of modern greats such as Samuel Barber, Wallingford Riegger, and Igor Stravinsky. I was in the best physical shape that I'd ever been, and I promised Mimi I would audition for a new ballet company scheduled to produce Tchaikovsky's *Sleeping Beauty* in the fall. Almost every ballet company had a version of *Sleeping Beauty*.

Our modern dance concert was a big success, and what we lacked in great technique we made up for in startling creativity. In true 1960s fashion, many in our audience dressed in stylish antique clothing and capes. The wealthy mingled with the poor and socialites were enthusiastic dance fans. Piece by piece, Elizabeth applied the parts of a huge spinning sculpture to her body. The program explained that each part of the sculpture represented a life-altering situation influenced by popular psychology.

During the climax, Elizabeth, dressed in this astonishing sculpture that took up a good 30 feet of the stage, sprang wildly to a pulsing electronic score. The audience enthusiasm was unanimous as the elegantly dressed Nob Hill set blended with the Haight-Ashbury crowd. Here we were - part of the sixties *avant guarde*. We were also delighted that Channel 9, now established as a successful PBS station, filmed Elizabeth's dramatic solos.

Around that time my dear friend Ruth invited me to her wedding. It was held on a Friday afternoon at the Zen Buddhist

Monastery not too far from the theater district a place I then called home. The building seemed more like a mosque than a monastery. The exotic Arabesque curved doors and painted pale blue ceiling reminded me of a movie set from Alexander Korda's movie, *The Thief of Baghdad*. Sandy and I attended the event and I examined every detail with great interest. Ruth was so down to earth about her mixed racial heritage that I hadn't known what to expect.

Once, she had joked with me, "If there was a riot here in the Fillmore where I lived, I couldn't take sides with the blacks or the whites because I'm both. My new husband and me would probably lie down in the street and make love!"

This idea made me laugh, so I wasn't prepared for the ceremony that was about to begin. As Sandy and I stepped through the doors of the monastery, we were enveloped by a wave of incense smoke and hushed voices. Sandy, who had been there before, was familiar with the place, and her big blue eyes showed no reaction. Heart thudding with expectations, I was ready for whatever drama was to come.

Suddenly the sound of a gong splintered the air and we all moved into a long hallway - the temple. The exotic atmosphere was also tender and touching. But to this day I can't remember whether or not the ceremony was even held in English. Still, the setting and its exotic details made this the most beautiful wedding I'd even attended.

At the end of the ceremony, the gong rang out again, now loud and strong. Ruth and her new husband embraced, kissed, then walked through the large, smiling crowd. It could have been an ad for the United Nations.

Sometime later, Sandy and I were talking excitedly about the appearance of ballet stars Margot Fonteyn and Rudolf Nureyev, scheduled to appear with the Royal Ballet in San Francisco. By that time, we had been to many theatrical events together and star sightings had become almost commonplace. We had spotted Agnes Moorehead walking ahead of us on Geary Street and seen the outrageously dressed Joan Blondell pushing her way down the sidewalk, wearing giant pink Lolita glasses. One day Tallulah Bankhead became the talk of town when she ordered a sandwich at David's Restaurant, across from the Curran Theater, wearing nothing but a mink coat. At this sight, the stunned waiter nearly let the bowls of hot split pea soup slide off his tray, held high above his head.

In earlier years, the entire neighborhood would anxiously await the arrival of the original cast of the show, *West Side Story*, at the Curran Theater. Carol Lawrence and Chita Rivera would make a quiet entrance while Larry Kert and all the male dancers would roar in on their motorcycles. This macho entrance did a great deal to lend a patina of masculinity to the image of the male dancer. Now, because of the original cast and the popular movie that came out later, young male ballet students didn't have to worry as much about being jeered at or beaten up because they studied ballet.

On a misty San Francisco day, Sandy and I entered the Opera House, excited and expectant. Even though they had a two-week run, we could only afford tickets to one performance of the Royal Ballet. By now we had seen the newsreel footage of ballet star Nureyev's defection from Russia and had heard stories about his escape, which had included leaping over cars. But we still weren't prepared for our emotions and the vision of these greats. Never in my life have I seen an audience respond to any performance with such enthusiasm. I found myself crying, applauding, and then becoming overwhelmed by the great coupling of the dancers Fonteyn and Nureyev.

Margot Fonteyn's delicate portrayal of 14-year-old Juliet was matched by Nureyev's great athletic strength. This was the first time I had heard the entire ballet score played live by a great orchestra. When the curtain came down, the audience stood and cheered for a full 40 minutes. Curtain call after curtain call came and went, yet the roar never stopped. I was more inspired than ever.

Fonteyn was in her 40s, and Nureyev was 20 years younger. They were perhaps the most famous dance couple in ballet history. Nureyev's rigorous technique and approach to ballet had raised the bar for all of us. Within weeks of defecting from the Soviet Union to the West, he was a ballet superstar. Even more exciting for the ballet school students of Jean Hart in San Francisco's Sunset District, the Royal Ballet needed dancers to play extras and small roles for their month-long run in Los Angeles. The first weeks would be performed at the Shrine Auditorium and the last weeks at the Hollywood Bowl. John Hart was the artistic director of the Royal Ballet of England and his sister, Jean, made the arrangements for us to appear in the production.

I didn't care that my participation would be as a soldier, a guard, or an undignified rat. I would be on stage with Fonteyn and Nureyev! Our dance troupe of extras stayed at the Roosevelt Hotel in Hollywood. One day in the lobby I spotted Ricardo Montalban. He was waiting for Michael Somes, a former principal dancer whom I had seen so many times on film. Later, I couldn't help wondering if Ricardo Montalban had in fact welcomed Michael to *Fantasy Island* in some unusual way. (Maybe he was a try-sexual: he'd try anything.)

I had a room with two other male dancers and the six girls who traveled with us were next door. We were so enamored of and amazed by Nureyev, that Nureyev Patrols were set up to scout the lobby and hallways so we could get a glimpse of him. We were becoming stalkers.

Alone in my hotel room one night I noticed a figure standing in his underwear in the window. His suite was directly across from my room. There he was, the great Nureyev himself! I quickly went next door and told the six female dancers. We all raced to my window, gasping with excitement. He still hadn't noticed his new audience.

"My God!" exclaimed my friend Mimi. I couldn't have agreed more as we watched Nureyev pull his T-shirt over his head and drop it on the floor. Another dancer swooned as Nureyev stretched his god-like body. Now he had stripped to his European briefs. Stunned silence settled over us as we hungrily explored that fantastic physique.

Then he looked toward our window and realized he had an audience. The great dancer stood still, staring straight at us, and with an exaggerated grand gesture, he bowed. Ever so slowly, he pulled down the shade - mimicking, perhaps not intentionally - a scene from *Giselle*.

The enthusiastic response to the Royal Ballet matched that of the San Francisco performance. The first week there were seven full-length productions of *Sleeping Beauty*. I played a guard during the last act every night, standing only 20 feet from dancers Svetlana Beriosava, Merle Park, and Nadia Nerina, in turn. The best part? On Saturday nights I got to watch Fonteyn and Nureyev dance.

That night, as usual, all of the principals stood in the wings to watch Fonteyn dance the role she had made famous in the United States 20 years earlier. Somehow, this made me forget the indignity of performing as a rat during the first act. Adding to my pride - this performance would be the very first to be transmitted by satellite to Europe from the U.S.

I was disillusioned with some of the antics of an older dancer who portrayed the king. Weary of playing that part night after night, and when his back was turned toward the audience and the camera, he'd look at Fonteyn cross-eyed and make ridiculous faces. Even after all these years in show business, I was equally dismayed to hear the sheer amount of swearing by the Royal Ballet dancers. I would watch the delicate looking fairies as they danced off stage, leaping with winged grace, and hear what came out of their mouths. Their picturesque swearing would have made Lenny Bruce blush. Their lightness of movements coupled with their British accents and those four-letter words seemed incongruous - even out of sync - with the beauty and spirit of the dance.

The dressing rooms were in the basement of the huge theater. As I showered after one of the performances, it occurred to me that I was not used to being totally naked in front of so many people. I had never seen my own father naked. That aspect of him was a mystery. My mother and sister had never hidden their bodies from me. While I was growing up, I frequently saw them naked. Did this make me a little warped? Certainly not. According to anthropologist Dr. Margaret Mead, had I had been brought up in Samoa, nakedness would be perfectly normal.

I had barely worked my fear out about my nakedness when 15 or so of the male *corps de ballet* entered the shower room. The scene was right out of ancient Greece, with these natural, yet sculpted bodies. They laughed at my gawking look of surprise as I took extra time to shampoo, washing my hair over and over until my intentions became obvious. I was enjoying their perfect nudity too much to leave. A nice, dark-haired fellow finally came over and asked my name and told me he was Petrus Bosman (who years later would dance many leading roles). By the time I came out of the shower some time later, my vision of athletes had changed forever. Petrus had remained totally objective, telling me what time I should arrive for that evening's performance.

After that, I bumped into Leslie Edwards, who played many character roles with the ballet. He said, "Why don't you come with us to the Hollywood Bowl? We're performing a new version of *Rite of Spring* and I'm sure I could find something for you to do."

We shared a taxi and he was smiling at me. "I doubt that Princess Aurora's fate in *Sleeping Beauty* was all that dreadful," he said. "What was so terrible about being pricked and then falling asleep?"

I got his drift.

"Alexander Grant loves blond young dancers," he continued. "Come back next week. I promise you won't regret it."

I found the offer difficult to resist, I so wanted to be around the Royal Ballet, but his veiled suggestions frightened me. Not that I was an innocent, but I couldn't bring myself to participate any further.

Obsessed with the world of ballet for so long, now I was even more taken with trying to become Rudolf Nureyev. His dancing feet, sweet smile, and love of the art merged so well with his dramatic flair. I, George Latimer, wanted to appropriate all of the elements I saw in him.

Around this time my parents appeared to be quite self-involved, although giving. Reflecting my psychiatrist's statement to the draft board – that I seemed to seek out parental figures – I became increasingly friendly with a middle-aged couple named Fay and Percy Nussbaum who ran the Navy Surplus Store at First and Mission in San Francisco. They had no children of their own and I fit right into their lives.

Fay was earthy and pretty, and Percy was a gentle Ernest Borgnine type, boisterous, but somehow sensitive. Their three-story San Francisco Victorian was startling to behold. The first time I walked through the front door, I was greeted with beautiful turn-of-the century antique furniture covered with plastic. The contrast between the delicate furniture and the garish plastic symbolized the warm eccentricity of opposites in their home.

Fay had warned me about the dogs. As I climbed up the gated stairwell, I heard the pitter patter of at least 52 feet. Then the doors opened to the second floor and at least a dozen Mexican Chihuahuas growled, barked, and greeted us with a sea of wet kisses.

"How are you, darlings?" Fay asked them. Percy smiled and knelt down as the dogs leaped around him looking back suspiciously at me. Eventually, I made friends with the canine crowd.

I couldn't understand why there was so much prejudice toward Jewish people. Fay and Percy had opened their home to me so many times. They also offered solace during my busy, confused life. They kept me in a supply of bright turtleneck sweaters and warm jackets, pretending to charge these items to me at their store but actually, they were giving me everything. When I left San Francisco, I wrote to them until the reply letters stopped coming. I still remember spending the night at their house, eating dinner, watching early, primitive television, and sleeping with at least six Chihuahuas pressed close against me. I wasn't sure where I fit into the scheme of things with them, but, to me, this was another home.

My father had given me enough money to go to Los Angeles, check out the local opportunities, and study ballet. The city was so different from San Francisco. I wore a clean white shirt as I explored the downtown area and soon discovered my shirt was turning gray from the city smog and whatever else was in the air. Never had I felt heat like that before.

One afternoon I met Carol O'Brien's husband Richard for lunch. I must have seemed nervous. Throughout the lunch we managed to have a good time, though. Turned out his real name was Edward, but the actors' union, then called AGVA, felt that his own name was too similar to Edmund O'Brien, and he was already an established movie star. So Eddie changed his name to Richard O'Brien. Eddie, alias Richard, drove me to Eugene Loring's Dance Studio on Santa Monica Boulevard. That was the last time I saw him other than on the street. During his career Richard O'Brien would appear in more than 500 movies and television dramas.

I nervously took my first class from Eugene Loring. He was cold but honest and a good teacher. I was impressed. A dancer standing near me during practice told me that Loring had choreographed many movies starring famous actresses like Audrey Hepburn in *Funny Face*, Cyd Charisse in *Silk Stockings*, and the French dancer Leslie Caron.

"Mary Tyler Moore is in the practice room right now," the dancer continued.

Our conversation was interrupted by Loring who asked me, "Have you studied long?"

"Three years," I answered.

"Well, you need to take more classes and to work with more concentration if you want to make it," he replied evenly.

This good advice was objectively delivered. I was so used to being babied. Criticism had always been delivered to me swathed in tact, so I was a little startled by his abruptness. I returned to the Bay Area a few weeks later fueled with more determination than ever. I knew I must take Eugene Loring seriously. (His *Billy the Kid* ballet with music by Aaron Copland was dance legend.)

Carol O'Brien invited me to attend a wonderful dinner and it demanded formal attire. The party was hosted by The Countess with Blue Hair, and was held at San Francisco's elegant Sheraton Palace Hotel. The dining room seemed made of glass. The huge ancient chandeliers contrasted well with graceful, draping ferns and dark green cushions.

Carol and Raoul Bettancourt had suggested I come along because some of the world's dance greats would be present, and this would be a great opportunity for me. But who was The Countess with Blue Hair? I was too shy to ask. She appeared to be a handsome older woman with beautiful demeanor and graceful carriage. She barely spoke louder than a whisper and nodded politely to all. Present were Anton Dolin whom I knew from his book, "Partnering Alicia Markova." Also present were John Gilpin, made famous for his interpretation of the Bluebird in *Sleeping Beauty*, and Raoul Pause, director of the early Oakland Ballet.

Then there was the young Ronn Guidi who charmed everyone with his sense of humour. Later, when Raoul died, Ronn became the director of the Oakland Ballet. James Starbuck from the Ballets Russe de Monte Carlo was a commanding presence that night. He would later become choreographer of the Bell Telephone Hour.

We dined on melon stuffed with crabmeat, green salad, and chocolate mousse served in an almond-studded cake shell. The champagne gave me a walking on clouds feeling and afterwards I could barely make it up the steps to my humble apartment. To this day, I wonder who The Countess with the Blue Hair was. According to dance historian Michael Smith, she was probably Catherine the Baroness D'Erlanger, a friend of Igor Stravinsky and patron of the Ballets Russe de Monte Carlo.

Chapter 12
My Age of Aquarius

The next four years were of vital significance to me. Many friends remained close, but as I zeroed in on my career and they devoted time to theirs, our visits became less frequent, especially since I didn't drive. Paul, a young, good-looking Italian dancer would give me transportation for a few dollars' worth of gas. Yona, his girlfriend, would take over the wheel when Paul got tired of the time-consuming traffic jams.

Paul and I performed yet another *Sleeping Beauty* with a regional ballet, while Lynette, Jake, and all of my dancer friends kept rehearsing for the big production in San Francisco. I somehow found time to attend group therapy with Dr. Joel Fort. The truth is that I was so grateful for the years I had spent with Dr. Patterson but could no longer afford the 50 dollars an hour. Money was tight. (I learned later that Dr. Fort was called to testify for the prosecution during the Patti Hearst trial.)

I guess my enthusiasm for psychology and therapy gave me certain privileges. One day our session was unexpectedly cancelled and the therapist downstairs, Gene Sagan, who collaborated on the popular book of the times, *Games People Play: The Psychology of Human Relationships,* by Dr. Eric Berne, let us join his group temporarily. He was affiliated with Stanford University and was a legalized expert on LSD, the latest hallucinatory drug, that 60s craze. When I went into the room, people were "sharing the experience," and there was more touchy-feely action in a group than I had ever experienced. They explained that they were having contact highs. This had increased their awareness about life and put them in touch with the glue that held the universe together. Needless to say, I was glad when Dr. Fort came back. I was the only group member at that time that attended both the wives' group and the separate husbands' group. I was sworn to secrecy. The only thing I did learn was that two people can see the same situation in totally different ways - a revelatory insight.

It was becoming expensive to live in San Francisco, so I moved to the more affordable Berkeley, getting an apartment at the corner of Ashby and Adeline. While walking home one night, I met Greg and Jane, my new neighbors. Greg was tall, handsome, of Armenian extract, super intellectual, with piercing, blue eyes that shined from under a mop of curly brown hair. Magnetic Jane was as rangy as Greg, unusual for a girl of the 60s. She had short black hair and a Greek statue-like body. We talked and both Greg and Jane seemed oddly curious about the life of a ballet dancer. I could not figure out their relationship. They lived in my building with Archie who was as handsome as Greg but shorter, more muscular. I found their openness comforting.

Country Joe McDonald whose band Country Joe and the Fish would later be a big hit at the huge music festival and peace gathering in Woodstock in the mid-60s, lived in the next building. My neighbors played Country Joe's latest songs on the stereo.

One night as I caught my cable car ride and as the tram started up the steep hill, I noticed a tall girl in a white pleated dress and high heels running up behind us. She began to push at the back of it, shouting at the top of her lungs, "Let's give the boys a hand!" Everyone began to laugh as she made an effort to push the cable car up Powell Street. I realized with a start that the woman was Jane! Charmed by her outrageous behavior, I asked her if she would like company returning home to Berkeley. She said, "Hello! Hello! Don't worry about me. I'm okay!" I tried to persuade her to come back to Berkeley with me. She adamantly refused and before I could get her to jump on the car, it left her far behind.

Greg and Archie were beside themselves with worry when Jane didn't come home for a week. Apparently someone had put

LSD into her coke at a party. Afterwards, Jane felt lucky to still have a handle on sanity.

I missed living in San Francisco, but being in Berkeley meant I could still get coaching from my close friend, Carol O'Brien. I could go to two groups a week at the Northern California Psychiatric Association with Dr. Fort. I also discovered Frank Shawl, Victor Anderson, and a creature of heavenly otherworldly qualities, Louisa Pierce. They all taught ballet and modern dance and Louisa had been with the Martha Graham Company.

My dancer friends Paul and Joey appeared with me – nearly nude – in Stravinsky's *Rite of Spring*, shocking not only the audience but ourselves. Ruth, who sometimes took three classes a day, caught us between performances and asked with solicitous interest, "Weren't you cold?" I remember that the director of the ballet got quite angry because we hadn't shaved our armpits. And, snickering, Paul said, "That made it more realistic!"

I was drawn more and more to both Greg and Jane. Somehow, the fact that Jane or Archie were always with Greg made the attraction stronger. I was feeling more accepted by them. I was the token artist in a group of intellectuals.

One time, Jane, Greg and I drove down the coast toward Big Sur. Jane almost swerved off the highway when she saw a small road that led off behind the huge arched bridge right before Big Sur. This magnificent bridge was used a lot in films and commercials. A picture of the bridge was also part of the opening credits of *The Sandpiper* starring Elizabeth Taylor, Richard Burton, and Eva Marie Saint featuring that haunting melody, *The Shadow of your Smile*. It affected the audience's mood and could even leave them feeling love struck.

Henry Miller lived in Big Sur, where he wrote several of his most famous books, including *Tropic of Capricorn* and *Tropic of Cancer*. Greg and Jane were Miller fans.

In one of our chats Greg told us he had discovered a book about Reverend Otis Gibson, Carole O'Brien's grandfather. He had frequently traveled to China, writing to the White House about the local political scene. Greg, who was majoring in History at the University of California, read us Reverend Gibson's diary. It included letters addressed to the president and many details about 19th-century China.

Jane parked the car under the bridge and we built a campfire in a nearby cave, near the crashing waves that nearly drowned out our voices. We heard the seagulls on the main beach echoing against the cliffs. As the sun began to set, Jane took off her clothes and ran down to the beach with a passionate energy. She looked like a Greek goddess.

As the fire faded to embers, we laid out our sleeping bags and blankets. That's when studious Greg left his intellect behind and moved closer to me than I would have expected. "You are so patrician," he whispered.

I didn't know what he meant, but as he pressed against me, I felt his heart beating faster than I had ever felt anyone's heart beat. There was another side of Greg that was not intellectual at all.

We seemed to share the awareness that this was a time we could never return to. Our bodies were probably at their peak of perfection and our heightened senses only increased because every taut muscle would also never again be this strong. Every touch created an increase in that electro-magnetic experience that bodies have as they dissolve into hot liquid. Our only rival was the pounding surf.

The next day Jane didn't seem to notice that tears came into Greg's masculine eyes each time he spoke to me. I could not believe someone felt that way about me. I intuitively knew that Jane was aware of what had transpired the night before. My reasoning was that I loved both Greg and Jane equally. Jane cared a lot about me, but she was in love with Greg. Where did Archie fit into this picture? I was never sure.

Over the next few years, I became more aware that I was experiencing a host of uncontrollable emotions. Reason had nothing to do with the way I thought. These wayward emotions were a clue to me that Greg was winning out and my intellect was being left behind.

Two months later, Jane, Greg, Archie, and our newest roommate, David, moved to San Francisco. The constant commuting would have killed anyone else, but my ambition to become a dancer kept me traveling from one side of the Bay to another. The four of us rented what used to be the Swedish Consulate at 16th and Castro Streets. The Castro area in San Francisco's gay district didn't yet flourish as it does today. We moved there quite by accident, innocent of what was around us.

Since neither Greg nor Jane had been to a ballet I decided to take them to a performance of the San Francisco Ballet's *Fantasma*, a new ballet starring Robert Gladstein, with whom I had danced in class. That night I wondered if I had made a mistake by not making the San Francisco Ballet my center of activity. I liked the Prokofiev score and the dancing, but, the *San Francisco Chronicle* reviewer felt the costumes had ruined it. According to him, the ballet looked like "sale day in a crêpe paper factory."

Jocelyn Vollmar with Roderick Drew as her partner was incredibly sophisticated in *Raymonda Variations*. Drew was almost as handsome in tights as he was in street clothes. The program rounded out with *Jest of Cards* with a young Terry Orr flying across the stage, hanging onto a rope attached from above, choreographed to the music of Stravinsky. The scene was a daring athletic performance and it brought the audience to their feet. Although Jane and Greg totally picked the performance apart afterwards, they

managed to appreciate some of its aesthetic. The choreography of
Len Christiansen was at its best.

Even though I was exhausted from our *Sleeping Beauty*
rehearsals I managed to keep my part-time Orange Tree job. This
daily routine gave me stability.

My unusual relationship with Jane and Greg continued.
When we went to see *Jules and Jim,* Truffaut's great film, we joked
that we understood all too well the meaning of the film. At the end,
when the *ménage à trois* drives their car off a bridge, the audience
gets the impression that these three would rather be dead than live
apart. But was that truly the meaning behind the ending?

I seem to find a rapport with almost everyone I meet. Once I
had a chance encounter with a religious man with whom I spoke
every morning when he came into the Orange Tree. I asked him what
religion he represented. He answered, "I am a self-ordained
minister." A few weeks later, after much casual banter with him, he
said, "I am quite tired. I flew to India last night."

"How did you find that kind of plane schedule?" I asked,
thinking that he was probably kidding me.

"I didn't take an airplane," he answered, "I had an out-of-
body experience."
I tried not to smile. Since then, I have learned much more about this
kind of experience and found that Eastern religions, including
Buddhism, claim there are people who can be taught to experience
many such out-of-body experiences. Many books have been written
about this kind of experience and are now being taken seriously in
the Western world.

Near-death experiences are based on the separation of the
body from its many electro magnetic fields of "skin," as they are
sometimes called. Perhaps the Western mind is simply too logical or
stubbornly indoctrinated to open up to such possible experiences,

although in addition to the public, there are scientists and theologians investigating this kind of phenomenon.

Many astrologers have predicted that during this century, mysticism and science will join together, enhancing our understanding of life on Earth. This is occurring during what is called The Age of Aquarius, a 1500-year period based on the slow turning of the North Pole and it will bring in a new direction for evolution on Earth. I see all of this new interest as a way to awaken the Western mind to centuries of ancient Eastern wisdom.

When the astronaut Edgar Mitchell returned from space he wrote a book called *Way of the Explorer*. In it, he revealed his own new perceptions and insights acquired while moving through space and time, insights that changed his ideas about life.

A few weeks after I had revealed to my intriguing minister friend that I was living in a house with seven bedrooms and three fireplaces but a minimal amount of furniture, he said, "My friend, Dr. Lawson, was on an island off Nagasaki after the city was hit by our second A Bomb blast. She saved many lives, endangering her own. She was a true heroine and one of my best friends. I told her about you and she wants to ask a favor. She has a fortune in beautiful furniture from the China mainland, but as a result of helping the people in Nagasaki, she now has leukemia and is afraid her furniture will ruin in storage. She thinks you could use the furniture."

Not believing a word he said, I replied carelessly, "I certainly could. It sounds wonderful."

He replied, "Are you going to be home Saturday about one?"

"Yes," I replied.

"The Christian Brothers will deliver the furniture around then," he informed me.

"You mean the ones who make the wine?" I quipped, half joking.

He abruptly answered with a curt "Yes."

I still didn't believe him.

I usually got home from ballet about one in the afternoon, but on Saturday I didn't hurry any more than usual. In fact, I had almost forgotten about our conversation.

Berkeley was an incredible place to live in the 60s. One day I witnessed a huge traffic jam. A large crowd of demonstrators had gathered, all of them singing *Blowing in the Wind* at the top of their lungs. Joan Baez was scheduled to lead a peace demonstration followed by a short speech, and her song, *We Shall Overcome*, was being played everywhere. Later that day my neighbor Country Joe sang some of his popular anti-war songs. He wowed the crowd with "Be the first one on your block to come home in a box."

As I walked up 16th Street I noticed a small crowd gathering in front of my house. About 16 men in long brown robes were carrying the most beautiful and elegant furniture I had ever seen right into my house. My life was full of impossibilities, I grinned happily to myself, as I added that amusing mental note, and maybe it was all due to my highly vibrating magnetic field.

I was also grateful to Dr. Lawson. I never met her or spoke to her and I probably could have kept this wonderful treasure indefinitely. Most of the furniture was made from cherry and teak wood with huge carved dragons and bunches of grapes around flying doves. So I say now, "Thank you, Dr. Lawson, wherever you are!"

Finally the new performance of Tchaikovsky's masterpiece, *Sleeping Beauty* opened at the Norse Auditorium (now long gone). While we were no competition for the San Francisco Ballet we all dreamed of a future Royal Ballet-style company for San Francisco.

Jake played the Prince, Lynette was Aurora, and all was going as expected. The Flouristan Trio, part of the ballet, performed well, and we all performed well. In my solo, I usually managed to do a safe two or three *pirouettes*, but I actually performed four complete turns. The audience burst into long, loud applause. In the wings, I toweled off my sweaty face.

"You must have done something really special," Mimi said, adding, "Congratulations."

Lynette smiled at me and nodded her approval, too. As my head was growing larger by the minute from such praise, Jean Hart came in the stage door and cried, "Margo Fonteyn had stepped into the theater!" The applause hadn't been for me after all.

The show was a success and a small tour was launched. Later, Jean told us that The Royal Ballet with its great stars, among them Rudolf Nureyev and Margo Fonteyn, were going to Los Angeles, to the Hollywood Bowl, for another three-week run after their San Francisco performance. I was very excited. Maybe I could go for a second time.

That night, a while after I returned to my large house with the beautiful furniture, strangers knocked at my door. Jane, Archie and I found ourselves being questioned extensively by FBI agents. I knew Greg had attended the Monterey Language School, but I was now finding out that he had a secret profession. We had lived together for almost three years and I was startled to learn that this secret profession involved working as an interpreter of radio messages from mainland China. It seems that he needed to renew his security clearance and the FBI was investigating him.

Concerned that we might say too much or too little we were nervous about answering questions. Greg's clearance was renewed, and I'm still amazed that he pulled that off while living with the four of us.

But things were about to change. Greg came home one day and announced that he was moving to New York. Jane was going to Africa to join the Peace Corps. They were both very excited.

My pleading with Greg not to leave had no effect and I began to see aspects of his personality that had escaped me before. He was an Army brat. His family was constantly on the move and impermanence was simply a way of life. The family eventually settled in conservative Glendale where he had been living on weekends when I first met him.

I felt deserted by Greg's announcement, but his leaving was more than that for me. I was devastated. Greg sarcastically suggested that I go to work in an erotic show that had recently opened in San Francisco. I was in the bathtub when he came in to take one last look at me.

He said, "I'll write to you." But, from the way he looked at me as I lay there in the water, I could tell he was conflicted.

I became deeply depressed. My dancing began to fall off. I could barely get through a class. I would lie in bed counting the cracks in the ceiling.

It was another 15 years before I saw Greg again, but in the intervening years I learned he had married.

My roommates, Jim and Archie, tried to cheer me up by carrying me blindfolded on their shoulders to the Peppermint Lounge. They then dragged me down the street to watch Carol Doda dance topless at the Condor in North Beach. Nothing worked, but I eventually got back to ballet classes. This time, I returned to The San Francisco Ballet and studied modern dance with Frank Shand and Victor Anderson in Berkeley. Carol resumed as my coach, and also tried to cheer me up. She was truly alarmed by my state of mind.

Chapter 13
Letting Go

As depression began to take over my life all my friends became concerned about my downward slide. I even went back to my psychiatrist, Dr. Patterson, and talked about being committed.

"Not a good idea," he said. "I can easily do that for you, but you might not be able to get out, especially if they give you insulin shock therapy or electric shock therapy. Those things have permanent, negative results sometimes. Go home, pull down the shades, and take two aspirin. You'll survive this."

The next week my father died. He had perfect health as a youth. He had studied gymnastics and was very athletic. Doctors knew little about heart disease at that time and, out of the blue, my father had fallen through a swinging door at the Wells Fargo Bank, grasping his chest as he experienced a major heart attack. No one found him for hours.

In those days there was no heart bypass surgery and there were no anti-cholesterol drugs. My mother called and informed me of my father's death. She told me in her matter-of-fact way that she was going to clean the house for the arrival of guests, but she sounded very odd. I rushed to my parents' home and found her cleaning and bravely holding back her tears. I was amazed at her ability to survive the greatest loss of her life. I was barely surviving at all.

Carol O'Brien, worrying about my inability to cope, decided to arrange an appointment with Gavin Arthur, the Bay Area's best known astrologer; the grandson of Chester Allen Arthur, a lesser known President of the United States. She told me he used astrology as part of his treatment. "Gavin will amaze you and be most helpful," she said.

At 80, Arthur had been published twice and impressed several University of California professors who had gone to see him in order to expose him as a fraud. After their visit they changed their minds. I knew this for a fact because these professors were Carol's friends.

I was willing to try anything to escape my pain. Because of my faith in Carol, I believed he might be able to help, encourage, and perhaps reveal something that would touch my budding interest in astrology. I felt anticipation, almost excitement, about my upcoming visit. Maybe astrology could help me with a new way of dealing with my life.

As I set out on my journey of possible enlightenment, she instructed, "Simply give him your place of birth, date, and time. Don't tell him anything, and you will be amazed."

Arthur, a feeble but still brilliant man, answered the door. The first thing I noticed was a huge photograph of Arthur and Oscar Wilde prominently displayed in his apartment. He noticed my interest and said, "We were great friends, but I only saw him when he came to the United States." He continued with a serious smile, "I'm sorry, I haven't been feeling well. You see, Anton LaVey, head of the Satanic Church, keeps sending me nightmares."

Unable to find a suitable comment following that strange revelation, I followed him into his study. He looked over my personal chart and commented, "Your chart is so like mine. Your Taurus sun is on the classic part of Friendship. You never meet a stranger. What do you plan as a career?"

I still continued to dream of becoming the next Nureyev, encouraged that Nureyev was only a year older than I and had begun dancing at 16 as I had, so I said, "I am a dancer."

"Oh," he replied, "You'll never be a great dancer."

My heart sank. As he discussed my chart, he seemed to know me too well, even though we were total strangers. He surprised me by saying, "You're soon going to be leaving this place (San Francisco.) You're like a pioneer."

Gavin pointed to my Aries moon conjunct Jupiter in my ninth house signifying much travel and the promise to live far from home while developing new ideas about the meaning of life. "Your greatest gift is creativity," he said, pointing to all the fiery Aries energy around the Moon and Jupiter. "You will have fame as a true original. Your career will be financed as if out of the blue."

I listened to every word with keen interest. When he had finished with my astrology chart, I found that I was impressed with this man. He knew me better than I knew myself and he had given me hope for the future. As he led me to the door, he added, "Oh, by the way, you had better remove your valuables from your apartment. Your house will be broken into this weekend. I hope to see you again. Your chart is so much like mine!"

That fact bothered me. Gavin Arthur had been married five times and nothing in his life seemed permanent.

To my amazement, one afternoon my apartment was broken into. Someone had trashed the place and many items were missing. Luckily I had removed my valuables as Gavin had suggested. I only saw him once more, while walking in Dolores Park. He gave me a strange, penetrating look that I'll never forget.

In retrospect, I believe what helped me get through my last year in San Francisco was my sense of irony. My mother startled me one day by knocking on my apartment door. When I opened the door and saw her there, I realized this person I had known all my life as all powerful now seemed tiny, fragile, and a little helpless. More than a year had passed since my father's death, and she realized that the time had come for her to stop being a recluse. She needed my help and from then on, every Friday night, with a few exceptions, I became her escort to the Ali Baba Ballroom in Oakland. My mother would dance from eight to 11 in the evening and she began to meet many prospective beaus. My mother was never aware what a physical challenge it was for me to become a dancer.

Raoul Pause, the director of the Oakland Ballet at the time, had danced with the Ballets Russe and the Paris Opera Ballet and brought from those years an emotional and dramatic approach to his company rather than the cooler technical style of the day.

It was here that I met Ronn Guidi, young and handsome, and usually the principal dancer in the productions. He appeared to leap and bound about the stage as if on springs. Later, as director of the Oakland Ballet, he brought many greats of the dance world to Oakland and received much international acclaim. Also in the company were Sven Norlander and Marc Wilde. Marc was known for his original choreography in the 60s and 70s.

The Oakland Ballet became known for reviving many of the ballets by Bronislava Nijinska. There were times in the 60s when we danced at the Woodminster Amphitheater, a difficult thing because it had no wooden floor. Somehow we survived without injury, but today dancers would never be allowed to take that risk.

After a modern dance concert at the University of California, Berkeley, I met with a well-known African American poet. He explained that he had attended every dance event at Berkeley, and he liked the fact that some of our performances had political content, but I admit that some of this political content went over my head. I was flattered by his attention and later was asked if I had any extra time to attend a gathering of African American artists, since he felt my experience as a performer would add to the affair. At that point, unless I was performing, most of my Friday nights would usually be spent with my mother. I was always looking for a new experience, so I quickly replied in the affirmative.

On a Saturday night, I attended a meeting in a large flat near Ashby on the Berkeley/Oakland border. There were tables stacked with books and plays by LeRoi Jones, Stokeley Carmichael, and other authors. There were many books and some pamphlets written by Huey Newton, considered a hero by many of his African American contemporaries.

I was in the midst of a suppressed group of artists and poets, and I became their supporter. During the meeting, I was asked by my new friend to tend bar. I knew I was not a good bartender, but many Saturday nights I volunteered anyway since my social calendar was empty.

A month or two later, to my surprise, I found myself learning to tend bar for a well-attended cultural meeting. One night, I was working, filling orders right and left, when suddenly a group of reporters rushed into the room taking pictures of everything and singling out my friend the poet. One reporter from *The Oakland Tribune* came over to the bar where I stood.

"How does it feel to be the only white person in the room and tending bar for the Oakland Black Panthers?"

Since I didn't understand the whole political picture at that time or the significance of his question, I smiled widely and replied cheerfully, "Fine. You say these are the Oakland Black Panthers?"

Later Trevor Edge, the poet who I had thought was truly one of my admirers, said, "If necessary I would kill your whole family if I thought they stood in the way of the progress of my People!" Well, so much for my revolutionary days. I never went back to tend bar for these cultural artists and poets again.

Beverly McComb who directed the Merce Cunningham-inspired Chance Dance Company took Carol O'Brien's class at the University of California at Berkeley (U.C.B,). She had arranged for Carol to teach there and I felt lucky to be her assistant. Back in 1966 my partner was Diana Kaftan, and we are still friends today.

One day while I was working as assistant teacher at U.C.B., Beverly McComb gave me a letter. "I know this probably won't interest you, but they need someone to be assistant director of the Memphis Ballet."

I was looking for a new adventure, and so I called the ballet's director, Nelle Fisher.

"It doesn't pay much, but it is a chance to perform a lot," she said. There are choreographic and teaching opportunities as well, and we tour the East Coast."

I got out a map. Memphis was half way to New York. Looking at the map again, it appeared to be even closer than that. I had heard that the Mississippi River bordered the western end of Tennessee, something I remembered from all the Tom Sawyer films. As a kid I dreamed about Huckleberry Finn and Tom Sawyer rafting and swimming along the Mississippi River. The possibility of being able to do the same thing fascinated me.

I was auditioned in San Francisco. They liked me and so signed me to a one-year contract. Then I went out and bought two swimsuits not realizing how dangerous it was to swim in the Mississippi River.

I had to say good-bye to the San Francisco Opera House, and I wanted to go to a performance of the Royal Ballet that included new works by Frederick Ashton and Kenneth MacMillan, but the ballet had been sold out so I found myself standing in the back of the theater, seeing a young Anthony Dowell perform. Who would guess that this dancer would become future director of The Royal Ballet?

Lew Christiansen, one of my teachers, and James Starbuck, whom I had met a year before at The Oakland Ballet, were standing near me.

I was in awe of Mr. Starbuck because he was the choreographer for NBC television's *Bell Telephone Hour*. He and Lew were critiquing the dancers loudly with comments such as, "he's sickling his foot." Lew mentioned Ashton's new work *Monotones*, saying, "It's the same old snake dance."

They were important figures in dance. Who was I to disagree? Anthony Dowell's dancing still inspires the audience when viewed on videotape and *Monotones* has since become a classic.

I was leaving! I was going to Memphis, Tennessee, halfway to New York.

Carol's actor-husband, Eddie, as I knew him, gave me about 10 neckties and drove me away from a smiling, moist-eyed Carol after we had said a long farewell. Later, my mother drove me to the airport and I felt a little like I was deserting her, but, after all, she was making a new life for herself, too. She looked tiny and helpless, waving to me from the window of the departure lounge as the plane took off. I thought about that image quite a bit during the long flight to Memphis. My plane took me forward two hours in time and when I landed there, it was four in the afternoon.

Can anyone look so innocent? In a play at Jack London Square Theatre. (Photo by Fred Kellogg)

Pas de deux was my favorite class at UC Berkeley.

Latimer's mentor Carol O'brien and husband Richard.

Ballet Bad Boy: My Life Behind Barres

Part III
Cornbread in My Tutu
(1967 – 1989)

Chapter 14
Cornbread in My Tutu

The flight to Memphis in 1967 was the longest one I had ever taken, and it gave me plenty of time to think. My two bathing suits were packed and I had thoughts of women in antebellum dresses meeting me at the plane. I carried a cordial letter from Mrs. Arnold Klyce inside my briefcase, inviting me to stay in her large home in midtown Memphis for an indefinite period. She was president of the Memphis Ballet Board and apologized that my salary wasn't lucrative. She didn't know how pleased I was to have a contract for a whole year. Also, I had a letter from Nelle Fisher, artistic director of the ballet. All I knew about her was that she had her own company in New York called The Littlest Circus. Even though Nelle was the director of the Memphis Ballet, she continued to have a touring company out of Memphis. These dancers were a mixture of local talent and guests from different cities around the country.

I had pictured Nelle standing in front of the Tara set of *Gone with the Wind* as dancers leapt down the long, white stairway accompanied by a chorus of slaves singing *Wait Til the Sun Shines, Nellie!*

Nelle had an elaborate dance and theater background and had been the understudy to one of my idols, Gwen Verdon, who starred in many Broadway musicals, including *Can Can, Chicago*, and *Damn Yankees*!

Instead of meeting the plane in some sort of old South apparel, she wore a white mini skirt, go-go boots, and a pink blouse. I was startled, but she made me feel at ease immediately. I was elated when I learned that I would be the assistant to a true professional whose background was associated with great American artists.

Many ballet supporters in Memphis didn't appreciate Nelle. True, she had not danced for the Bolshoi, but worked on the original *On the Town* for Jerome Robbins and Leonard Bernstein and was close friends with Cole Porter. She had danced with the original 1931 Martha Graham Company and then for Agnes de Mille in the original *Oklahoma!* for much of its record-breaking run on Broadway. I suddenly realized I knew her face. She and Bambi Lynn were the lead dancers in *Your Show of Shows* with Imogene Coca and Sid Caesar on NBC.

Nelle and her sister, Dorothy were originally from the Cornish School of Music and Ballet in Seattle. Maybe I was closer to the basics of classical ballet, but knowing Nelle's background, I could hardly wait to start working with her.

I also learned that Mary Byrd Klyce's interesting southern accent came from her Virginia heritage. Later, I discovered my mother's long-lost relatives had descended from Virginia plantation owners. Living around southerners, I came to realize that people from different states in the South spoke with varying dialects and used a variety of colloquial expressions that were totally new to me.

When we reached the Klyce's stately home, we were greeted by one of her daughters. Mary Byrd made the introduction, saying proudly in her slow drawl, "I want you to meet my daughter, Ellen. She's a beautiful, young dancer and you must give her private lessons."

Ellen smiled at me and quipped, "You know, I once attended a dance camp in Bar Harbor, Maine where I studied Indian Dance with a Hindu homosexual! Can you imagine, a Hindu homosexual?"

Believe me - that was the last thing I had expected to hear on my first day in Memphis.

Our conversation was interrupted by the honk of a car horn announcing Nelle who was taking me to the Memphis Symphony. As the front door of the Klyce mansion opened, I was almost knocked down by the intense heat that rushed at me. It reminded me of the sensation experienced when opening the door to the steam room at the San Francisco Embarcadero YMCA.

I looked down at my charcoal gray suit, perfect for San Francisco, but much too heavy for Memphis nights. The sidewalks were literally steaming as we went outside and we shared it with some sort of reptile who slithered past us on our way to the car. A voice inside my head whispered, "Toto, I don't think we're in Kansas anymore!"

Nelle and I were fashionably late for the symphony. Bobby Gentry was the guest artist and Vincent de Frank, the conductor. I was struck by the excellence of the musicians, not knowing at the time that Memphis was considered one of the country's musical jazz and blues meccas and was very big in the recording industry.

Nelle was wearing another white mini skirt, go-go boots and a blouse dotted with silver sequins, topped off with a white feather boa. We made quite a couple. Nelle - with a blonde Shirley MacLaine haircut - and me, with my hair hanging down to the length of a princely ballet dancer. I felt handsome.

As I worked with Nelle, I quickly learned that she became outrageously outspoken when she drank alcohol. That night, apparently having had a few, she began to talk to me in a stage whisper that could be heard over Bobby Gentry's rendition of *Tallahatchie Bridge.*

Referring to a dancer seated in the audience, she said loudly, "She has no talent. She only has delusions of grandeur."

She loudly whispered another tidbit in my ear, "Mrs. Brown, one of the parents of a Memphis dancer, thought she had contributed quite a lot to the ballet, but she could have afforded 50 times as much."

"Who is Mrs. Brown?" I softly whispered back, hoping she would follow suit and lower her voice.

Ignoring the question, she continued on as my expression became blanker by the moment, "Suzanne Farrell and Conrad Ludlow will be coming to Memphis next fall. I've already gotten permission from Balanchine in New York. I introduced Balanchine and Suzanne Farrell. Now, she's the love of his life."

She continued her roll of information and gossip in her blasting stage whisper while I desperately wanted to become invisible. Apparently unaware of my discomfort, she continued, "I'm not sure people here know Suzanne Farrell, but they will! She's one of the new stars of The New York City Ballet."

One thing I discovered about Nelle is that she never lied. Everything she said, whether one was ready for it or not, was true. At the moment, Memphis was as familiar to me as Oz. I felt like Dorothy and to prove it, the next day I experienced my first taste of grits, turnip greens, and the great southern staple, pulled white meat barbecue.

On the way to Bill and Jim's, a popular restaurant on Madison Avenue, I managed to respond to peoples' stares with my usual cool. I couldn't understand why African Americans practically jumped off sidewalks to let us pass. I was almost ashamed to be white. I had been told that Memphis was about 50 percent African American, but despite their deference to the white population, I was to find that these black Americans had their own proud culture and heritage. They could be genuinely warm and friendly despite the southern prejudice and lack of opportunities offered their race back in the 60's and earlier. I was finding that the South was a little like the way many of my friends in California had envisioned it to be.

Nelle, her close friend Nancy Gause (a strong ballet patron) and I ate more southern cuisine as we indulged in fresh cornbread, greens, and field peas topped off with banana pudding. As we ate, I realized that my Memphis experience would include learning about racial relationships all over again.

Nancy began to explain the local attitude by saying, "Prejudice comes from fear here, not from hatred, George." I absorbed that bit of information and realized I'd have plenty of time to find out exactly what she meant.

Thankfully, my room at the Klyce home included a bathtub. After dancing all day or teaching, my muscles tightened into possible *rigor mortis* in the evening and I was so grateful for my big bathtub.

As time went on, I enjoyed living with the Klyce family. Looking back now, the atmosphere was sort of a blend of George Kaufman's parody on life, *You Can't Take it With you*, as a bright yet zany mother and the Klyce children were all very individual characters. I began to teach Ellen privately for a while. She was full of youthful energy. Kathy was quiet and thoughtful, and Emily bright and intellectual. Henry was polite and masculine. Lisa was the most like Californians, open and friendly toward me. Arnold, the father, was rarely seen. He would always look up from his chair where he was reading and nod faintly, smiling. The *You Can't Take it With You* kind of atmosphere was actually superficial. They were a warm, friendly family and made me feel very much at home.

My life in Memphis gradually became a soap opera, reminding me of Lillian Hellman's play, *The Little Foxes*. I was constantly being pulled into the plot. There were power struggles in the ballet company that would rival episodes of *Dynasty*.

The Memphis Ballet was looking for a permanent home while our classes were being held in the Memphis Armory. Fifty feet outside our door was the Memphis Belle, the airplane William Wyler had immortalized in his Academy-Award winning World War II documentary. This aircraft attracted many tourists.

Nelle's house was diagonally across the street from the Armory. She appreciated the convenience, but it came with the task of bravely removing any snakes found among her clothes. As I watched in amazed terror and with a certain reverence, she would gather them up, take them outside, and throw them into the vacant lot next door. She did this task calmly as if she was taking out the garbage or doing the dishes. We were a lot closer to nature during those days, and I found Nelle to be very courageous. Why did southern people have so many experiences with snakes, I wondered? The Klyce home had an anaconda mounted on their living room wall. According to them it had once been a family pet owned by a relative when they had owned a rubber plantation in Honduras.

Each day when I returned from teaching or rehearsing, Mary Byrd asked how things had gone. I always gave a positive answer for I loved to teach and made no secret of my enthusiasm.

I enjoyed listening to my southern hostess as she sang her traditional songs. I also remember the day Mary Byrd gave me a private concert of English folk songs. One melody was particularly haunting. The first line went like this: "The joys of love are but a moment long. The pain of love will last you a whole life long." Her plaintive voice seemed to know exactly what the ancient lyrics meant.

Nelle asked me to teach all the classes, about five a day. With this schedule, she had time to do the choreography and public relations.

I began to know my students by names that sounded strange to me, such as Mary Lee and April Flower. But children are children everywhere and their response to ballet was joyous, gleeful, and highly energetic. I must have seemed a dashing worldly figure back then because the mothers' response was appreciative, kindly, and even flirtatious.

Lillian Gordon was one of the mothers who ran the desk in the area near the ballet entrance and helped me keep the records straight. She surprised me with her little comments. One day following my grateful praise, she said with a wink, "You can call me Raquel!" followed another time with, "Our daughters love you!"

There is a delicate and fragile femininity about southern women. Like so many dramas, I wondered if their sensitivity and sweetness might hide a darker side. Were these women protected from the harsher realities of life, ignoring some of the more troublesome aspects of reality?

Would they change their southern heritage if they could?

Many of these women treated me like a Prince Charming. I worried that I was not worthy of their kindness. Southern women appeared to have high moral standards, and I became concerned that the life I had led in California gave me a guilty - almost unworthy - feeling.

Would they reject me if they had any inkling of my unconventional lifestyle?

One day Mary Byrd asked me, "How are you getting along with everyone?"

"Fine!" I replied enthusiastically.

Then Emily asked a puzzling question, "Do you really think Nelle is a fine teacher?"

I blinked. Where was this going? Then I answered earnestly, "I'm fine with her. In fact, I'm in awe of her knowledge."

This conversation would foreshadow the negative attitudes toward Nelle that increased as time went on. If I viewed myself as "the prince," I was reminded to be a little more humble by one of my older students. Laura Shindler had become a friend and she was developing into an excellent Memphis ballet star in her own right. With a glint in her eye, she told me that "the prince" came to ballet class each day with a hole in his tights. I thanked her for that observation but, actually I wasn't that embarrassed. Yet, that hole in the back of my cotton tights must have provided dinner conversation for weeks.

"I'll gladly sew up your tights," offered Lillian, looking up from her record keeping at the desk, then added, "or Janet or Pam can help you since *they are already grown-up little ladies.*"

"Thanks," I replied, measuring my words. "I didn't realize I'd caused a problem. After all, who would be looking at my behind?"

"You would be surprised!" Lillian laughed, half seriously, half joking.

I was astonished that, despite her many triumphs and friendships with well known artists, Nelle was not changed by this notoriety. I suppose that was why she was willing to come to Memphis to further ballet and the arts. Nelle and Nancy Gause had literally saved the ballet in Memphis.

Four years earlier, before Nelle's arrival, Memphis Ballet had brought two of America's great ballet directors to the city's historical Peabody Hotel for the Southeastern Regional Ballet Festival. George Balanchine was famous and impressive enough, but Robert Joffrey was an incredible coup. This combination alone was a great educational accomplishment for the community. Unfortunately, the sophistication of the performance was only matched by the incredible amount of money the ballet lost.

As soon as the artistic staff began leaving, Nancy, representing the Memphis Ballet's Board of Directors, traveled to New York in search of new blood. Meeting Nelle and seeing the results of her work with her New York company, plus her background in ballet and dance, Nancy talked the reluctant Nelle into leaving the Big Apple and coming to Memphis to put the Ballet back on its feet.

Nelle had a great sense of humor, and would entertain Keith Grosjean, one of the dancers, and myself, for hours on end with her stories about a wild and talented Cole Porter, Sid Caesar, and

Imogene Coca, in the early television broadcasts of *Your Show of Shows*.

Leonard Bernstein and Jerome Robbins, then relatively new talents, produced *On the Town* and *Wonderful Town*. Nelle had many memories of working as a young dancer with these showbiz greats.

The Memphis Ballet sponsored the American Ballet Theater (A.B.T.) during the Fall of 1967. Nelle graciously made sure I was introduced to Lucia Chase, their longtime artistic director. She had the reputation of being a queen bee, but was polite to us. One of the dancers, Elliot Feld, introduced himself to me. With his slicked black hair, he looked like one of the young hoods in the gang he was part of in the movie *West Side Story*. He was not at all like the regal ballet director he is today. Bruce Marks, another dancer, was an incredibly handsome talent and somewhat seductive toward both men and women. He was more than the formal prince he tended to play in the A.B.T. productions.

That night they performed Copeland's *Billy the Kid*, a literal interpretation of the pioneers of the American West. I began to believe that the ballet's parents and students were appreciative of what I had to give them as a teacher. I realized that the students had an excellent knowledge of dance vocabulary. Both current and past teachers had contributed to this, as well as the fact that Memphis was only an hour and a half from New York by plane.

I helped them to correct their posture using the head and eyes in connection with breathing techniques. I was also a task master in helping them develop the brute strength that all dancers need. I was the first to touch them instead of using a pointer to correct posture, and some of the old school found this inappropriate.

Due to the hot, humid southern climate dancers here were able to be more limber because they were able to practice extreme stretching exercises. By practicing in the steaming heat they were able to create unusual flexibility within their physical bodies.

Lowell Smith of the Dance Theater of Harlem and Sandy Baldwin of the Pacific Northwest Ballet are both talented dancers who came from the South. Sandy was like a lanky filly, but with practice became a graceful dancer over a period of several years.

In my early days in Memphis, Nancy Shainberg and Laura Shindler were beginning adolescent dancers. They later helped bring a great deal of credit to Memphis as a leading dance center. I was expressive and innovative and developed a following of students who felt the love of music and movement as I did. My internal conflicts never interfered with this part of my life. When the music played, these conflicts evaporated.

Nelle Fisher invited me to join her touring company comprised of promising students. Our schedule that winter allowed the company to dance with the Hartford, Connecticut Symphony, with Arthur Winograd conducting. We returned to Memphis before our next performance with the Buffalo, New York Symphony with Lukas Foss conducting. Nelle's ability to create such an up and coming dance company was impressive for three short years.

Her dancers included the highly talented Suzanne Farrell and Yuri Chatal. When Nelle introduced Suzanne to Balanchine, one of the great careers and love stories in American ballet was launched.

I always knew I was a good dancer, maybe not a great one, but the ballet *Coppelia* gave me a chance to show off my expressive high energy abilities. My partner, Deborah Henry, was 12 years younger than I and still in high school. She alternated in the role of Swanhilda with Stephanie Smithy, an animated dancer in her early 20's. Later, Deborah Henry (known as Debbie) took over Ann Reinken's part in *A Chorus Line* on Broadway and Stephanie Smithy became the choreographer of the Starlight Theater in Kansas City, Kansas.

I had never seen snow before and the sight of it in Hartford, Connecticut was thrilling. The only other time I had seen it was from afar, in the California Sierra. I danced well in Hartford but when I returned to Memphis, I reacted poorly to the intense cold. One of the largest snowfalls the city had ever seen occurred in that fall of 1967. By the time we left Memphis and reached Buffalo, New York, I had a temperature of 104 degrees. Charles Dowling, a kindly and handsome Memphis doctor, sent a supply of antibiotics and cold medicines with me. I managed to perform fairly well but almost fainted during the curtain call and the audience knew something was wrong.

"Did I need to hold you up?" Debbie asked, with wide-eyed innocence. I was embarrassed. Still, I owned most of MGM recordings by Arthur Windgrad, and Lucas Foss was considered one of America's most respected modern composers. Despite my illness, I got to perform under these famous conductors' batons!

When Debbie finished, she left for the Royal Winnipeg Ballet in Canada. Although she was considered too athletic for that company, I believed her qualities would have been appreciated in Europe and she might have been a star there, but her destiny was to move away from ballet and become a Broadway dance star. *A Chorus Line* (in which Debbie took over Ann Reinking's role of Cassie) became a huge Broadway hit and ran for years, fostering numerous touring productions. Along with *Oklahoma!*, *West Side Story*, *Damn Yankees!*, and *Chicago*, it inspired so many dancers of the time.

The people of Memphis did not know me very well yet. Any notoriety I gained had come from being Nelle's escort and friend. Eyebrows were raised when by accident, I created a scene at the Memphis Opera production of Verdi's *Aïda*.

Among my many new friendships were Craig and Nancy Gause. They had patiently taught me about southern customs and manners. I had also developed an unexpected friendship with an unconventional young woman from Arkansas who had transcended her country upbringing by studying art in New York and Europe. Her name was also Nancy and she was my date to *Aïda.*

Because it was the most expensive production The Memphis Opera had produced to date, there was fervent media coverage focused on the huge set that included pyramids and a giant sphinx along the shores of the Nile. These sets had all been flown in for the event. Later, Memphis was to become one of the four cities to have the Ramses Exhibit direct from Egypt and New York. After all, Memphis was the namesake of the original ancient Egyptian city, our spiritual sister city.

The rented red carpets were rolled out for the guests of honor. Spotlights focused on the various important guests as they arrived. Terry Bill, a radio and television personality, interviewed us as Nancy and I entered the theater. I didn't own a proper tuxedo so I wore a dark suit. As we approached Terry, Nancy dropped her Oleg Cassini stole from her shoulders to her arms, revealing her new ensemble. I immediately noticed the surprised expression on people's faces and they turned to look at us. Terry stumbled on his words but kept on going with manly courage. When we were inside the theater, I became aware of Nancy's beautiful, but transparent blouse.

She whirled around, saying proudly, "This is the latest trend in New York. Do you like it?" She saw my look and explained, "I'm not supposed to wear a bra with it, so I didn't." She whirled again as alarmed Memphians glared.

"Do you like it?" she asked again.

All I could manage was a mumbled, "Yes," as I unabashedly studied those amazing breasts! Nancy was ravishing in the transparent gauzy blouse. Her nudeness was incredible. We received almost more attention than Queen Amneris and Ramses, who were the starring roles in *Aïda.*

I was a little embarrassed by our off-stage spectacle but respected Nancy's right to fashion freedom. Who would guess that a wealthy girl from the Arkansas countryside could be, in her way, another daring Isadora Duncan? If Memphian art patrons hadn't talked before, there was little else that they found themselves doing in the days following the opening of the opera *Aïda*. All I knew was that the Pharaoh himself would have been proud of all the pyramids on and off the stage that night.

Chapter 15
Front-page News

As we advanced into the New Year, which would be Nelle's last, another kind of politics was beginning to brew, and it would be played out in the city of Memphis.

An interlude of violence was unfolding in the city. For years there had been a long fight to raise wages for city garbage workers, most of whom were African American. The situation came to an impasse when a worker was accidentally killed by a garbage truck. The city was wracked with emotion.

Mayor Henry Loeb refused to meet the wage demands, and a battle raged in the city council as well as on the streets. Black residents of the city urged civil rights leader Dr. Martin Luther King to come to Memphis and help negotiate, and he did.

On April 4, 1968, Nelle, Nancy and I had been invited to a party not too far from the Lorraine Motel. There was an abundance of southern food, something I was becoming accustomed to eating with great relish. There were Memphis barbecue sandwiches, made of pulled pork white meat, cole slaw, and dill pickles. We drank various drinks, many made with Southern Comfort whiskey, and ate black bottom pie, an exceptional treat, for dessert.

Everyone dined, uneasily discussing the garbage strike and the fact that Dr. King had marched with angry protesting workers in downtown Memphis amid jostling crowds of black and white Memphians. Mayor Loeb, by not giving in to the unions' demands, had become a controversial figure, and curiously enough, there was a reporter present from the *Tri State Defender*, a newspaper that usually wrote about minority causes and found itself at the center of social unrest. Irma Laws, the reporter, was the paper's society reporter and a big ballet fan.

Nancy seemed alarmed that Irma wanted to have her picture appear in the next issue with Nelle and me. Always gracious, Nelle posed with us near a huge table of food while Nancy stood by. After our pictures were taken, the falsely jovial atmosphere quickly changed as a grim-faced, wild-eyed young man announced that we should all quickly return to our homes.

"Dr. Martin Luther King has been assassinated and violent riots are beginning to happen around the city!" he said. King had been felled by a nearby sniper while he stood on the balcony of the Lorraine Motel in downtown Memphis, right nearby.

The Lorraine Motel was about eight blocks away, so we were feeling a bit panicky. As we left the mansion where the party was being held, muffled sounds and flashing pools of light where fires had been started broke through the April night. We could hear rioting in the distance and someone told us that automobiles were being turned over. The sounds of the explosions of social change had only begun.

For the next 10 days all rehearsals were cancelled. A few days later, The Gage Mansion, where all the Memphis Ballet costumes were stored, erupted in flames. Oddly enough a figure was seen fleeing the site of the fire and more than one person commented that the description of the arson suspect fit me! They described him as having reddish brown hair, an athletic build, and appearing to be about 29 years old. Of course, I was not the arsonist. Totally detached from Memphis politics, my only love was for the ballet. The long curfew that went into effect was difficult for me. When our rehearsals finally began again, I was exhausted from rescuing the many costumes that had been drenched in mud and water when the firemen attempted to save the Gage Mansion.

Of all the young dancers, Amanda Aldridge was the sweetest. She tearfully told us a story that was hard to believe. Her father was a minister at the Union Avenue Presbyterian Church, had taken the silver cross off the pulpit to march down Main Street in the sad peace march that took place a few days after the assassination. The pastor didn't feel he needed permission from his superiors, but according to Amanda, he was immediately fired, and her family was to relocate across the country. The dancers and our teaching staff were her best friends, so her departure in the middle of the ballet season was painful for all of us.

Tears and confusion filled the sweaty air of our rehearsal hall. The media (*Time* or *Newsweek*) had written that Memphis was "a sleepy river town," that some Memphians thought implied a painful lack of sophistication, and a lot of anger was expressed about the magazine's description. That's when I learned that *Damn Yankees!* was more than a Broadway musical.

****

Later that year, the Royal Ballet from Great Britain was scheduled to dance at the 4,400-seat North Hall on the banks of the restless Mississippi River. Securing ballet stars Fonteyn and Nureyev, the elaborate sets, and the top box office draw in the world was a crowning achievement for Memphis. People could look forward to this artistic event to last for a full three days.

The three-day event immediately sold out. Almost 14,000 people would attend. Both *The Commercial Appeal* and the *Memphis Press Scimitar* sent their best critics to review all three performances. But to everyone's horror, the unsophisticated headline writer, totally unaware that a world class event was in his city, wrote in the *Press Scimitar* the day after opening night: "Royal Buffet was Excellent."

The red-faced newspaper staff rushed to retrieve the papers already on the newsstands, and delivered to thousands of homes. But, after experiencing one of the most deadly serious and transcendent events in American history, many of us enjoyed this moment of humor.

I soon found that Memphis had much in common with the tropics except for the fact that snow fell there in winter. Despite some of these weather extremes, I came to love the people and the city. Midtown Memphis, the area where I was staying, lay between suburbia and the downtown area bordered by the Mississippi River. Filled with quaint, old two- and three-story houses and mansions, and lush with pink and red azaleas, their streets were lined with tall, stately elms and oaks. Among these historic homes, some dating back to the turn of the century, a few were national monuments, steeped in the atmosphere of the old South's bygone glory.

In the summer, residents shared outdoor space with heat-seeking snakes wiggling out of the shade, and making pathways toward the searing heat radiating from the sidewalks. When pedestrians walked through nearby Overton Park, police warned them to look where they were stepping because a moccasin snake might be slithering across their paths.

Prior to my arrival, my knowledge of the area stemmed from MGM's Tom Sawyer and Huckleberry Finn movies that I assumed they were made near Memphis. In my naïveté I had planned to do some swimming in the Mississippi River, and I brought with me several new swimsuits. (I still have the red one that I had discovered was reversible, one side plaid, the other a dashing red with white checks.) I quickly realized my error in thinking had occurred when a gruff cab driver looked me over one day and informed me that September was open hunting season for "Damned Yankees." He then gave me some good pointers about swimming in the Mississippi.

"You'd better be a great swimmer - not only a good one," he said. "The current is mighty tricky and if you don't drown, the quick sand'll get ya. And if you make it back to the bank alive, it'll be teemin' with water moccasins!"

I took that information to heart and never swam in the Mississippi River. Later, my friend Judy Freeman and I went out to Shelby Forest, a large camping and picnic park, that flanked the river. Twice we saw huge snakes hanging from trees along the river banks. That same month, Gloria Kolesar discovered a diamondhead rattlesnake in her backyard.

Snakes seemed to be everywhere. One day Donna Benitone's gardener reached down to pull out some weeds from the moist earth and came up with a moccasin, its fangs embedded in his hand. Jerry, her husband, raced the man to Baptist Hospital where he received emergency treatment. Another arrival at the hospital, Harold, a Hell's Angel type, was bitten out in Shelby Forest. He had quickly cut off the snake's head, dramatically pulled its body through his belt, then raced to the emergency room where he frightened most of the people in the waiting room before he was taken in for urgent treatment.

Across the Mississippi, in Arkansas, snake handlers tested their religious faith during a snake ceremony by passing poisonous snakes from person to person. If you got bitten, it was a sure sign that you were being influenced by the Devil. I am not fond of snakes and found out much later, to my relief, that snakes usually leave most Memphians alone.

Memphis was built on a bluff surrounded by semi-tropical land, and this influenced the flora and fauna. While walking home with a friend near Summer and McLean Streets one afternoon, I almost tripped over a gigantic dead reptile stretching across the street. Being so well versed in local snake lore by now, I said, "That snake is not from around here."

My friend thought I was crazy, but I continued, "That's a deadly snake from some place like Africa or the South American jungle." He laughed and gave me several big pushes into the bushes along the way to my apartment, not realizing that this could have been a dangerous thing to do. When I arrived home I turned on the television. The news broadcast reported that all the snakes at the Memphis Zoo had been accidentally released from their cages and some had been seen on the very street where we had been walking a short time ago.

***

Nelle had arranged for me to appear with Deborah Henry in George Klein's Saturday musical show on Memphis' Channel 5. Although I was slim and muscular I felt as though I had been poured into my costume. Hers was a flowing gown.

George was famous all over the South for his close friendship with Elvis Presley and had a huge audience, so this was great publicity for us. As we left the studio some young women drove by. Spotting me, they slowed down and leaned out their car windows, shouting and waving at me, "Paul, Paul Newman forever and ever!" I couldn't believe my ears. Maybe I really *was* attractive, after all!

By the next day everyone who had tuned in to Channel 5 knew who we were. Debbie was unusually muscular for a classical ballet dancer at that time. Since the thin, anorexic look was becoming so popular, it got tough to break into classical ballet with a more robust body. A few years later, she took over the much coveted role of Cassie in the Broadway production of *A Chorus Line*. She had found her niche and would finally know what it was like to be a star.

That December in 1968, Nelle Fisher produced what we thought was the first *Nutcracker* in Memphis. Other than on television, the Tchaikovsky warhorse was still relatively new for many local audiences. The event was sold out. I was the male lead in the *Waltz of the Flowers* and also appeared with several beefy dancers in the Arabian variation. Sadly, despite our success and the fact that she and Nancy Gause had literally saved Memphis ballet, the Memphis Ballet Board voted not to renew Nelle's contract. They said they could find a director with a more traditional classical background. Others felt it was time for a change. Many ballet people talked of behind-the-scenes politics.

Annabel Yeldell, Adelaide Dowling, and many others, including Robert Jennings, the drama-dance critic, expressed their regrets. The dancers, the parents, and numerous patrons showed their disgust at the board's lack of appreciation for Nelle's years of sacrifice.

With Nelle's contract not being renewed, I felt that the Ballet's existence was tenuous at best. Behind the polite and superficial social graces that marked my encounters with Emily Klyce, I was aware of being catered to and being carefully questioned. They wanted to know my position on Nelle. Would I take a strong stand on her credibility as a director? Even though my ego had been hurt at times in dealing with ballet problems, I was absolutely fair and honest in my opinions. The truth was clear to me that the board was mistreating Nelle. Besides, I felt indebted to her for all that I had learned from her.

The leader of the Let Us Find a New Director Committee seemed to be Emily Klyce, whose intelligent, calm, and steady manner were impressive and persuasive. Still, I held my own with her, and Emily's disappointment was apparent when she found I could not be manipulated. The Memphis Ballet Board, made up of parents and influential citizens, asked me to take the witness stand. I did and said with great sincerity, "Nelle, like all of us, is not perfect. As long as someone works with her as a team member, her gifts as a teacher will benefit us all."

At this point, I was only speaking for myself. No one person can do everything. Nelle was a spontaneous choreographer and teacher and I supported her by moving slowly and carefully. My position drew disapproving looks from a number of board members. Winning approval from them was not easy. Nevertheless, Mary Byrd continued to remain a friend and later we would develop an even better understanding.

Nelle vanished from Memphis without fanfare and, suddenly I realized I, too, was out of work. Before long I was hired by the Memphis Junior League. They had a lot of power in the Memphis artistic community and they used that power to produce Prokofiev's *Cinderella*. I asked Mary Byrd, who was still president of the Memphis Ballet Society, whether she thought I should leave town too. But she urged me to stay. That's when a dramatic and occasionally comical search for a new director began.

"We think a married couple would really be suitable for our city," one board member publicly announced.

I watched and listened and told some friends, "I want to dance until I'm 40 or 50, and so the board's search doesn't disturb me that much." I knew Memphis was not the only place for serious dancers.

At the end of the summer, *The Commercial Appeal* published a long story about Nelle, stating that she had been hired by the San Francisco Opera as the choreographer for the 1969 fall season. I was happy for Nelle. Now I had another problem. The minute I stopped performing I began to gain weight and so began a long struggle to keep the pounds off.

Nelle had once introduced me to Suzanne Farrell who was connected to Balanchine. He was so well known for his artistic contributions to ballet and I had been impressed with Nelle's connection to the great choreographer. Once, she even called him while he was in a stage rehearsal to arrange for Farrell's appearance in Memphis. Balanchine apparently was in love with Suzanne despite their age difference and she seemed to feel indebted to Nelle for this introduction.

When *en pointe*, Suzanne was taller than I and I was five feet 11 inches. She could have been huge and ungainly. When I asked her how she kept the weight off she had replied warmly, "Toast and orange juice for breakfast, salad for lunch, and a dinner high in nutrition."

If she could do it, I could, too, I thought. Following her instructions, I succeeded for many years until I realized that more than a few of my students didn't conform to the diet but were also superior athletes. I rationalized that weight was protection for my lack of confidence and I began to think big was better. But diet or no diet, I was aware of my weakness as a dancer.

I missed Nelle and her stories about dealing with the city's wild creatures. I remember being in her house one Saturday night right after Easter Sunday when she told me another Memphis animal story. One night she awakened to the sound of a giant bird crashing through her kitchen window. Somehow, the bird found its way out and Nelle calmly duct taped cardboard over the broken pane and went back to bed. For a New Yorker, she had adjusted rather well to the fact that Memphis' intruding nature rarely remained totally outdoors.

One evening, Nelle had invited me to dinner with another dancer, Keith Grosjean. I stuffed the turkey with cornbread, clams, cherries, and parsley while nervously looking over my shoulder for another bird or snake to arrive.

Nelle cheerfully offered me a cocktail, sensing my unease. As she proceeded to regale us with stories of New York, I kept wondering how her career had led her into this unusual Memphis world.

After Nelle's departure, I did less performing and became choreographer off and on for Opera Memphis. In another big career step I became entrepreneur and director of my own company, Ballet South. I chose that name because I wanted my company to represent not only the Mid South, but the entire South. It was more than egos at work. Every dancer needed equal opportunity.

A search for a new artistic director continued and I was asked to attend monthly meetings at the Brooks Art Gallery. The energy at these meetings ran from benevolence to archaic narrow mindedness. The Whites, a couple from the East Coast, were being considered for the job. While they were being interviewed, they had to make long-distance calls to Russia and Cuba. When they came back into the room, some of the board presumed that they must have had Communist connections. They were excellent teachers, but somehow that didn't matter. They were excused and the witch hunt was on again. Many were interviewed, but the committee judged none to be the right people. This committee now seemed to run things for the board. Over a year passed before a new director finally was hired.

I decided that the best thing for me to do was to leave town, after all. I was still a good dancer and Nancy Turpin told me that my choreography seemed quite original. She also let me know that the board was hiring dancers from Chicago. Keith Grosjean, who was still with the ballet and had become a close friend, suggested that we go up North to the so-called land of opportunity. I called Mary Byrd who assured me that if I didn't leave there would be a place for me in the new ballet hierarchy.

As time went on and nothing happened, I threw myself into my own ballet company that began to progress and gain attention. One of our Memphis Opera performances was *Walpurgis Night*, from the opera, *Faust*. This performance had made headlines the year before in New York for its lascivious representation of hell. The choreographed scenes were said to raise the audience's prurient interest. Dancers appeared near naked and sensuously slithered across the stage. The performance left little to the imagination. Ballet South's performance the following year was a bit more conservative, although it was rumored that Jerome Hines, famous for playing Mephistopholes, had threatened to boycott any future productions containing the same overt sexual material. Still, there were some shocks and surprises in our production.

After a program of classical excerpts, Danny Buraczeski and Laura Shindler performed W.C. Handy's *Memphis Blues*. They were sizzling.

Of course, we had to have an Elvis ballet with choreography by Danny who would later have his own New York Jazz Company. We ended the program with Isaac Hayes's music, *Shaft*. Isaac had given freely of his music and his fame. The performance was called the *Memphis Trilogy*, and I choreographed none of it. Yes, this time I could finally stand back and not be the choreographic star.

We repeated the performance at the Overton Park Shell. Elaine Jekels choreographed Prokofiev's *Piano Concerto No. 3* for herself and Lowell Smith. In the middle of the performance, a gust of wind blew off Elaine's skirt, adding a bit more improvisation to the performance.

"I know I have now added to the controversy over Ballet South for being modern and obscene," quipped Elaine.

I replied earnestly, "Elaine, your ballet has become even more beautiful, believe me!"

We loved dancing outdoors. In the early summer before the August heat, we performed Stravinsky's *Rite of Spring*. Jeff Stuart (more about him later) and Carlton Johnson, our lead male dancers, paired with Anna Palmiere and Julie Morrison. They had never been more athletic. Peggy Howard was the dramatic Chosen One and the ballet was successful. Many in the audience commented that the ballet was as though "from another world - primitive, sensual, and yet spiritual." The stark, raw choreography made it memorable ballet history for Memphis. The dancers were the music.

A great new friend, Albert Edelman, once said musingly, "I played in the premiere performance of that piece. Tomatoes were thrown at us. No one understood the music or Nijinsky's choreography in Paris in those days."

Certainly Stravinsky was recognized as a great composer. I began to quickly do my addition in my head. The youthful Mr. Edelman must have been in his 90s by then, and I was grateful to have him help me interpret the difficult rhythms of this great ballet score. To know him was like finding unexpected treasure. And to think that after living in Europe and New York, he had chosen Memphis, of all places, to settle in his later years.

In 1969 when I opened my ballet school in Memphis, a woman named Vi took my night classes. I'm still not sure whose friend she actually was, or who referred her to me. Her body was thinner than thin and her clothes could only be described as ragged. Despite that, she had a pretty middle-aged face, a quiet nature, and great piercing blue eyes.

Everyone whispered that she was the girlfriend of a man called Sweet Willie Wine. I would learn later that he was a civil rights legend. Interracial relationships were still fairly rare in 1969 Memphis, and I wondered who this "Sweet Willie" was.

"You're obviously not from around here," my new student told me in a voice that had a distinct country twang to it. She paused. Uncertainty and possibly fear shadowed her face. "I do hope Willie is all right now. As far as I know, he's still in jail in Forest City, Arkansas," adding in confusion, "or maybe it was El Dorado, Arkansas. You know, he and I led a protest, one of many, against the police. They still discriminate against all blacks in Arkansas." Her blue eyes snapped. "We aren't going to have it that way any more! They threw all of us in a jail cell and used fire hoses on us."

"Did that hurt?" I asked naively. I was only 30 years old, from California, and not knowledgeable about civil rights matters and cruelties.

She glanced sideways at me, showing sadness and pain in her eyes, "Yes, it hurt, it hurt real bad. The only thing worse were the horses. The police had horses. Two of my friends were killed!" I led her to a bench and sat down beside her, not knowing what to say.

One of my students, Randy, later explained to me that Sweet Willie Wine was most likely a folk hero. The newspapers were full of stories about this scruffy and courageous character who had made his own civil rights headlines back in Arkansas in 1969.

Recently, I was given a computer sheet by my friend, Samuel Flint who had found it in the archives of former president Bill Clinton's huge library and museum right outside of Little Rock, Arkansas.

The article, accompanied by a photograph of a group of angry African Americans back in 1969, had the headline: "The Long Walk to Little Rock."

It read:

"In 1969 a *poor people's* march from Forrest City to Little Rock was scheduled for August 24-26. The march was meant to dramatize outdated conditions black people are forced to live in throughout the State of Arkansas. Although Governor (Nelson) Rockefeller negotiated with the March organizer, Reverend Cato Brooks, to postpone the march and allow him time to find some solutions, the march took place as scheduled."

Renamed a "Walk against Fear" the march began in West Memphis and was led by Lance "Sweet Willie Wine" Watson, the leader of a militant Memphis group called the Invaders. Watson had been in Forrest City to help organize a summer boycott of white businesses by the town's black population. The marchers were to be escorted by plainclothes state policemen."

***

Early in my Memphis stay I was nervous about how I'd fit into this truly southern city and I became very lonely. Unlike the thriving night life of Memphis today, back in the 60s, the city shut down tight at night. Around this time, I met a handsome British man who told me his profession was making medical films. He had honey red hair and turquoise blue eyes and he told me that he, too, felt a little out of place at times. He seemed interested in my career and said he had subleased an apartment on the banks of the Mississippi River. He invited me over for dinner and I discovered that he was a good cook.

As we talked, we slowly and sensuously ate the meal he had prepared. At that time, I tended to believe what I was told. He was perhaps in his early 40s. The wine flowed like the Mississippi, which we could see out of the huge windows on three sides of his bare, wooden loft apartment. Artwork and photographs hung everywhere. I was impressed, as I usually was with people older than I.

A huge old-fashioned bathtub had been placed in the center of the main room. After dinner, he filled the tub with some masculine scented bubble bath and began to disrobe. He asked me to join him. I had rarely been so intoxicated. But it wouldn't have made any difference. I was more than a little lonely and this Brit was beautiful. Under his formal suit was the body of a young athlete. I was definitely fooled by his formal British manner and his cool charm. He had kept his lascivious drives well hidden.

We both sat in the warm, bubbly water and I forgot that I was in Memphis. I was so relaxed and gave in to his skillful seduction.

The formality disappeared and I experienced a truly erotic experience. I got drowsy. My eyes shut. Sometime later, while in a state of hazy half sleep, I heard a noise, and looked up to see another man get up from the far, dark corner of the room and tiptoe toward the door. He went out and the door swung shut behind him, but not before I had caught a glimpse of the movie camera the Brit had mentioned.

To my chagrin, I understood. The man wasn't filming medical films at all! To this day, I wonder if an X-rated movie is floating around Britain or some parts of Europe where I am the intoxicated sleepy-eyed star. I never wanted to see Mr. Britain of 1969 again and never did.

Memphis was full of surprises then and there would be more to come.

Chapter 16
Solving a Problem Called Me

My life has always been full of reality checks. Because I have such an active imagination, there has always been something or someone who brought me spinning back down to earth again. Dr. Illardi was such a force. He was a Memphis therapist with his own private practice, but he also was a psychologist in residence at Shelby County Penal Farm. Dr. Illardi was recommended to me by my friend Keith Grosjean who was also one of my students.

My problem was intimacy. The idea of being more than close friends with my students was impossible. They had lives of their own. My life was the school. When it closed for the day, I was left with a lot of lonely time on my hands.

I was distracted from my loneliness by the talent I had attracted to the school. The dancer named Keith and another, Pam Taylor, were my best students at the time. Later, Pam would move on and become a principal dancer with the Atlanta Ballet where Robert Barnett, Atlanta Ballet's longtime artistic director, would describe her as being "luscious." I found that expression an apt description for someone whose dancing abilities were a delight to the audience's senses. Pam's talents eventually helped her to become director of Ballet Hawaii.

Elaine Amis was an invaluable married friend, but she had a nice family and her own ballet school. In our many conversations about ballet, I found that Elaine's gift was the ability to communicate her dancing skills to her young dancers. I would have loved to talk for hours with Elaine about this subject and others, but I couldn't ask her to go to events or even dinner during the evening hours. Her busy schedule was full, with both personal and professional demands. So I was glad to find Dr. Illardi. I needed to talk with him about this growing feeling of isolation.

I was heading toward an identity crisis, and Illardi had a calm and reassuring manner that kept me grounded. During the day, I taught ballet at three different locations, the primary one being a new theater and dance school at Union and Rembert Streets in midtown Memphis. My classes were growing in size, and the Royal Ballet of England, coming to Memphis for three days, had inspired many Memphians to take up ballet.

One day I went to my class and, as usual, found my students waiting for me to open the doors. Searching my pockets, I realized I had left the keys behind and we were all locked out. What to do? I remembered there were portable barres stored in the back shed, so I decided to get them out and have a limited exercise class on the front sidewalk. The novel idea appealed to my students and they began to go through their ballet positions and do their stretches at the barre. As we continued to practice, two things happened. Both a light sprinkle of rain and the evening rush-hour traffic began about the same time. As the sprinkle turned into a drizzle, the traffic began to slow down and we realized that the occupants of the cars were enjoying our impromptu performance. As the vehicles continued to creep by, the drizzle turning to rain, turning a misfortune into a great publicity stunt! The NBC affiliate, Channel 5, came over to film the dancers for the evening news and in the weeks to come, my class enrollment doubled.

Evening was a difficult time for me. I felt acutely alone after the school closed every night, even though I lived in a strange but attractive attic apartment at Alexander and Central. I took to walking down to the Normal Theater on Highland Street each evening to relieve that lonesome feeling. The theater had recently begun to screen all 20 hours of the Russian film masterpiece, *War and Peace*. I think Bill Kendall, who ran several theaters in the area, brought the movie to Memphis as a public service and it certainly was one for me.

My experiences seemed to bring certain bizarre kind of
excitement. I was in my third autumn in Memphis and darkness
filtered in early, curtailing any kind of dusk. I chose the longer route
down Southern Avenue to the theater so that I could view the
Chaney mansion where movie star Lon Chaney's family once lived.
In those days, Lon Chaney, Jr., was a big horror movie star. Passing
by his mansion with all its dark shadows and crevices, was part treat,
part therapy for me because I had never been allowed to watch any
horror films until I was a teenager.

As a child, even the previews of *The Mummy* with Boris
Karloff and "The Wolfman" with Lon Chaney gave me nightmares.
And so, perhaps with some hidden anticipation of what I might hear
or see in the dark shadows, I continued to walk up Central and down
Highland Avenues to the theater.

This evening there were no people walking along the streets.
The night was particularly dark and windy and autumn leaves lay
thick and piled up along the uneven sidewalks. At times, I found
myself knee deep in leaves. There was an area of woods across from
an old church that I usually passed, and I was always careful to look
where I was stepping due to the amount of leaves and my snake
phobia. My eyes had been downcast, but I suddenly looked up. High
on an extended tree branch, the body of a man swung gently in the
breeze. I came to a halt, staring upward in immobilized shock.

The scene had the distinct atmosphere of a horror classic. The
dim moonlight, the rustling of fall leaves, a body swaying. I gasped,
my breath caught somewhere down in my windpipe, and I looked up
again. *A body was swaying up over my head on the limb of the tree.*

I turned and hurried down the street toward the distant lights
of the movie theater. Once there, struggling to breathe, I told my
story to the startled staff who immediately called the police.

Suicide is a tragic event, and the dead man had chosen, for
some unknown reason, an eerie Stephen King-like setting for an

unforgettable visual image of his suicide. Needless to say, from that night on, I began to take a different route to and from the theater.

One night as I arrived at my apartment, my eccentric landlady met me near the steps at the front entrance. Her hair was shooting out in all directions, rather like someone who had recently been electrocuted.

"We don't like female visitors at night," she urgently croaked at me, creating bullfrog sound effects straight out of an Edgar Allen Poe tale. What could she mean? I was always alone at night. Puzzled, I followed her glance upward. At the top of the stairs stood the figure of an attractive young woman blending in with the moving shadows of densely colored fall leaves. A nearby street light cast her first in light and then in shadow.

Her name was Liz Green. She was a decade younger than I. Once I had heard her sing at a waterfront club near Front and Main Streets. She had an incredibly expressive voice. Her long, straight, honey-colored hair fell to her shoulders and gave her an extraordinary theatrical look.

Liz had taken my ballet classes on the weekends. She had driven me home after classes once or twice. Right now, she seemed as distraught as I was. I learned that she had come over to my apartment because that night she had walked in on her husband and his secret lover. I comforted her as best I could and we began to meet nightly, walking to the Normal Theater together, or having dinner in some quiet, relaxing place. I thought I might be falling in love with her. I knew I wanted that. She continued to be distraught because her marriage was falling apart and I was a sensitive friend she could trust.

Liz had a pretty body, without an ounce of extra weight. I only weighed 165 pounds then, and it was easy for us to blend together, both physically and emotionally. The landlady growled at us each time I brought Liz home. One night at the theater, we had seated ourselves near the parents of two of my young African American students. The film was Swedish and contained much romance and nude sex. All of us giggled self consciously while we watched the movie and I realized that they were as self conscious as Liz and I had been, to be caught watching an artistic, but X-rated film.

The sexual relationship Liz and I developed was probably a natural progression of our close friendship. Physically, we seemed made for each other. At that young age and unattached, we were ready for love. Liz would look at me with those eyes of hers - an unusual turquoise seen only in Impressionist paintings. I found her beauty breathtaking sometimes. When we were making love and I hesitated, she seemed to know exactly what I was experiencing and would reassure me.

"It's okay," she'd say, knowing I needed her gentle reminder that she was not my mother or my sister.

The psychological aspect of every close and emotional event in my life, including this relationship with Liz, brought back old feelings that had to be revisited. When I felt lost in these moods, I was lucky enough to be able to turn to my counselor.

I experienced something new with Liz. I had never had sex with a woman with the lights on! Despite some of the outrageous situations I had participated in back in California, I guess I was a real prude at heart. But Liz would always put me at ease. She'd say, "Even though you're 10 years older than me, your body is as young as mine and as exciting!"

Liz was exactly what I needed in my lonely life and I always felt comfortable with her. We practically lived together even though my landlady constantly threatened to call the police. Eventually, we moved to a small house where no one threatened us. We comforted each other during those days. But, as good as things were, I began to feel I needed to take a short trip back home to California.

My hunch proved correct. My mother and I had always written letters to each other, mainly because she thought of long-distance phone calls as a luxury. By June 1969, I hadn't received a letter for several months. On a Monday morning at eight sharp, I called her at a number we had used all of our lives and heard a strange man's voice on the other end of the line. That caught me by surprise. My mother finally came to the phone, giggling like a school girl. She proudly announced, "We were married yesterday! I was meaning to write to you!"

Although startled and curious as to who this new husband of hers was, I felt very happy for her. I knew she was cautious when it came to men, and Joe had to be the right one for her to have married him.

Joe, back on the phone, informed me happily, "Your mother's new name is Susan Teran. She wants me to tell you that we flew to Las Vegas over the weekend. Your mother has strong ideals, you know. She wouldn't sleep with me until we were married. She is very old fashioned!"

Joe Teran was a nice man. He owned a shopping center and his home, and came from a huge Spanish-speaking family. My mother loved to travel and she and Joe had gone abroad together, flying from Spain to the Casbah in Morocco, and then to Acapulco, Mexico. Joe was lots of fun and he had a great sense of humor. He was nothing like my father. My mother said that Joe reminded her of one of her film idols. She had always loved Valentino and Ramon Novarro. Later, she had added Anthony Quinn, Gilbert Roland, and Caesar Romero to her list. Joe continued to live in his house and my mother in hers. She never learned to speak Spanish. With their close relationship, I realized almost wistfully, it wasn't necessary.

In California, my mother gave my brother Bill and his wife, Gail, and myself directions to Joe's home. What followed was a jolly, fun-filled dinner, and I marveled that things could suddenly change so quickly and in such a wonderful way for my mother. Mother was 57 and Joe was 75. He was proud of his Spanish-Mexican heritage.

That they were from different cultures didn't bother either of them.

"When you're happy, nothing else matters," Joe said, giving me a wise look.

Later, my old friend Bob and I drove to San Francisco and on the way, he informed me, "Your stepfather Joe said he was the painting contractor for many years for the San Francisco War Memorial Opera House and that's how he was able to buy the shopping center in East Oakland."

"Maybe he was," I answered, adding, "What's that old expression? Never look a gift horse in the mouth?"

Bob and I had dinner at a restaurant called Jackson's and I found that I still felt self conscious in restaurants that were primarily gay. I later realized that what I was feeling, the uneasiness, was some sort of self hatred.

Frances Fay, a singer I had heard about before, was the evening's entertainer. The fact that she could joke about her own experiences between songs made me forget my inadequate feelings and even laugh at myself.

Afterward, we went to a nightspot called The Gilded Cage where Charles Pierce was fast becoming a mainstream performer in the San Francisco entertainment world. The great thing about Charles was that he was a wonderful mimic. All he had to do was stand with his back to the crowded Cage audience, dressed in a black velvet gown, then lurch around with a bright spot picking up his image, and he would proclaim in that throaty Davis voice, "What a dump. It's me, Bette!"

The audience howled, cheered, and applauded. Not only was she/he hilarious but the banter included all the news that never made it into the newspapers. People went to see Charles not only to be entertained but to be informed. He used to repeat that famous line from the movie *All About Eve*, "Fasten your seatbelts! It's going to be a bumpy night!"

This was the San Francisco of old when some popular local talent would communicate the legal, political, and moral tragedies of the times. When Charles left the stage that night, three mock nuns from the cast of *The Sound of Music* stepped out of the wings singing, "How do you solve a problem like Maria?" Then they lifted their skirts high, revealing chains and leather boots. The audience loved it all!

At the end Charles came out dressed like Jeanette MacDonald. Perched on a flowered covered swing, he flew out over the audience, singing, "San Francisco! Open your golden gates!" Then he invited everyone to join in during the final extended verse and we did with appreciative gusto.

I had a few more weeks in California before returning to Memphis, a city I had begun to think of as home. Bob worked as a manager at the restaurant at Pier 13 and I went there a number of times and had the thrill of watching the huge S.S. Oriana pull into dock, a sight well worth seeing.

I confided in Bob and told him about Liz and how I was having trouble in accepting male promiscuity as a lifestyle.

"We're not all promiscuous," Bob stated. "Only the Twinkies are!" He meant the young unsettled people. He never seemed to have the same kind of internal tug of war I did.

One night before I returned to Memphis, we went to dinner and had an experience straight out of *The Twilight Zone*. I was actually learning to feel comfortable about going to nightclubs, especially if they had a show. As I later discovered in Memphis, shows with real talent were attended mostly by a broadminded audience that wasn't exclusively gay.

That night, after our meal in San Francisco, we went to the Fantasy Lounge off Sutter. A Nancy Sinatra impersonator came out in front of a black curtain and began to sing, *These boots Were Made for Walking*. "One of these days I'll walk all over you!" Halfway through the song, the curtain parted, revealing five handsome men in revealing underwear. The impersonator grabbed a whip and imitated the moves of a dominatrix. The show was funny in a satirical way.

Then the MC announced, "Next on the stage, the Fantasy presents Doreen Desire, the Snake Goddess. Knowing how I hated snakes, Bob laughed. I couldn't tell if Doreen was a man or a woman, but she or he resembled Yvonne De Carlo. As the dancer spun quickly around with a 12-foot boa that I hoped was tranquilized, the music, possibly from *Serpent of the Nile* with Rhonda Fleming, grew louder and more intense. Each time she spun around, the snake would lean out further from her. I wanted to leave. Then, I noticed that with each spin, the snake's head was being bashed into the music stand. This didn't happen once, but over and over again.

"She's killing her snake," shouted Bob who jumped onto the stage, thus preventing the snake's untimely demise. The next day, as I had my morning orange juice at The Orange Tree, I read a startling story in the *San Francisco Chronicle*. After the show, Doreen Desire went back to her apartment and was giving her boa a bath. (I guess to calm its nerves after the experience of being a battered dance partner.) The phone rang and Doreen stepped away from the bathroom to answer the call. When she came back, the snake had disappeared. She glanced at the open toilet in time to see the tip of its tail gong down the bowl. Doreen grabbed for the snake, but she was too late. The boa had slithered on down the pipes and out of sight.

Meanwhile, her innocent neighbor in the next apartment had taken that moment to attend to his private needs and was sitting on his own toilet seat. When the snake's head appeared between the poor man's legs, everyone in the entire apartment building heard his piercing scream. Now Doreen had a lawsuit on her hands and the public was laughing for days about the unbelievable story. Doreen and her neighbor stopped speaking to each other.

A week later, I was ready to return to Memphis. I missed Liz. Carol, my former ballet coach, was planning to come to Memphis to help me with a performance of Debussy's *Sacred and Profane,* French composer Albert Roussel's *The Spider's Feast,* and Béla Bartok's *Romanian Dances.*

Eddie, Carol's husband, was performing in a fine Arthur Laurents play, *A Clearing in the Woods,* with Priscilla Pointer, who was Amy Irving's mother. Five different actresses played the same woman during different periods of her life. Eddie was the dominating father, causing the heroine to doubt herself and lower her self-esteem. The plot was resolved in a touching and meaningful way. Of course, the development of a person as they grew into adulthood reminded me once more of that old saying, "as the twig is bent, so grows the tree," but with a touch of Freudian analysis thrown in.

Chapter 17
Those Men in Tights

Memphis hadn't changed much in the month I was away. Our school was doing well. Liz and I we were fine when we were alone. We shared some good times with our friends Barbara and Carter Tarkington, but deep inside I knew I was living a lie. This was especially true when we socialized, and I was forced to discuss the latest football maneuvers and star athletes with Liz's friends who were mostly sports-minded young couples. I was trying too hard to fit in.

We had a huge adult ballet class every night with at least 20 to 35 women who had been inspired to attempt ballet by the Royal Ballet's recent visit. Pam Taylor, whom I mentioned earlier as one of my first students, came in with a strange story about being asked to step back from the wings in the Dixon Myers Auditorium during one of Nureyev's rehearsals. This huge theater housed the Metropolitan Opera and held 4,000 people each performance. The public was kept away from backstage, but Pam always had powerful connections. The stage manager had asked those privileged enough to be backstage to move further away. A young medical student named Jeffrey Stuart was sitting on a folding chair in the middle wings. Pam saw him get up and start to move back, but the great Nureyev flexed his hand in a motion that blocked the young student's exit.

Nureyev shouted, "No! He stay!" Jeff was surprised but returned to his chair. Pam wondered who this young man was and why he was so important. After all, the other onlookers had been asked to move back from the wings during the practice. Pam and Jeffrey never spoke while backstage together, but eventually they became dance partners, not only with Ballet South, but with the Atlanta Ballet.

Nureyev, by then the world's greatest ballet star, had met Jeff in the historic Peabody Hotel lobby. They had struck up a conversation while watching the famous Peabody ducks swimming in the large lobby fountain, a daily event that always attracted a crowd.

Nureyev's English was very limited and Jeff didn't speak Russian. Nureyev found this country-bred ballet aficionado as irresistible as Jeff was in awe of the world's greatest ballet star. Later, some of the Royal Ballet dancers followed them as they walked together down Front Street, yelling "Rudy! Rudy! What does he have that we don't have?"

Fonteyn and Nureyev's magic was world renowned and Memphis ballet patrons were thrilled to have them perform in their river city. Perhaps only the Beatles caused more mass hysteria.

Jeff, I learned, was working his way through the University of Tennessee Medical School by assisting in research at St. Jude's Children's Research Hospital. Nureyev had said to him, "You have the feet of big ballet dancer. Why you no take ballet class?"

Jeff was only 22 and did harbor a secret desire to try the serious world of ballet after tapping, clogging, and jazz dancing his way through his teens. Now, finding himself on intimate terms with the world's most famous ballet star and seeing him perform *Swan Lake* with the great Margot Fonteyn was like giving heroin to a junkie.

Rudolf Nureyev told us that he found Jeff's southern accent amusing and he liked having him around. Years later, when I asked Jeff what Nureyev was actually like during those weeks in 1969, all he could do was shake his head and say, "Incredible!"

Nureyev transformed ballet for all dancers. He was the first male dancer since Nijinsky to emerge as great a star as any ballerina. He raised the standards for all male dancers. Men now had to be as limber as their female counterparts. Male dancers could no longer perform pirouettes with the foot at the opposite ankle, and the standing heel low to the ground. Now, we had to pirouette with the leg in a high *passé* and push up hard on the *relevés* as the females did. The myth that flexibility would make one physically weak was thrown out altogether. Nureyev was the greatest artistic athlete of his era and he paved the way for future talents like Baryshnikov.

So inspired was Jeff, that within a month he had secretly quit medical school and even changed the spelling of his stage name in hopes of keeping his new career direction secret from his family until they were ready to accept it. Pam and Jeff became friends in my advanced ballet class. He attended class in a medical shirt, sweat pants, and short cropped hair, unlike the other long-haired would-be dancers in my class.

Nureyev continued to find Jeff's accent hilarious and ended up asking him to complete the Royal Ballet tour with him as his guest.

Jeff declined. He was still devoted to research and the many projects at St. Jude. One of them involved growing leukemia cells in a glass flask, a project he had not yet completed.

We all became good friends and had dinner together after class. Liz wanted me to be happy no matter what that meant. And even though we began to understand that our paths were soon to diverge and we lost the degree of intimacy we once shared, to this day we're friends.

Dr. Illardi said that I was intellectualizing my life. "Follow your feelings," he said, "you still have time to be anything that it's possible for you to be. Don't ignore the things that seem beyond reason!" Still, I couldn't see where I fit in. So I stopped trying.

The Memphis Arts Council had received a special grant to present the arts to the Shelby County Prison. Although they had ignored me in the past, I suddenly seemed perfectly eligible to put on this performance. Later on, some members of the council called our performance obscene, even though I thought it was quite ordinary. They criticized the dancers for wearing ballet tights, some saying it indicated immoral behavior. The comments seemed like a joke and I laughingly asked myself, "What else do dancers wear?" Despite their continuing cooperation with Ballet South, the Memphis Arts Council still refused to recognize any of our dances as artistic and socially important.

AP Wire Service carried the story about how Ballet South had danced to some classical pieces by Vivaldi and to pop music behind bars. The story got a favorable response from the prison staff and the prisoners themselves. We were so pleased that Ballet South was receiving positive news coverage all over the United States.

One day Jeff asked if I would like to see the lab at St. Jude's where he worked. It was spring of 1970 and I held my breath the whole time we were at St. Jude's because I had recently read a theory about cancer in *The New York Times*. The story indicated that cancer could be caused by airborne viruses.

As I watched Jeff going through his routine with the test tubes, I must have distracted him for as he meant to blow into each tube of Leukemia cells, he reversed his actions and instead, he sucked the air out and swallowed! We both panicked. Not knowing what protective action to take, he rushed over to a bottle of Clorox and gulped down more than an ounce. He repeated that process several times, swallowing water in between while I watched, horrified and fascinated.

Not remotely a scientist, to this day I wonder whether or not Jeff and I owe a debt to the Clorox Company for saving his life. Some of the executives are our friends here in Oakland and I have meant to ask them about the possibility.

Chapter 18
Tempests in a Teapot and the Dead Elvis Party

My first production sponsored by the Memphis Junior League was a full-length Cinderella, music by Prokofiev, starring Alice Cartwright and Carrie Jeanne Wilson. With the support of so much talent, I was able to create a sweet yet dramatic version of the classic.

As a result of this success I was invited by the Memphis Opera to choreograph the ballet in their upcoming production of Faust with Jerome Hines in his signature role of Mephistopheles. In pre-production talks I was encouraged to not hold back on the somewhat erotic vision I shared with them for the ballet.

Unfortunately the ballet proved to be a bit much for the locals. A small war erupted in the newspapers, and we were preached against in church pulpits all over the city. Mr. Hines, decided not to perform Faust again if this ballet were included.

We did have supporters. Defending our ballet in which the dancers wore body stockings dipped in tea to resemble flesh, Edwin Howard, the television and newspaper critic said, "The only thing dirty about the production was the tights worn by the dancers rolling on the floor."

Jeff and I had begun living together in an apartment a block from Overton Square where Kathy Bates, as yet unknown, was then working at the theater ticket office. She greeted me one day with a sarcastic, "Here comes l'enfant terrible!" Her wit and unpretentiousness already apparent, she confessed she found the "tempest in a teapot" quite amusing.

Luckily, while working for Frank Holeman, I had met Peggy Henders at his theater dance school. Peggy knew we needed a new school and rehearsal space and, like magic, she made this happen for us. We moved to 3355 Poplar and soon were dancing on both the top floor and in the basement.

Memphis was replete with talent in those days. "You have some real celebrities in your classes," Peggy said. There was Dixie Carter, for example, who had married Hal Holbrook, long before the television show, *Designing Women* became a hit TV series. And there was the wife of Rufus Thomas, a nationally known rhythm and blues celebrity, who also took regular ballet exercise.

The Memphis music legend Isaac Hayes would pull up in his limousine (with a television on in the back seat - unheard of then) so that his daughter, Mia Hayes, could take my ballet class. Ralph Abernathy, famed civil rights leader, had grandchildren enrolled. Larry Riley (who later died later of AIDS) later played the role of Memphis in *A Soldier's Story* with movie star Denzel Washington. Larry was extremely shy when he took class. I thought his being extremely handsome would have boosted his confidence.

Michael Jeter, Tony winner for *Grand Hotel* and nominated for an Oscar for his roles in movies *The Fisher King* and *The Green Mile*, lived a block from me. What a fun person he was. None of us could have predicted the exciting futures of these performers.

A few years later, Warner Brothers rented our school for the movie, *This is Elvis*. Jeff Stuart played Pricilla Presley's ballet instructor. I held onto our paycheck, not cashing it for years.

I'll never forget the macabre and hilarious southern sense of humor. Bill Kendall, who owned the Guild Theater, was arrested many times while expressing his right to freedom from censorship. The night we saw the Swedish movie, *I Am Curious Yellow*, the line of moviegoers stretched almost around the block. A friend of Bill's, a character whose real name I have yet to find out, was known to all of us as "Mother Nature." He could be seen walking around midtown carrying an armload of gladiolas that he would hand out to people as he walked. He came to the movie premier dressed as Scarlett O'Hara in an antebellum gown complete with a huge hoop skirt. As his car headed down Poplar Avenue toward the theater, the heel of one of his high-heeled shoes got caught under the gas pedal, making the car go out of control, and he crashed into a police car. As the policeman got out of the car Mother Nature realized she was about to be arrested and made a mad dash toward the line of customers in front of the Guild Theater. She did a spontaneous hand stand, revealing to the crowd that Scarlett had forgotten to wear underwear that night. Seeing the policeman in hot pursuit, the crowd came to her aid, hiding her under the customers' feet as they sat in the theater awaiting the movie's start.

The angry policeman broke through the line of ticket buyers, searching for the person who had crashed into his car. He went into the theater and found Bill, and asked him if there was someone in the theater dressed like Scarlett O'Hara.

Bill replied very loudly, "I didn't know Vivian Leigh was supposed to be in attendance tonight, but frankly, my dear, I don't give a damn!"

The policeman, totally frustrated, grabbed Bill by the arm and carted him off to jail. Just one example of the many times Bill was arrested for showing films some in Memphis thought obscene. When the judge reprimanded him for showing an obscene film, Bill replied that Jackie Onassis' picture had been in *The New York Times* showing her emerging from a New York theater that was screening the same film. Glaring at the judge, he said, "People here would not know art if it bit them on the ass!"

One event that never made the society pages was the Dead Elvis party on Front Street, parallel to the Mississippi River. As the party began to swing, a coffin rolled along in a funeral dirge around midnight and out jumped an Elvis impersonator singing, *You Ain't Nothin' but a Hound Dog!*

Another time, we gasped at the glaring example of bad taste shown by the tribute to country music singer Patsy Cline, but we laughed at the outrageous humor of the scene. To the accompaniment of the Patsy Cline song, *I fall To Pieces*, out came a coffin bearing a drag queen dressed as the deceased Miss Cline. The impersonator held a giant propeller in her arms and lip synched along with the song. Her costume was made of burned fabric, reminding us of Patsy's untimely death in a plane crash.

Chris Ellis, our stage manager, who later went on to have a very successful movie career, said, "My God. All your taste is in your mouth!"

***

Southerners have a wicked sense of humor. Isn't it always better to laugh than to cry? At George's Bar and Truck Stop I learned to appreciate popular music once again. A lot of gay icons had already died by then. James Dean had been gone a long time, but as people suspected, his conflicts were all too familiar. Judy Garland was dead, so was Marilyn Monroe. Bette Davis would obviously soon be gone, too – she had suffered a devastating stroke.

We were all preparing to attend the annual Dead Elvis Party. I had been to it once before. Because it was Halloween, we were all expected to wear costumes. I went as an animal trainer, wearing a handle-bar mustache, a blue velvet cape, and carrying a whip. Jeff was dressed as a masculine lady bug – he had exaggerated wings, a red and black skull cap and antenna, and he teetered along on platform shoes. Stan, an athlete, explained what a huge boost in self confidence he got by occasionally becoming Barbara Streisand. No one mentioned to Stan that Barbara had never been six feet tall. But, tall and confident he was!

The party was held in a deserted warehouse above The Magazine, a well-known dance supply store where dance students and even Cybil Sheppard bought everything from leotards to toe shoes and one-of-a-kind jewelry pieces.

Upon arrival we were greeted with peals of laughter and we went into a state of high amusement when we saw everyone's imaginative costumes. At midnight a coffin was carried in and out sprung the best Elvis impersonator I had ever seen. Later that night, Judy Freeman, Stan/Barbara, Jeff and I, more than a little tipsy by now, walked up Front Street feeling the cool embrace of fog and mist rising off the Mississippi. Jeff the lady bug, a little off kilter in those platform shoes, accidentally stepped on a pile of glass and cut himself so had to be taken to Baptist Memorial Hospital. He tactfully snuck into the emergency room without us, knowing we might have caused a small riot.

While sitting in the car that night I heard a radio report about the fate of a friend. A college professor, well respected by everyone in Mississippi, he had one fatal flaw. Although married, he was compulsively attracted to handsome young men. Against his better judgment he had followed the young man into a public park. The man went into a public restroom stall and closed the door. My friend then went into the next stall. Through a hole between the two stalls the young man gestured for the professor to insert his flaccid penis. Unbeknownst to both men, they were at that very minute being observed by a state trooper who, in a booming judgmental sounding voice, asked them to step out into the open.

The professor was unable to move. By now his penis had become erect and he couldn't pull himself out of the hole. Even if he had have pulled out, the state trooper had obviously discovered the two men in the middle of a sex act.

The men were arrested and hustled into a police car. After that night the professor's productive teaching career was ruined. The younger man switched colleges and left the state for good. In those repressive days, erotic feelings could lead to these kinds of desperate acts.

Well, let's be honest. For closeted married men, things haven't changed that much.

Chapter 19
With Jeff by My Side

For the next 15 years, I had many adventures with Jeff by my side. Because he proved to be ambitious and restless, maybe my lifestyle was an exciting challenge to him.

Lack of funds and the disapproval of the Memphis Arts Council found me frequently digging into my own pockets to fill the constant financial needs of Ballet South. Since Ballet South did not follow the traditional rules of the Arts Council, all would-be dancers were welcome. The company made its own rules as artistic opportunities presented themselves, and we gave free range to any truly creative talent. I had to do this. Even so, we did have some money left from classes and other sources, but our personal finances were generally unstable and became the main reason Jeff and I moved a lot.

Jeff liked nothing better than to transform a mediocre environment into something beautiful. Now and then we had landlords and others who understood our plight and helped us in our artistic pursuits. But the conflict between the dream and the reality, the fantasy and practicality, seemed like blind ambition. Ballet South was always my first consideration and my own comfort came second.

The Paige family had a huge mansion on Belvedere Street. This Memphis neighborhood was one of the oldest in town and had great historical value. At one time, Russian immigrants had lived at the mansion, a fact that seemed odd to me. The image of Russians in the Paige mansion was strange. The building was large and stately, but didn't look southern at all. But neither did it look like the home of Russian immigrants.

Maria Paige, Anne Paige's daughter, studied with us. As long as I paid the rent, Mrs. Paige, whom I found to be very beautiful and intelligent, didn't mind if I was late with the payments from time to time. Marguerite Piazza whom I had seen countless times on *Your Show of Shows* and *The Bell Telephone Hour* lived right up the street.

We loved the mansion's carriage house next to the swimming pool, and it provided an atmospheric abode for us. We lived there longer than anywhere else. We also lived in some other memorable places in Memphis.

The Barracks, which looked like an army barracks, was located in midtown one block from Overton Square, the center of many interesting venues, including a bookstore, many restaurants, and several eclectic little shops. The Barracks was pleasant enough during the day, but when we turned out the lights at night, we discovered a huge cast of cockroaches reminding us, in their huge number, of the entire cast of *Ben Hur*.

I remember the wonderful cottage across from Audubon Park on Goodlet Street, also in midtown, and the night a huge rumble of thunder was followed by a big ball of lightning that came streaking through our front door. We saved our lives by diving quickly to the floor and later found that all of our appliances, including the television and lamps, had shorted out during that one dramatic and frightening moment.

Then there was the upstairs loft at Bingham and Broad Streets. From the moment I moved in I felt uncomfortable living there, despite its privacy and spaciousness. At one point, I became deathly ill. On the wall were drawings of pentacles (a five-pointed star used in magic) and mounds of black wax. There were drawers full of old dried plant leaves and flowers, and a wooden carving reminded me of the devil. When I was alone in the loft, eyes seemed to follow me everywhere. The place reminded me of the movie, *Rosemary's Baby*, so full of black magic symbolism.

My students Shirley Silver and Debbie Faber agreed that we needed an exorcism to get rid of the loft's bad vibes. So we scrubbed down all the walls with Clorox. Then Debbie found a drawer full of animal collars, again fuelling our imaginations. We played music at full blast and Shirley shocked us as she went into a wild dance to the music *Doin' the Devil In*. Laura Lacy joined us and soon we were all laughing hysterically and had forgotten we were supposed to be scared.

When I became acquainted with Sare Van Orsdell, a well-known astrologer who lived in Memphis, she turned away when I told her about the apartment with the black wax and pentacles.

"I know who lived there before you," she said. "Did he have a pet ocelot?"

"Yes," I muttered, wondering how a spotted wild cat could be someone's pet.

Sare looked at me long and hard. "George, you're from California and you can't know about southern black magic, and what I mean by "black" is negative energy that has taken place in and near this town, especially down along the Mississippi River banks and in towns all the way down to New Orleans."

"Memphis is known to have had the largest slave block in the South where slaves were brought up river in irons and sold by powerful men who made huge profits," she said. "The terrible fear, agony, and pain of those African American people and the uncertainty of their families' futures, probably caused a psychic doorway to be ripped open allowing deep levels of emotional anger and hatred to seep into the consciousness of the city, blacks and whites alike. I can feel it when I walk down the streets of midtown and along the waterfront. Energy had been left here by the things whites have done to blacks, as it has in many southern cities. It's dark magic energy. It's the legacy of Memphis."

I wondered, "Black magic...In my apartment?"

"Do you know who lived in that apartment before you, George?" She didn't wait for an answer. "It was the head of the Mid South Satanist Church. No wonder you have felt ill. The vibrations must have been quite intense for someone as sensitive as you."

"What should I do?" I asked innocently.

"Move," she said.

This information colored my imagination further, and every dark thought was confirmed when I found another wood carving in one of the drawers, looking even more satanic. The more I learned, the stronger my conviction became. I would not be ruled by this energy. My own positive disposition would overcome my anxieties.

I eventually became seriously ill despite my age and attitude, and I was forced to move.

We lived in another beautiful place for a few years, in a condominium we shared with Peggy Howard. She was a truly inspiring dancer and a great person. She and Jeff danced the leads in *On the Waterfront*, a beautiful modern ballet I choreographed. We performed on the banks of the Mississippi River for the Memphis in May Festival of 1979. This lyrical ballet was about the youth of Memphis rising up against racism by recognizing the universality of the humanity that connects us all. The ballet was a big success and the Leonard Bernstein score was vibrant and meaningful as the music echoed out over the rushing waters of the Mississippi.

All our hard work and efforts garnered us national attention and we didn't know about it until years later. One day while visiting New York, Jeff saw a picture of himself that neither of us had known about in an art gallery. There he was with his partner, Rose Barile, standing together in front of Alex Jankowski's stark sets and the Memphis-Arkansas Bridge arching gracefully in the background.

I loved living with Peggy and Jeff. Together, they inspired my best work as a choreographer. We were renting from Lyman Aldridge, a young developer and entrepreneur who had become an officer on our Memphis Ballet Board of Directors. I could see that he wasn't quite sure what he was getting into. Lyman tried to be broadminded about his tenants. He was an officer in the Overton Square Complex – Memphis' new entertainment center which included a theater, fine restaurants, and much more. The local prohibition laws that require people to brown bag their alcoholic beverages had been repealed, and Lyman was on the cutting edge of a new look being developed.

Then there was our unpredictable friend, Stan Allen, who was terribly shy, very polite, but lacking self confidence. When his alter-ego, Barbra Streisand emerged from time to time, though, he blossomed into a talented, aggressive, temperamental performer, one full of drama. His life reminded me of *The Three Faces of Eve* with Joanne Woodward. As a male, Stan was tall and handsome and had a winning smile. At first I couldn't imagine why he needed to become Barbra but I came to realize that his entire personality changed dramatically when he heard her music. Stan as Barbra was larger than life and he felt strong, happy, and more genuine. I treasured knowing Stan.

One fateful night, as Stan pulled up in front of the house to park, his car horn got stuck. The loud wail from the horn woke up the entire neighborhood, and eventually a big crowd of neighbors gathered around the car. He hid his face in sheer embarrassment as he crouched down in the car seat as far as his large body would allow. When he emerged from the vehicle after much coaxing he stunned the crowd with his full Barbra Streisand make-up on display. Peggy giggled with glee, "They all know we're different now!"

Our most memorable apartment was the huge one at Vance and Cleveland, in one of Memphis' most controversial areas. We had six big rooms on the second floor. A cat wandered onto our window sill one day and Tootsie soon became our pet. What I didn't know at the time was that every night at least 50 stray cats ate dinner at the

Sports Stadium across the street and slept under our apartment complex.

One day the electricity went out in our building and Memphis Light, Gas and Water (MLG&W) sent out a serviceman. He had been down in the basement awhile when we suddenly heard him frantically knocking on our door. We let him in and were stunned to see that his legs were covered with a mass of fleas. We immediately sprayed him with flea spray and he thanked us and asked if he could take the can back with him to the basement.

We learned to live with these frequent power outages. We kept the spray can handy for the service man and we religiously avoided the basement ourselves.

I remember seeing a beautiful African American woman standing on my corner night after night, going off in cars with total strangers for quick sexual interludes. She always smiled at me with reticence, apparently unable to quite believe how non-judgmental I was. I recognized many of our city's elite who were picking up this beautiful woman in her 40's, and taking her to the back parking lot. I felt sorry for her standing out there every night in the snow that winter and, in my mind, I imagined the children this woman might be supporting with her nightly take. One night, as Jeff came home from a night of dancing in the city's all-night discos, she stopped a mugger who jumped out of the shadows, ready to bash Jeff's head in and rob him.

"He's a friend," she told the burly man.

The next night was Christmas Eve, and in an effort to thank her, I went out to the street to take her a glass of hot Christmas brew, and she shyly accepted it.

As usual, we had an unconventional Christmas. I was reminded that Jesus always had a loving attitude towards prostitutes. So, why shouldn't I?

Chapter 20
Under an Electromagnetic Field

Ballet South's board president Mrs. William Farris (affectionately called Jimmie) had planned a big gala occasion to present one of the Democratic candidates' wives, Mrs. Walter Mondale, to the Memphis Arts community. Her husband was the head of the Democratic Party in Tennessee. I was honored that Mrs. Farris was our board president that year. I would never have thought back then that the intense conflicts between Republicans and Democrats would one day erupt into an all out vicious power struggle.

Like the richly sprawling Tara mansion in *Gone with the Wind*, the Farris home was stately and imposing. Jimmie always radiated a commanding presence that made one think of the country's First Lady, Nancy Reagan.

My Memphis friends and board members comprised a mixed political bag. Orma Henders, a Republican at that time, was married to a Democrat, Peggy, and I thought that was rather interesting. I came to care a great deal about them for they were in some ways like my own parents even though they were only a few years older than myself. I, too, thought like a Democrat, although my father always voted for the candidate he liked best and not along party lines.

Nancy Kopald was one of my most loving friends. She would give money to help a struggling dancer or to establish a scholarship fund, and she saved my neck more than once by giving me money for rent and doing other good deeds. While she always spoke her mind, she had the demeanor of a modern Joan of Arc. Her father was head of the local chapter of the Republican Party in Tennessee. Jimmie was very political. She knew her way around powerful people and she was clever.

She greeted us at the door and we looked forward to the elaborate reception she had planned for Mrs. Mondale. Visiting Jimmie was such a treat and I told her, "Your house is always so beautiful!"

She replied, "This will be a great event, George. The publicity will help the ballet and promote the Democratic candidate, too." Then, with a charming innocence, she added, "I don't know why people make such as fuss about me, because I'm only a simple country woman, you know!"

I grinned. There was something about her statement that didn't ring exactly true. She had already helped me so many times and I enjoyed a friendship with her daughter, Laura, who was a dancer with the ballet, and her son, Jimmy, an extremely interesting and intelligent fellow. I knew there was nothing country or simple about Mrs. William Farris. She always had great aplomb.

The food was abundant and the champagne flowed. Mrs. Mondale was scheduled to speak later. Alis Goldate and her husband Jim stood with me at a table the length of a football field, covered with elaborate dishes of exotic food and favorite southern finger foods.

"I'm so glad we didn't eat dinner before we came," Alis said, while Jim began filling his plate.

Everyone, including Mrs. Farris, was dressed up for the occasion. Following Mrs. Mondale's speech, Mrs. Farris raised her champagne glass and we all gave the guest a toast, wishing her and her husband, Walter, the best of luck.

The next speaker was the Vice President of the Memphis Arts Council (M.A.C.). I watched him expectantly. Over the years, the caliber of my work had finally succeeded in getting Ballet South some council funding. This was an achievement because, despite whispers about my personal life, the money came. Also, many Memphians thought I was color blind due to my promotion of black and white students alike according to their talents. When the Memphis Arts Council vice president stood up he credited Mrs. Farris for her involvement with the arts, ballet in particular, but before he got started, he gallantly raised his champagne flute and gave a personal toast to Mrs. Mondale.

Courtney Lewis, my great friend and ballet guild president that year whispered to me, "Next will be a long deserved tribute to you, George. You have worked for many years, not only for the ballet, but as a social worker in Memphis working to bring us all together."

All 200 guests waited patiently for the coming speech. The Vice President began, "I would like to thank Mrs. Farris and Michael Tevlin for the progress the Memphis Ballet has made in the last few years. *The Nutcracker* with the Memphis Symphony is superb, as were Baryshnikov's many appearances during the ballet season."

Alis, who was ordinarily warm and tranquil, bolted to her feet. Jim reached up and placed a hand on her arm, but she wouldn't be stopped. She stared angrily at the MAC vice president and cried, "I can't believe our own arts council is not aware of the amazing accomplishments of Ballet South and above all, George Latimer. The Memphis Ballet and Michael Telvin represent an entirely different organization!"

The MAC vice president turned pale and swayed, then, in embarrassment, he stumbled back into his seat.

Alis continued, "George Latimer has done more for ballet than any other person in this city and the professionalism of the ballet in Memphis is largely the result of his sacrifice and struggle!" She paused, and then added vehemently as she turned to face the guests, "And he doesn't even have a pot to pee in! I am outraged!"

You could hear a pin drop. Mrs. Farris courageously moved into the void as she began to smile and nod at everyone in true perfect hostess fashion, pretending that the evening was a joyful experience, while Mrs. Mondale looked startled and confused.

Apparently awed, Tricia Ochs whispered to me, "Alis Goldate is my friend forever, but I didn't see that coming!"

"I'm truly sorry," gasped the MAC vice president, acknowledging his mistake to the crowd. He sank down, stunned and unable to continue.

A few days later my friend Sare, the astrologer, said, "George, you had some disruptive energy going on that night… lots of misinformation and confusion. If people took astrology seriously, many personal, social, and business interactions could work out with greater smoothness. You're lucky. Things could have been much worse. The energy was bringing things to a head!"

"You can say that again," I said. I always listened to Sare and hoped that I would never again find myself in as vulnerable a position as I had been that night, under that astrological aspect.

I was depressed after the Mondale dinner. Was this the week from hell? Not entirely, but it had its highs and lows. I kept thinking of the opening words of Dickens' novel, *A Tale of Two Cities*. "It was the best of times - it was the worst of times."

Only I knew about my inner war. I called my brother, Bill, who never failed to make a joke.

He said, "Remember, on Dad's side, we come from a long line of British vaudeville comedians. They always found a way of coping. Remember what Mae West said, 'Why make an issue out of a little bit of tissue?'"

I couldn't help but laugh as I hung up the phone, but my surge of relief was interrupted by some shattering news. Dancer Roderick Drew had committed suicide. I never realized how conflicted he had always been. I had followed his career with great envy. First, he was the star of the San Francisco Ballet, and later, along with Finis Jhung and Lawrence Rhodes, he headed the team of artistic male dancers at the Harkness Ballet. I still envisioned him as the playful figure on the beach at Point Reyes, California when he was in his 20's. Now the person I so admired was dead, and by his own hand.

***

Sare had the style and wit of a quiet comedienne and the sunny looks that could have come from an imagined emerald isle. When speaking in front of her students, a self-confidence and strength emerged. A certain kind of sophistication surrounded her, and we were all transfixed as she translated the ancient language of astrology to us. I became a student as soon as I could and enrolled in her classes at Overton Square Bookshop. I had almost no religious training, but I believed that all humans were important and represented a basic part of the wheel of existence. But Sare was also spiritual.

I had always been puzzled by religion. The philosophy that is a part of astrology made intuitive sense to me: *all positive strengths and frailties in people represent the reasons we fulfill and need each other so much. All people's energies throughout their many lifetimes are found in the entire spectrum of human experience recorded in the electromagnetic field flowing throughout the universe.* Astrology show us that life is logical and perceivable, and that in each lifetime Spirit sends the soul to experience the potentials of organic, sensory, emotional, mental, and spiritual existence.

Sare was like no one I had ever known. She could sound like Scarlett O'Hara one minute or a little girl the next, and then she'd be immediately transformed into a European gypsy. Perhaps the real Sare was the writer and lecturer who inspired me to study with her and for a while to become her part-time assistant. My existence expanded and opened up to an entirely new world of people and parts of nature I had never experienced before. I realized as I met her followers and the new-agers who came to her lectures that I wasn't the only one in awe of this knowledge we were being taught through the ancient science and art of astrology. We were learning a concept that explained how energies in the solar system influenced the personalities of people on earth.

Whenever I think of Sare, I think of Jane Wyatt standing in the middle of Shangri- La on the Asian set of the film *Lost Horizon*. Birds are flying all about her as a Max Steiner score soars in accompaniment - truly an unequaled presentation of tranquility.

Chapter 21
Acts of Freedom

Ballet South got a jumpstart the day Peggy Jalenak called me regarding the Memphis appearance of Valery and Galina Panov in Memphis. It was a *cause célèbre*.

Valery had been imprisoned in Russia because he was Jewish and refused to abandon his religion. Galina, his wife, not a Jew, had steadfastly stood by him and people the world over sympathized with the stand they had taken against their government. Sir Laurence Olivier, Paul Newman, Joanne Woodward, and many other stars rallied to free Valery Panov. Their efforts were rewarded when the Panovs eventually got their freedom.

Since Ballet South was the most progressive dance organization in Memphis, we were chosen to co-host the Russians' appearance in our fair city. There were only a handful of performers throughout the entire United States who had made history like the Panov dancers and, to everyone's shock, all 4,000 seats in the Dixon Myers Hall were sold out in less than a week.

Rumor had it that Emily Klyce, who had become outspoken about how I had betrayed the local arts community by successfully funding Ballet South as the city's second ballet company, was amazed that any ballet event could be sold out in such short order. She tried to downgrade the event by commenting, "It sold out, like a football game."

Walter Diggs and Beverly Sousoulas planned the reception at Brooks Art Gallery. There was Russian caviar galore and steak tartar, a tasty concoction of raw steak, mayonnaise, chopped pickles and olives and, of course, plenty of vodka. Everyone looked forward to meeting the two great stars.

With our illustrious guests, we performed three ballets in different styles with a live orchestra performing classical music of

Shostakovitch, Debussy, Rossini and Gounod. But it was Galina who amazed us with her classical *Fouette,* changing her spot four different times so that she turned from corner to corner and eventually with her back to the audience, then returning to her original spot and faced the crowded theater with a brilliant smile. When not performing, the two Russian dancers, unlike most other great stars, stood in the wings when not performing, and in their broken English gave our dancers encouraging comments like, "Don't dance to the music - *be the music!*"

Beverly Sousoulas, a vice president of the MacDonald's corporation in Memphis, was in charge of public relations. Discovering that the Panovs were tired of caviar and Russian food, she arranged for the famous dancers to get a taste of MacDonald's hamburgers along with champagne, and an area was screened off at Brooks Art Gallery for the occasion. To the Russians, the hamburgers were a rare gourmet treat and a luxury.

Author James Michener, whose books include *Tales of the South Pacific*, was present that night. After the Panovs ate dinner, we all celebrated the visitors and their new found freedom.

Later, the ladies of the Jewish Community Center served the Ballet South dancers a traditional Russian meal at our rehearsal hall. They were kind to us, treating everyone as "important" artists. I later heard that the Panovs made their final home in Israel, where I believe they still reside today. They are also honorary citizens of New York City and San Francisco.

Beverly Sousoulas had many other talents besides being in charge of public relations at MacDonald's. She took over the production of Prokofiev's *Beauty and the Beast* for Ballet South. The newspapers, both of them, appeared to point out the differences in what they thought was the unusual creativity of our productions along side the technical elegance of the Memphis Ballet Company's Spring Concert.

This kind of press would mark the prelude to a proposed merger of the two Memphis ballet companies. Since Nelle's departure, Memphis Ballet had continued under new artistic direction for the most part in the classical mode. On the other hand, my own company, Ballet South, had experimented in different media and had developed strong, athletic and interracial creative dancers. Some of our African American dancers of note were Lowell Smith who went on to real fame, along with Marsha Peete, Denise Betts, and Sheila Bradley. And then there was Carlton Johnson who danced strong lead male parts and later formed his own company. Mari Lewis became an equestrian dancer for the Ringling Brothers Circus.

Then, as always, there were many funny little moments that lifted us briefly out of the anxiety and fear we all faced about the future of Ballet South. For example, one day when we were into our last full production of Ballet South and at 7:30 p.m., Jeff began to practice his press lifts with Laura Shindler (formerly Lacy). Peggy Howard and Laura were Jeff's partners most of the time. Laura and Jeff began to laugh hysterically over the fact that our guest artist from The National Ballet of Canada had just performed the same lift. The main difference was that the famous ballerina had an explosion of gas just as her partner pressed her above his head in a high arabesque. The expression on her prince partner's face changed from serene to horror. Their classical form and regal demeanor remained unchanged. One of the dancers turned to a stagehand and whispered, "I'm glad the orchestra is playing loudly!"

With the last Ballet South performance started and as talks of the merger increased in intensity, I found myself attempting to form a friendship with Michael and Judy Tevlin, directors of the Memphis Ballet. I was lonely for other dance teachers and artists, and I guess I was feeling that things were changing and nothing would ever be the same again. Although they were friendly, it wasn't enough to quell my uneasiness. After all, I had shed blood, sweat, and tears with this company over what was about to be taken from me.

Before that evening's performance, a line had begun to form around the theater. We sold out that night. The next day Alis Goldate called me to say, "You're not really going to give up your independence by merging with the Memphis Ballet, are you?"

Alis thought my willingness to merge was mainly about money for me. This wasn't the case. I felt that my reputation would be ruined if I ignored the efforts of some very important arts patrons who were working harmoniously to bring together one strong Memphis Ballet Company. The feeling was that this merger would give Memphis real national attention. I was naïve and later realized Alis's comment had been right on target. I began to understand the depth of resentment directed toward me for having created a successful second ballet company, Ballet South, and having integrated it with African American and white dancers while also experimenting with progressive ballet.

The merger went ahead and after six months the Board of Directors of the merged companies fired us all. Mike Tevlin wasn't surprised, and he and his wife, Judy, soon left town.

I stayed on in Memphis, holding on, and in a final gesture of artistic need mixed with hopes for a last-minute reprieve, I began to start a new company, Tennessee Ballet. This company, I soon realized, was not a new beginning but the beginning of an end, as I defiantly fought my way back through the dark political intrigue that surrounded the Memphis ballet world. Strong feelings were surfacing in me and I admit that I had equal parts of a new artistic ambition and deep-seated revenge in my heart. It was not over for me yet, I told myself, but events that eventually led to my leaving the old river town loomed on the horizon with deadly certainty.

***

As time went on, I found I still needed therapy. I was dealing with the same old conflicts and felt that I didn't fit in anywhere except at the school, with the dancers. I decided to find the best therapist I could locate to help me deal with my continuing guilt.

Surprisingly, I found a former nun, Sandra Pera. If looks were any indication she was an angel. Her sweet oval face exuded peace and acceptance. I learned a great deal from her.

One day during a session, she had me stand on a bench in her office. "Imagine that you are on trial below the bench of this great judge who is also you. After all, judges always are elevated higher than the person on trial. Now give me a summary of the crimes you have committed as seen by you, the judge."

I gravely rambled on for about 10 minutes or so.

Sandra sighed, "I wouldn't want to be in your courtroom. You are one harsh judge."

When I left her office at McLean and Union Avenues I had an altered attitude. Somehow, I was going to have to learn to love myself. In a way, Sandra Pera had given me permission.

Chapter 22
Another Side of Memphis

Before I finish the story of my life in Memphis, I realize I haven't written much about the dark side of the city, and before I do, I want to say that I truly learned to love southerners. Over all, they were the most emotionally expressive of all people I had ever met. I could understand why Carson McCullers, William Faulkner, and other southern authors wrote with such passion. I wondered if the movie, *The Firm*, based on the novel by John Grisham, which was shot in Memphis while I was there, was inspired by a law firm that I was more than familiar with. The movie was even filmed in the same building where the law offices were located - where Mrs. Farris arranged for our Board meetings to be held.

Many of the warm-hearted southerners I knew held deep prejudices, not out of hate, but out of fear. They thought I was color blind when dealing with Memphians. I want to say here that most people followed their higher, more idealistic sides when dealing with the ballet and with me. A few who were secretive and dishonest made my life a living hell, but now I look back on that time with a sense of humor, and, still wonder if Memphians were aware of the dark underbelly of their society during that time.

Memphis' gay community, which flourished every weekend, produced great shows. Sometimes as many as 3,000 people would attend and sing along with some of the top female impersonators, comedians, and serious performers. A gay bathhouse opened up in midtown and then closed after only a year. The establishment was complete with rooms, lockers, dance floor, and exercise equipment. Rumor had it that a powerful city official, leading a double life, agreed to look the other way. The location was just a few blocks from the medical center and the statue of Nathan Bedford Forest, the founder of the Ku Klux Klan.

Jeff, along with one of his dancing partners, Pam Taylor, left for the Atlanta Ballet. Dancing there would certainly give them both a career boost. Jeff, soon after arriving, danced as the Waltz Boy in Balanchine's *Serenade* and Pam played the dramatic heroine in Todd Bolender's *The Still Point*, New York City Ballet staples.

While I was glad for them, my nights were sometimes sad and lonely with only our dog Greta as company. Out of sheer boredom one night I went to the school which at that time was forced to close because of freezing weather. Marcus, a troubled friend, called me, and together we went to the Memphian Theater in midtown. He was always in the middle of one of his fantasies, and at that time he thought he was meeting Brooke Shields in the astral world for regular sexual encounters. I felt sad for my friend, who was simply a child in a grown man's body.

He asked me, "Do you want to see *Behind the Green Door*, you know, the movie that made Marilyn Chambers the most famous porn star of today?"

"Why not?" I replied, and off we went.

A movie palace that Elvis had rented for private screenings of his first-run films for friends, The Memphian Theater had once been an elegant movie palace. A porno theater in downtown Memphis was a fact that many people did not want to allow into their consciousness. After all, this was the Bible Belt.

A scruffy-looking young man took our money as we stepped in from out of the snow. He also met us at the door to the auditorium and tore our tickets in half, motioning us into the darkened theater.

Marilyn Chambers delighted Marcus. She looked truly innocent while behaving in the manner of Lucretia Borgia. Known for her commercials for Ivory Soap, she gave a new meaning to 99/100 percent pure!

Abruptly, while the picture was being screened for about 10 people, the same young man who had sold us the tickets and then torn them in half, began to dance down the aisle, sensuously removing all of his clothes. I guess we were supposed to respond in some welcoming way to this frolicking "extra" performance.

Marcus just said, "I may throw up."

Our ticket taker was beyond presumptuous, in my opinion. Elvis would have, at that very moment, just turned over in his grave and screamed, "Stay off My Blue Suede Shoes!" and I am sure that at least half of the Memphis Junior League would simply have fainted.

When I got home that night, the weight of snow on the roof over my apartment had caused the ceiling to collapse, and now the place rivaled Edgar Allan Poe's *Fall of the House of Usher*. Piles of snow, dirt, leaves and other debris were on my bed. Squirrels were running around in my apartment and my dog was going crazy. I moved out immediately.

Chapter 23
Tour de Force

We were quite inspired in those months before September 1979. Lee Wright, who took care of the Orpheum Theater, had lent Ballet South a key to the theater. This gesture was partly because I was working night and day writing a grant to C.E.T.A. to hire the unemployed.

"Remember dancers and related artists are usually always unemployed," I kept reminding everyone.

No one was more surprised than I was when we received a $79,000 grant. In 1979, that much money in Memphis was like $500,000 today. I thought we finally could hire a business manager, a staff of dancers, and scenic and costume designers. Lee said, "You need a home now," as he handed me the Orpheum's stage door key.

We eventually hired Karen Mason, a fine local actress, to be our manager. Karen immediately developed a caring but critical mother/son relationship with me as the undisciplined child. Actually, Karen liked the ballet a great deal, but in some ways, she added to the image of my being out of control. I can still hear her saying, "George, less is more!"

Mary Reynolds, our costume designer, worked in the Orpheum's spooky basement despite the ghost stories of Mary, the little child who died along with her vaudeville parents in a theater fire 50 years before. Vincent Astor, who had a voice like Peter Lorre, was the organist. He had told of the many ghost sightings he had witnessed at the Orpheum.

In a scene reminiscent of *Phantom of the Opera*, a month or so later, Vincent rose majestically out of the orchestra pit, playing the grand old organ that produced a volume so loud the walls shook. Then the organ music came to a crashing halt and he turned to the audience, covering his eyes from the blinding follow spot and cried out, "There she is!" pointing toward the first set of boxes. "Mary is visiting us right now," he wailed. The startled audience began to twist and turn in their seats to get a better view.

That act was hard to follow, but after the uneasy silence, Jeff, with his partner Laura Lacey Shindler, both exquisitely dressed in white from head to toe, came onto the stage to perform Mahler's *Adagietta*. Later Rufus Thomas sang and brought down the house with his risqué blues song, *In and Out*.

After the audience had calmed down and the applause subsided, Alis Goldate who had produced "Memphis Night" at the Kennedy Center in Washington, D.C., came on stage and read her silky poetry - ensuring an effective mood shift in that "Afternoon of Memphis Artists" benefiting the Orpheum.

Later, I met Alis backstage. She was a tiny woman with huge energy. Her chiffon dress was of a subdued color, which made her brilliant blue eyes seem all the more intense. I explained to her how we had been trying to get Mikhail Baryshnikov to come to Memphis, but I had just about given up.

"Giving up is not the thing to do. You can always get major stars if you play it right!" Alis declared, adding, "Who is his manager?"

"Someone named Sheldon Gold."

"Oh, Shelly, we were friends before I met my husband Jim. I don't see why you can't have Baryshnikov. I'll get right on it tomorrow."

A few weeks later we were announcing the upcoming appearance of Mikhail Baryshnikov, Peter Martins and Friends, and stars of the New York City Ballet. Fifty cities wanted them but only 15 cities got them. Thanks to Alis, we were one of them.

"George, bring Jeff and a guest Sunday afternoon to the home of Richard Lightman. They have their own movie theater and also own all the Malco Theaters," said Alis.

We went over the next Sunday and saw a private showing of *The Turning Point*. The movie was a showcase for Baryshnikov and it was obvious why the Russian dancer, along with Pavarotti, were the biggest box office draws in the world.

The night of the performance, Ballet South made a $200,000 profit. Otherwise reserved people called my house at all hours, naïvely wondering whether Baryshnikov had a place to stay or if he would like to attend "a quiet and private dinner."

What they didn't realize was that Baryshnikov was like a rock star. The demands in his contract were not unlike that of Mick Jagger or the Beatles. Also, Peter Martins was a great dancer destined to take over the New York City Ballet after Balanchine's death. But the public didn't know that yet.

Rudy Jones, who unselfishly donated hours of his time, hired police guards at the Orpheum to hold back the crowds. The night of the performance, a girl who had hidden backstage was literally dragged from the theater because she refused to leave. She kept screaming, "I just wanted to give him a red rose!" That mixture of passion and sobbing, called "celebrity hysteria," colored her voice.

Such strong emotions echoed through the mass of bystanders and ticket holders that we feared fans might accidentally suffocate Mikhail. All tickets were sold out 10 days before the performance, and the 4,400-seat theater was packed. There was absolutely no doubt that everyone was mesmerized by that night's brilliant performance.

The old Peabody was the perfect location for the reception. The Belz family had been slowly renovating the hotel and was bringing the beautiful old building back to life. The reception was to take place in the magnificent lobby and a long reception table for the dancers would include caviar (only the best), Perrier water which was relatively new then, and lots of vodka.

Judy Freeman, Jeff, Peggy Howard, and I dressed in the

Romeo and Juliet Suite high up in the Peabody. I wore a black tuxedo with a bright cherry red tie. Judy, always vivacious and strikingly beautiful, wore a dress that was a favorite of mine. It was layered with champagne-colored chiffon, dotted throughout with softly sparkling amber colored rhinestones.

Judy and I held each other up going down the long staircase, but we tripped on the second step - actually falling and bouncing on our rears at least half way down to the lobby. Jim Goldate, Alis' husband, had done some very imaginative decorating and people were so enthralled with it and the expected after-performance appearance of Baryshnikov, that they didn't notice us at all. We regained our composure before anyone saw us and made a regal appearance on our way to the dining table.

Jim had dressed my friend Gloria Cummings in a nude body stocking, covering her with fruit and baskets of fine chocolate. The more people ate, the more of Gloria's beautifully sumptuous body would be revealed.

"This gives a whole new meaning to the term "center piece," Judy and I laughed.

Gloria said, "Thank God the cream cheese is at another table."

All the people I loved were there, the Thomas McLemores, Walter Diggs, Beverly Sousoulas, Tricia Ochs, Peggy Jalenak, William Huettle, Sandy Hanover, Courtney Lewis, Sarah Pratt, and Ollie, her mother, Orma and Peggy Henders, and the great Ballet South board members themselves. The board had fought against Alis having so much control over all aspects of the performance, but I knew we needed her experience to make the event happen in this exciting way.

The public was not disappointed in Mikhail's mixture of great dance techniques and fiery sensuality along with the performance of many of Balanchine's great ballerinas of the time.

Judith Fugate's delicate strength and femininity only brought out the male dancers' masculinity. There was an audible gasp of delight when Baryshnikov leapt into the air and then unexpectedly changed directions.

Both Martins and Baryshnikov had reputations with women, and stories preceded them into Memphis. They arrived exhausted, looking as though they had survived an evening of intense lovemaking (but we knew better!) and were taken to the Peabody where they were to stay.

Mikhail Baryshnikov and Peter Martins will always be remembered as two of the great artists of our time.

Chapter 24

Disrobics, Frail Children of Dust, and Other Memorable Events

The next decade consisted of one amazing brush after the other with those who were artistically successful as we held workshops whenever a great teacher was passing through Memphis.

Conrad Ludlow, who had been Suzanne Farrell's partner, came through to teach classes and to set Bizet's *Carmen*, usually the opera, but now a popular ballet. He casually mentioned how lucky I was to have a company with high standards, good financial support, and the freedom to succeed or fail. If I could raise $30,000 a year, he said he might consider becoming an associate director of Ballet South. I was impressed. After all, Conrad was a fine teacher and choreographer and Balanchine himself had chosen him to work on many roles. One was as Prince Desire in the first American production of Tchaikovsky's *Sleeping Beauty*. I am still sorry we could not raise the money, but at that time in Tennessee, $30,000 seemed like a fortune to my Board of Directors.

George Zoritch of the Ballet Russe de Monte Carlo was an excellent teacher with an amiable personality, and he visited frequently. Dame Sonia Arova, whom I had seen perform years earlier, charmed everyone who saw her dance. During one of our conversations she explained that she was sometimes mistaken for Gina Lollabrigida and that Marlon Brando had been obsessed with her. Her charm had a driving ambition behind it, and she was already the director of several companies simultaneously.

Mary Van Dyke who had once been Sonia's student, relished the idea that Sonia might become our artistic advisor. Mary, Jan Heatherly, and Susan Crosby McCloy stood around Sonia's table listening with rapt attention as she told of dancing with Nureyev and directing the Norwegian Ballet.

Ted Cunningham lived in Canada and managed and arranged tours for the great pianist, Glen Gould. Ted gained a foothold in the Memphis arts scene by managing the Memphis Symphony. Miraculously, we gained support from the National Endowment for the Arts because of Ted. He took time away from his position with Estelle Axton at Stax Records to work for the ballet. Ted was a Memphis arts gem and always kind and knowledgeable.

To most people at the time I seemed carefree. Dona Benitone commented one day, "Your bad moods are better than most people's good moods, George!"

Judy Melton Wingate and her coworker at Willow Road Community Center, Janie, asked me to give a lecture on "The Male Dancer" for an audience of 400 dance enthusiasts. I was a decent speaker and had traveled to many cities to give visually enhanced talks. I accepted. With a VCR at my side and the very supportive efforts of Judy and Janie we set up a speaking event. At the appointed time, Janie and I tirelessly pushed the gigantic television which was big for the times, into the center of a room filled with excited families and bordered by tables of refreshments. I began to talk, showing films of Nureyev, Baryshnikov, New York City Ballet, and *West Side Story*. Then by accident, I picked up a film called *Disrobics* which showed men doing an aerobics class totally nude, prancing and dancing, body parts flying every which way. The situation went from serious to hilarious with me scrambling for the Off switch. My friend, Susan Keller, had given me the tape as a joke. We were good friends and she shared my offbeat sense of humor at that moment, and I was glad that most of the audience did the same.

Perhaps our most unusual accomplishment was a "happening" we all put together in the early 1980s. It was the end of summer. Bobbie Dodge, Judy Melton, Bill Westerbrook, Berverly Sousoulas, and I created the longest chorus line in the history of the United States. Over 10,000 people contributed their time and talent, coming from several states to participate. In one very long line we all sang and danced to Rufus Thomas's interpretation of the classic song *Beat Your Feet on the Mississippi Mud*. It was covered by CNN that day with helicopter views that captured the whole event for the world to see.

We began the touring months. Many people had never seen live ballet performances or, for that matter, much theatre at all. They were in absolute awe. The children were wide-eyed and speechless when, after the ballet, we mingled with the crowds. The highest character qualities of my dancers came out when their tutu costumes were tremblingly caressed by the children's eager little fingers, their eyes wide at the feel of such soft and colorful costumes. Some of the audience stared in surprised at the close- up sights of the male dancers' muscles and the girls' long, false eyelashes and make-up. Our troupe was interracial and I never gave it a thought even though, at the time, feelings were running high in some of the southern states, especially Alabama and Mississippi, whose state lines ran close to Memphis, Tennessee.

Ted especially warned us not to wander off by ourselves in Philadelphia, Mississippi. This had been the scene of the murder of three civil rights workers a few years earlier. I found myself hardly believing that the people we were meeting held such hatred for those of a different race. Everyone we met was so polite and generous.

When I returned to Memphis, with very odd timing, I was invited to the movie premiere of *Mississippi Burning* with Gene Hackman at a theatre near the Mississippi state line. I couldn't believe that where we had been the day before was the actual site of the violence that had erupted between the American Civil Liberties Union workers and local Mississippi residents. The murderers were not brought to justice until many years later. By then they were elderly.

The only other really frightening tour experience occurred

three weeks later near Selmer, Tennessee, just south of Memphis.

The school where the performance was to take place didn't look sinister at first. One clue was the small dirt road that wound around and onward for miles from the main highway. It was humid out, but when we arrived at the school, the building was almost frigid with exaggerated air conditioning.

We were performing excerpts from Giselle with our usual integrated cast. The school teachers at this school seemed to withdraw a bit when they saw us emerge from the bus, but the children loved us. During this performance by my interracial composition of dancers, the teachers became even more distant – unfriendly, actually. After the first half hour and during a break, we were met with frowns, hushed voices, and suggestions that we all wear sweaters over our ballet costumes. We stared at them in disbelief, then looking at each other with mixed emotions, we made a mutual silent decision after completing the performance and decided to leave this negative atmosphere. Following my lead, Michael McCadden, Brenda Meece, Carton Johnson, and Laura Lacey Shindler stopped only to gather up all our equipment before heading for the bus.

The next school was even further off the beaten path, and the road became more primitive and foreboding as we traveled. Even the sky turned darker as daylight gave way to a false night. We found the school at last, only to be greeted by a group of angry-looking people. The group stood on the front steps of the building and called to us over and over, "Go away!" while shaking their fists over their heads. Needless to say, crestfallen and hurt, we never left the bus but turned around and rode back down the long road to the main highway. We were all in a state of shock.

I had grown up with movies of the 1950s where alien beings with malevolent intentions were always trying to inhabit the bodies of ordinary people. This was a common science fiction plot in movies like *Invasion of the Body Snatchers,* and it now seemed real. We had just seen people assuming the garb of school teachers who were barely hiding their angry racism.

My imagination kicked in. I wondered if things might go further than what happened in Philadelphia, Mississippi, where on the surface all appeared to be benign. I leaned forward and asked Michael to drive a little faster. The skies continued to darken and gusts of wind threw road dust into the air. I looked back, envisioning a murderous mob chasing us down the road. As time went on and the drive back seemed endless, I found myself becoming extremely nervous, as were Carlton and Laura. We all brightened up immediately when we reached the main highway. Someone turned on the radio to break the mood, and the news was on. A tornado warning was in effect. That seemed appropriate.

I had never known fear to overcome a whole group of people before and we couldn't laugh it off. We were, as Elvis put it, All Shook Up!

At home that evening, my mood changed from mild terror to hilarity when Marion Peete came by with her beautiful daughter, Marsha, one of my African American dancers. The two were giggling as they walked in the front door of my apartment. Marion was a few years older than I, but one would never know it. She held her favorite drink in her hand, white wine mixed with Sprite. And she had news.

Once again someone had failed to close the doors of the Overton Park Zoo. The monkeys had taken over Idlewilde School, where Marion taught. Some 30 wild-eyed and mischievous monkeys now ran and hid along the rooftops and in the shrubbery. For three weeks following the event their faces would suddenly appear at a window, causing great hilarity.

Marion grinned, "It's hard enough to teach them darlin' babies. A lot of them come from homes where trouble is no stranger.

Well, I guess it's good for them to laugh." Thirty days later the last monkey was retrieved and returned to the zoo.

Later that night, after Marion and Marsha returned home, I received a call from Lorraine Bell. I had always enjoyed our encounters, as she and her husband, Raymond, were sophisticated in a delightfully unexpected way. Their daughter, Tammy, was a student at the school, and Lorraine's visits were like a breath of fresh air. She asked if I could bring the ballet to Father Betram's school to help celebrate Dr. Martin Luther King's birthday. Also, they wanted to present me with a special award in honor of this great African American leader's birthday which had not yet been made a national holiday. I was deeply honored.

Despite the fact that we were in a gym, not a theatre, the dancers gave one of their best performances. I received the award with dignity and pride and treasured it for years. (California's infamous Oakland fire of 1991 destroyed it).

Following our trip down into Mississippi, we were exhausted from traveling and dancing under such stressful circumstances. At the studio, Brian Brother and Cynthia Bailey were rehearsing on what must have been the hottest night of the year. Lynn Gillick had written a ballet but with an unconventional music score, using Coke bottles. She had opened the top of the piano and strung the bottles inside the area. The piano music and the clinking of the glass bottles combined quite pleasantly. Sare Van Orsdell wrote the libretto, inspired by the 12 astrological signs.

The dancer's bodies were wet with perspiration because of the terrible heat that evening. I realized with a start that these "god-like" youth were now wearing transparent leotards and tights. The sweat of their dancing bodies had made the light colored costumes into see-through garments and my dancers appeared naked before their audience! Ah, well, I thought, all is in the eye of the beholder.

I felt a personal and spiritual closeness to my dance family and a great love for the romantic, emotional, and sometimes, even the devastating experiences of ballet in this place called the South. My closeness with Elaine Jekels Hoffman and Dona Bentone was typical as we performed *American in Paris*. Our choreographic collaboration with the Memphis Symphony was a highlight.

Meanwhile, Alis Goldate had been busy. She had arranged for yet another Baryshnikov benefit. This time, his group would come from A.B.T. The world premiere of Twyla Tharp's *Sinatra Suite* would be seen for the first time anywhere, in Memphis, with Baryshnikov and Elaine Kudo dancing the leads under the patronage of Ballet South. Anna Kisselgoff of *The New York Times* and a bevy of critics from around the world would also be present.

The ballet was a resounding success. Somehow, *Strangers in the Night*, *One for My Baby*, and *One More for the Road* worked beautifully together as a showcase for Twyla, Baryshnikov, and Elaine Kudo.

Alis, knowing that we were performing Tchaikovsky's Holiday Classic, *The Nutcracker* with the Memphis Symphony, mentioned this fact to Misha (Baryshnikov's nickname for those whose know him well). Alis also arranged for A.B.T.'s most recent Nutcracker sets and costumes to be sent to Memphis. This was very exciting because the previous December the entire beautiful production with Misha and the great Gelsy Kirkland had been televised on PBS. But besides the obvious blessing, there was a strange curse that began with the production in Memphis, which I will mention later.

The set was almost too large for the North Hall Stage at the Dixon Meyers Auditorium, but the overall impression was stunning. David McNaughton and Melinda Roy of New York City Ballet danced our Sugar Plum and Cavalier and looked in the magnificent in their costumes they brought with them from New York City Ballet production. Jeff was thrilled and honored to wear Baryshnikov's cavalier costume in the snow scene at the end of Act One.

The giant tree that grows after the battle between the mice and the tin soldiers was over 80 feet tall. At Lincoln Center, the tree worked perfectly as if in a dream. In Memphis, the giant tree was awe-inspiring, and the night of the dress rehearsal, the orchestra, under the direction of Vincent De Frank, out-played themselves. The Snow Queen and King were about to dance the elegant *pas de deux* when Jan Heatherly and Jeff looked high above to the tree growing inside the proscenium arch and were horrified to see that billowing clouds of smoke had begun to spill outward, spreading across the arch.

Jan screamed to the dancers, "Run, little mice!"

Jeff yelled, "Run, little soldiers for your lives!"

The dress rehearsal came to an abrupt halt as the stagehands put out a fire at the top of the tree. We opened the next night and during the holiday run, performed before 40,000 children and 15,000 adults – truly an awesome sight. The attendance was increased by 30 percent partly because of the front-page newspaper headlines that read: "Ballet Almost Destroyed by Flames."

Ironically, Henry Klyce performed in the string section of the Memphis Symphony that night. I knew Henry fairly well as I had lived in his room for six months after he moved out of his house, and later we would meet again under unusual circumstances.

After a few months, a newspaper story was headlined, "Snow Queen marries Drosselmeyer." Our *Nutcracker* star, Jan Heatherly, had married the kind and masculine Mike Henry who played the mysterious magician in our production.

The odd curse was that no one else would ever see this production again. There was a warehouse fire in New York and the same stage elements had turned to ashes. Another act of irony took place when our warm and caring stage crew packed about 20 costumes in the wrong trunk. A year later I gave them to Cynthia

Gregory and Clark Tippet who needed them for a tour. Clark and I were shocked when they turned up in our costume room. We finally shipped them back to New York by Federal Express.

A few years later this fine dancer, Clark, joined the ranks of the many ballet dancers and directors who died of AIDS. I was deeply saddened. He was a real prince on stage and in life.

During this time the Memphis Arts Council brought in Walter Terry, the famous dance critic of *The New York Times*, to evaluate the choreography of the two Memphis ballet companies' artistic directors - Michael Tevlin of Memphis Ballet Company and myself for Ballet South. Some people secretly hoped he would find my work atrocious. Luckily, he was honest and gave us both good reviews with only some reservations. Other than the rudimentary facts, art is a subjective matter, after all.

About this time, I had started hearing from my brother that my mother was so arthritic, he felt she needed some help. Was it time for me to go back home to the Bay Area?

***

Although Lynn Gillick thought I had real talent as a composer, she was the one who had great talent as a composer, having written two ballets my company performed. My students, Sandra Gatlin and Susan McCloy, loved the modern sound when Lynn strummed the inside of the piano like a harp.

While Sandra had always treated me like an equal (young students often do not), Susan saw me as her godfather. Susan's mother, Suzanne, and I would often exercise by going for long nature walks. She became my close friend and she seemed like the daughter I would likely never have.

We flew to New York (only an hour and a half by plane from Memphis) together and within one week attended five ballets, four musicals, and six films.

I was also enjoying my relationship with Sare. For the first time I thought I understood the natural flow of all energy through the teachings of astrology. It helped me feel at one with nature.

Lynn played the piano for our master class series that included some of the all time dance greats. During one of our classes she whispered, "Aaron Copland is coming to Memphis for a special celebration. Dr. Fruchtman told me they're going to ask you to choreograph *Appalachian Spring*!"

I was so excited to hear this news. I knew dancers come and go, but great composers are remembered forever. I loved his music, and he knew I loved the classics and modern music equally. What an honor!

Later, Martha Graham, who owned the rights to *Appalachian Spring*, gave us special permission to use the original 16-instrument score which was longer than the popular *Suite* from the piece. This information about *Appalachian Spring* was relayed to me as Efrim Fruchtman talked to her on the phone.

"I have never let anyone use *Ballet for Martha* before," Martha Graham said. It's Aaron's 80th birthday celebration, so you can use the score, but you must change the title."

We wracked our brains for weeks. One day Laura Lacy Shindler opened an ancient Bible in an old church down on the Mississippi River Bluffs. Her eyes were drawn to a phrase, "frail children of dust." That was it, the title we had been looking for.

The program was successful. The Opera performed Copland's *The Tender Land*. Memphis Ballet bought in Norbert Vesak for the Clarinet Concerto and the program ended with *Appalachian Spring* alias *Frail Children of Dust*. We all shared a bow with America's greatest composer.

The local newspaper loved the entire program but added that my ballet was a musical "menage à trios." I had taken the plot of one of my favorite French movie, *Le Bonheur* (translation: Happiness). The story was of a dying woman who truly loved her husband and encouraged him to take a mistress so that he would not be alone. I thought this heartfelt selfless sentiment was well displayed and very beautiful.

Beverly Sousoulas, Efrim, and I had dinner with Aaron on his 80th birthday. There I learned the art of a backhanded compliment. Aaron wrote a note on a poster that was kind and personal. He then added, "Your ballet was very interesting." Well, I thought no one could compete with Martha's great originality.

When I met Peggy and her husband, Orma, they had already become involved with the ballet. They loved the arts, partly because they loved me, and partly because, as Peggy had said, "A lot of dancers would have no place to perform if it weren't for George and his humanitarian Ballet South Board of Directors."

Meanwhile, Alis Goldate had once again worked her magic, and Peggy, Orma, and I were off to attend yet another Baryshnikov fundraiser for Ballet South. Orma was in a dark tuxedo and Peggy wore a beautiful evening gown, bedecked with amazing jewelry for the occasion.

We piled into Orma's car and I thought we were on our way when Peggy cried out, "Orma, stop the car! I have to feed the babies."

To my surprise, Peggy disappeared into a seemingly deserted building. A few minutes later she came out with a large tray holding recently opened cans of cat food. Being careful not to trip, she balanced the tray as she walked, evening gown, high heels, and all into what appeared to be a deserted field. From out of nowhere they came, first one cat, then two, then 10, then 30. The meows of appreciation were deafening.

Peggy smiled, "Well, that's done. Now we can go."

I would often spend the night with the Henders. There was Peggy and Orma's house, which was professionally decorated, and then there was the house for the dogs. I often stayed in the dogs' house, which was elegant, too. (At night the dogs would go outside into their little dog houses where music was piped in for them.)

Peggy and Orma were true animal lovers. The special dog residence was across the street from their home, and Henry, who was the Henders' loyal helper and jack-of-all-trades, would let a chef in to cook fresh chicken just for the dogs. Peggy and Orma's hearts went out to all in need. Luckily, I was included.

I loved my Memphis Country Club class. When I walked through the doors, I put all politics behind me because there were many fine people whose friendships I still value today.

I will never forget the day that I complained about the fact that Jeff Stuart, Peggy Howard, and I were totally out of food and money. We had eaten coconut sandwiches the night before and in desperation, fed some sunflower seeds to the new parakeet Jim Farris had given us. The bird died the next day, and I felt just awful about being so uninformed about what birds can and cannot eat.

Justine Smith, hearing about our frustrated hunger, invited us to come to the world-famous Justine's Restaurant for dinner anytime we were hungry. Often Justine and her daughter, Janet, would meet us there for the best food we had ever eaten. No wonder it was the favorite restaurant of the Metropolitan Opera Company in the South.

In another *cause célèbre*, the City of Memphis had sued porn actors Georgina Spelvin and Harry Reems for obscenity in their movie, *The Devil and Miss Jones*.

My recently divorced friend came to the class daily. She met the infamous Harry Reems at a party and offered to cook him a southern meal. The cornbread was baking, a pork roast was cooking, the salad was in a large glass bowl, and the greens with ham hocks were boiling on the stove when she felt his hands grab her waist with an exaggerated sense of urgency. The salad hit the floor along with the cornbread. But nothing could stop Harry. There they were with food all over their partially clothed bodies. The sight was truly comical, something right out of the movie *Tom Jones*, had it been X-rated.

Chapter 25
Of Dancers and Ducks

As I look back over my Memphis years, I now understand how some events took on great symbolism for me. As I mentioned, The Memphis Arts Council had asked us to perform a program of ballet excerpts at the Shelby County Penal Farm. We felt our performance was a big success, especially when the Associated Press covered the event as a story about the revolutionary idea of bringing ballet to prisons. I received calls from California and New York the next day because the release was such a positive story it ran in most national newspapers. The ballet was well received and was followed with compliments from both prison personnel and the inmates. Curiously, a blackout had occurred during the performance, but my high-spirited dancers had walked in an orderly fashion to the center of the gymnasium and patiently waited for the lights to come back on. In retrospect, I believe this lighting failure was a premonition of things to come.

The Arts Council did not agree with the national coverage claiming our prison ballet was a positive event. The very people who asked us to carry it out called our performance "obscene." They unfairly punished us by holding back our funding for two years. (During that time, I thought, well, maybe ballet really was obscene. After all, I would rationalize, did I really know whether the prisoners were whistling at the female dancers or the male ones?)

We had performed a jazz ballet in brightly colored leotards. Innocent enough, I thought. I began to ruminate on the situation and wondered if it was the integration angle, not the sexual one, that disturbed them so. At that time, we were the only ballet company in the region that had a black dancer. Or perhaps there was a bias toward me because I wasn't born a southerner and had a mysterious and private personal life.

My courageous Ballet South Board of Directors responded to the Arts Council's cutting of our funds by staging a fundraiser at the historic Peabody Hotel. This hotel had been mentioned in the film of Tennessee Williams' *Cat on a Hot Tin Roof* with Paul Newman and Elizabeth Taylor. Writer William Faulkner had once commented that anyone who was socially important was sure to be seen from time to time at the famous lobby fountain which was the daily destination of the Peabody Ducks.

For years, these well-trained mallard ducks would web-foot it down from the rooftop via the elevators, which opened onto the lobby and then march out single file past crowds of people, lining their walkway. They would head for the huge fountain in the center of the lobby and jump in for their lively daily swim. The Peabody Ducks were an inspiration.

People like Rudy Jones, Beverly Sousoulas, and Courtney Lewis went beyond all our expectations and secured Memphis Slim, Rufus Thomas, Ma Rainey, and Phineas Newbern, who rarely performed at that time, and Sid Selvedge who volunteered his services.

Rufus Thomas was by now famous for Doing The Dog and The Funky Chicken. His daughter, Carla Thomas, and many other stars also took part. The *crème de la crème* of the Memphis Blues Community donated time to what they thought was a worthy cause: the reopening and refurbishing of the Peabody Hotel and the survival of Ballet South.

When I think about it, strong feminist women have always surrounded me. First, my mother, my friend Irene, and then Carol, my dance instructor, who counseled and guided me throughout my career and to whom this book is dedicated. Carol used to say, tongue in cheek, between *pliés*, *pirouettes* and *grand jetés*, "A woman's place is in the house!" Then under her breath she'd mutter, "in the House and the Senate!"

Judy Short Freeman, one of my dance instructors, had never bothered to burn her bra, but declared her feminist freedom in many other ways. Judy had divorced her husband and become a member of the feminist organization the National Organization for Women (N.O.W.) and had begun to support the ballet. I remember one of our guest artists saying that Judy wore him out. Then he would smile mischievously to show he loved every minute of her company. Judy would come to support the ballet, with all her heart and soul. When the dancers had nothing to eat, we would all go to her house and project movies on the wall while she filled our stomachs with huge plates of pasta, grated cheese, and salad.

***

I wanted to add our own touches to make the ballet at least, in part, our own. Dona Bentone was moving everything extra out of the way and into the Overton Square studio while Courtney Lewis helped alleviate some of the financial strain by selling ads for the program. We were excited that we could rent the entire Boston Ballet production of this Tchaikovsky classic (*Sleeping Beauty*) and it soon arrived in two huge moving vans.

Our Aurora, meaning "beauty," was to be danced by Suzanne Goldman who was bringing her own costume from American Ballet Theatre (A.B.T.) where she was a soloist. Baryshnikov himself approved of her appearance. Ethan Browne, Leslie Browne's brother, was going to be her partner as the dancer, Prince Desire. I remembered seeing Ethan perform amazingly well as Shirley MacLaine's son in the film *The Turning Point*.

Elaine Jekels Hoffman and I formed a choreographic bond during this performance, and would work together frequently.

Suzanne had brought seven other dancers from A.B.T. for the performance. Alexander Bennet, formerly with England's Royal Ballet, staged some of the solos, while Elaine and I, along with Nancy Shainberg, cleaned everything up. This was a true venture of cooperation in the arts in that we all created the choreography together.

While all of this was going on, Alis, who always came through for us, had arranged for Baryshnikov and members of A.B.T. to perform yet another lucrative benefit on our behalf, and the sold out the house.

A benefit dinner was to follow in the ballroom of the Memphis Country Club. I had worked there in the mornings teaching ballet exercise for almost 20 years. I knew that many, many racially mixed groups had rented the ballroom. The rumor was, and it often appeared to be true, that old southern traditions about color would not easily keep pace with the changing times. Yet, Memphis grew more cosmopolitan. Courtney had also made an encouraging comment about the country club when she said, "My father was Jewish and he became a member at the club."

What we didn't know was that Baryshnikov had heard some rumors about racial discrimination at the club. We found out that he was not in a good mood when he entered the establishment.

After the performance the entire troupe of A.B.T. dancers came in to an elaborately staged dinner at the Memphis Country Club. I sat with Suzanne Goldman, Ethan Brown, Dona, Carlton Johnson, beautiful Marsha Peete, and Alis and Jim Goldate. Suzanne whispered in my ear, "Something is going on."

Misha and Bernie Lawrence, Steve Lawrence's brother, seemed very unhappy. Something was upsetting them.

All at once, every dancer, every staff member, along with Baryshnikov and Bernie Lawrence, stood up in what appeared to be a choreographed motion. As a gourmet dinner beyond my imagination was about to be served they headed for the door. Alis had great instincts as to what to do in a crisis, and she raced Misha to the door. "What is happening?" she demanded.

Misha responded with anger. Apparently, he had heard

something that provoked him to it. He said, "We protest the Memphis Country Club's attitude toward minorities. Half of my company are minorities."

Alis pleaded with him, "Don't do this to George and Ballet South. Just look at his staff and company!"

"All right, Alis, for you, George, and his dancers we will go back to the dinner. But first all media, TV, newspapers, everyone must be called."

Alis gave a sigh of relief. "Thank you."

My friend Shelia Peace, a reporter, was already there partying with us. She, being African American, was sympathetic toward the situation, but I was worried, knowing that all three television networks would soon be there along with more reporters.

Baryshnikov addressed them. "My dancers are Asian, Jewish, and African American," he began. His words took me completely off guard because by now, many kinds of people were County Club members, and rules of the club had been established a long time ago. Still, at this time, there were no African American members.

The story went national the next day.

Chapter 26
Good-bye, Memphis

Imagine this scene: Alexander Godunov dancing in an intoxicated frenzy with his dance partner in spirit, Justine Smith, on the dance floor at Blues Alley. Although they each had their own space they were dancing together. We had dined that evening at Justine's Restaurant where our hosts went into the wine cellar and brought out two bottles of 50-year-old wines. Godunov was not only a great dancer, but had just appeared in the critically acclaimed *Witness* with Harrison Ford. There was also the much-publicized romance between Godunov and Jacqueline Bisset, mind-blowing at the time.

Later in New York, we realized that the Godunov who excited us so on stage in the ballet *Spartacus,* loved to dance as much offstage as he did on stage. Jeff and I watched him dance his way down the street to freedom, followed by a stream of photographers, cameras flashing.

What excitement for ballet around the world the day Godunov defected from Russia and the Bolshoi Ballet. We had watched the local events from our room at the Empire Hotel across from Lincoln Center in New York. Tragically, only a few years later, Godunov, one of the greatest dancers in the world, would be found dead in his Los Angeles apartment. Many said that he had been under a terrific strain from trying to combine his dancing career with his new movie career. Alcoholism was rumored.

As for me, my days in Memphis were now numbered now that my mother back on the West Coast could no longer walk. I spent many wistful hours going over in my mind the all of the Ballet South highlights of the last 20 years.

Lowell Smith, my former student, was causing a sensation at Dance Theatre of Harlem in *A Streetcar Named Desire*. I could still

see him leaping high above the students' heads in our tours of Shelby
County and Memphis City Schools. Agnes De Mille requested that
Lowell perform in the Russian tour of Dance Theatre in *A Rose for
Miss Emily* based on a Faulkner short story, as well as her classic
Fall River Legend. Jeffrey Stuart out-performed himself as the tragic
clown in *Petruska.* Barbara Dodge drove daily from Arkansas to
play Jeff's mysterious gypsy nemesis. Carlton Johnson was not only
our dancer then, but became associate director at Ballet South. In his
ballet, his performance was a vivid *Adam* to Marcia Peete's *Eve.*

During this time, Sheila Bradley was our most flexible dancer
and electrified everyone in the Ruby section in *Beauty and the Beast.*
Carlton had become a taskmaster and the girls found that they had to
work harder for him than for me.

Liz McLemmore said, "I love him like a brother. But it is like
being in the army."

Brenda Meece had come back to ballet and found a new joy
in performing the Snow Scene in *Nutcracker* even though the
costumes looked horrible up close because they were made partly of
plastic. Our new studio was in Overton Square above the old ice
rink. Dona Bentone to whom I owed a great debt, had courage and
daring and she loved ballet. Jeff, Carlton, Dona and I took many
risks with overall exciting results. Dona would often reach into her
own pocket to make sure the school was thriving with artistic vigor

One day, Tiffany, Dona's daughter, arrived in a very excited
state. "Cary Grant is eating lunch across the street at Paulette's
Restaurant!" She cried, "My heart is beating a mile a minute!"

Grant was performing in a one-man show at the Orpheum.
The manager of the candy store beneath our studio quickly handed
Tiffany a huge brightly wrapped bag of gumdrops and told her to
take them to his dinner table.

As far as they were concerned, Cary Grant was the most
romantic figure in films and she had heard he was addicted to

gumdrops.

Later, as she was closing down the shop and on her knees cleaning a sticky spot of ice cream off the floor, she felt hands covering her eyes. She was pulled to her feet and found herself staring right into Cary Grant's large, expressive eyes. He quickly kissed her, thanked her, and left the store.

"I think I'll never wash my face again!" she said, sighing and placing her hands over her heart.

A suitable ending for my stay in Memphis would be the scheduled appearance of Rudolph Nureyev. He would appear in a Wednesday-night performance with members of Paris Opera Ballet, sponsored by Memphis Cablevision. One of my dreams was about to come true because since my 20s I had felt my spirit had entwined with Nureyev's. He was the inspiration for all my intense ambition.

Then we received two psychological blows. One month before the performance, Rudolph's manager announced we would have to rent a special dance floor from the Boston Ballet for $20,000. This was a lot of money back in 1986. At the same time, a week earlier, Cablevision withdrew its support. That was no mystery. An unhappy former dance board member was also on the Board of Directors at Cablevision.

Dona said, "We can do it anyway!" And she was right. Billie, Abbie, and Richard who were my friends as well as members of the stage crew, worked hard to find a dance floor. All the stage hands, dressers, union members, seamstresses, and other union hands saved our lives and I was forever grateful.

Billie had shown me a basketball court in the storage area above the theatre and the day of the dress rehearsal the crew moved the basketball court onto the stage that they covered with our Marley floor, a covering that all ballet companies take with them when they travel. The Marley is essentially a vinyl covering that goes over the regular dance floor. The seamstresses Joan Richardson and Ollie

Lewis concealed the edges with black material.

Beverly Sousoulas contacted her close friends who sold antiques to fill the rather plain main dressing room with $25,000 worth of antiques and her heirloom Persian rug.

The great Nureyev, by then 50 years old, seemed really pleased with everything. He told Beverly, "This is the best dance floor on my whole U.S. tour. Now I don't worry about injuring myself."

In 1986, Nureyev's fee was $50,000. We were also responsible for $30,000 in other expenses, including advertising, theatre rent, and union crews.

Nureyev's manager said, "Rudy won't go onstage unless he is paid in advance." Two hours before the performance we were still $40,000 short of the $80,000 we needed.

Peggy Henders, Dona, Jeff, and I helped run the box office, and by 8 p.m. we had sold $40,000 worth of tickets. At 7:30 p.m. Orma found $20,000 for us, all cash. He had saved the day for us so many times before, going out on a limb to get backing for performances or to pay our dancers.

As an act of love, I refused the money. I didn't want him to feel used and I wanted him to know he was valued as a person, not just as a benefactor. Orma was just a few years my senior but I loved him like my father. Needless to say, we raised the money.

Meanwhile, across the street, the Crowne Plaza Hotel staff was preparing a sold- out $250-a-plate benefit dinner where the special guests were to be Nureyev himself and the Mayor of Memphis, Dick Hackett.

After the performance, Nureyev who had truly mellowed in the last few years, sat down to eat with the rest of us. He was quite nice to the elderly ballet fans that in earlier times he might have seemed aloof or pompous towards.

The critics had criticized him all over the world for not being in his prime as a performer. But we all recognized the greatness that was Nureyev in Balanchine's *Apollo*. After dinner Mayor Hackett, Dona, Jeff and I stood on a makeshift stage in front of 500 guests. All the microphones were on. Everything that was said was heard full blast by the audience.

Dick Hackett said, "Mr. Nureyev, we welcome you to the City of Memphis. Here is the key to the city." He handed a large key to the dancer.

Nureyev glanced at Jeff, Dona and me. "What ees thees for?" he asked in a thick, almost comical Russian accent. Mayor Hacket continued, "This is the key to the city, Mr. Nureyev. It will open many doors."

Nureyev stared around at everyone and then replied, "I just hope eet will open a veree tight asshole!"

I thought the mayor seemed to have trouble breathing and we all stared in disbelief at our great star. A moment of stunned silence fell over the audience then, to our relief, they recovered and burst into loud applause. I don't believe they really understood what he had said.

The dancer's unpredictable response to the Memphis mayor that night reminds me of another startling Nureyev moment. Alis Goldate had arranged for a group of 40 jovial travelers made up of Ballet South personnel and other Memphians to travel up to St. Louis. She had scheduled them to see the Monet exhibit and a performance by Nureyev and the Dutch National Ballet.

On the bus, there was much champagne drinking among the revelers and some were secretly smoking pot in the back of the bus. Many were wealthy and well-known high society Memphians. I kept my mouth shut, not wanting to legislate morality.

After the ballet performance, Jeff headed backstage to see Nureyev once again. The great star was holding court while standing totally nude. He showed no embarrassment, and as Jeff came up, he greeted him in a cordial and friendly way.

Leaving Memphis was painful, to put it mildly. All the dancers were like family to me, and my friends had become as close as relatives. Finally, I received a terrible phone call from my brother who said, "Either come home to help out or our mother will go into a nursing home."

Suzanne Brown and I had just returned from one of our three-mile exercise walks which were aerobic and consciousness-raising at the same time. I found this news of my mother heartbreaking and felt myself literally breaking down. Suzanne had become one of my closest friends and we were always throwing each other a challenge with new ideas or new ways to exercise. So with tears flowing down my cheeks, I turned to her slowly, threw back my shoulders sounding somewhat like Arnold Schwarzenegger, and flung out to the world my own gritty challenge: "I'll be back!"

I kept quiet about leaving. It would have been impossible to say good-bye to everyone I knew, but I did allow some friends to come by. Jennifer Tyson, Holly Hopper and Violet Redfern were just a few of the people I had come to love while working in Memphis. They all knew what I was going through, despite my efforts to keep it quiet.

It was hard to leave Kris Hanley, our costume designer for many years, and Carlton Johnson, who became the artistic director of his own company. I would miss Marion Peete, (Marsha Peete's mother) who always reminded me that my tuxedo needed ironing and I would find myself standing in the wings of the theatre before many a performance in my shirt and underwear while she ironed away. They all came to me say their sad good-byes. By now all three of them have passed away and live only in my memories.

Country Lewis, my guild president, dropped by, saying, "You're going to miss Miss Ollie's (her mother's) cucumber sandwiches!"

I nodded sadly.

Jeff and I were packed up and ready to leave. As we got in the car and drove away, in a gesture to new beginnings, Jeff threw away his last pack of cigarettes with a vow that he was through smoking.

As we drove by a lake that was part of a national monument, I said, "Jeff, let's stop. They have never found the bottom of this lake." I knew to not take his response seriously.

"Who gives a damn?" he said, and just kept driving.

Even more shocks and transformations awaited me upon my return to California.

Stephanie Smithey **George Latimer**
Coppelia

Buffalo, New York, 1967

Integration was startling and controversial in the South. (1975)
(Latimer with Peggy Howard, Marsha Peete, Debbie Greenfield, Laura Simmons)

Carlton Johnson - Associate Director Ballet South

Jeffrey Stuart in Rite Of Spring
(Photo by Suzanne Brown)

Jeffrey Stuart with Julie Morrison in Romeo and Juliet
(Photo by Stanley Rodgers)

Jeffrey Stuart with Laura Shindler in Poem of Ecstasy
(Photo by Stanley Rodgers)

— Staff Photo by William Leaptrott

Baryshnikov Comes to Memphis

Baryshnakov, Alis Goldate, Latimer

On The Waterfront performed on the banks of the Mississippi.
Inspired by the youth of Memphis. (1980)

**Controversial performance of Walpurgis Night from Memphis
Operas production of Faust (1971)**

Part IV

Return to My Roots
(1989 – Present)

Chapter 27

A Shaky Re-entry

My mother really needed us. The apartment we rented in Sunnyvale, in the heart of Silicon Valley, had us driving to Oakland three times a week to try to meet my mother's needs. One day our schedule came to an abrupt halt when we were told that we couldn't drink the water or use the shower in our new abode. Such daily activities, it seemed, were dangerous because the complex was built over a toxic waste dump.

Before Jeff grew two noses and all my hair fell out, we moved to Oakland across the street from my mother's home. The neighborhood had been considered countryside during my childhood and had by now become home for a wealthy new suburban class. As they say in real estate parlance, the house we rented was a 1930s Spanish-Moorish- style charmer.

Jeff and I went to work for the well-respected Oakland Ballet where my childhood friend, Ronn Guidi had by now been artistic director for nearly three decades. It was our job to sell subscriptions for the Oakland Ballet, by then one of the more inventive companies in America.

About six months after we arrived, Baryshnikov, on a public television special, endorsed the Oakland Ballet for preserving many works from the Diaghilev ballet era. Especially noted were those of Bronislava Nijinsky. Bronislava had been a true original, as was her brother Vaslav. Only a few of Vaslav Nijinsky's works had been preserved. His most famous choreography included *Afternoon of a Fawn* and *Rite of Spring.* Each of these performances, at first controversial, made ballet history when originally produced. He is considered the first superstar of ballet and known for his incredible leaps that seemed to suspend him in mid air. Sadly, this ballet genius died in a mental institution.

Largely through Ronn Guidi's efforts, Bronislava's *Le Train Bleu* (The Blue Train) and *Les Noces* (The Wedding) have been preserved in their entire original form. The Oakland Ballet's ticket sales soared.

Our hearts were still torn between Memphis and our new home in Oakland. I began creating a new family by reuniting the people I had come to know in Oakland with my own relatives. Among my new friends were dance teacher Bonnie Sita, whose recollections of her father's friendship with Arthur Miller and her meeting Marilyn Monroe color her childhood memories.

Patricia Allen Hunter danced with the late Patrick Swayze before the star made the movie *Dirty Dancing*. She expressed amazement after touring with *Disney on Parade* that, Swayze, the Don Juan of the Disney *Chorus Girls*, had developed into the romantic movie hero he played in *Ghost* with Demi Moore and Whoopi Goldberg.

Careers can quickly separate people. For example, Patti headed for Mexico City, to do aerial work for Disney. At one time, she had put her life on the line nightly in stage crew leader Larry Hunter's strong hands. Now she is one of most popular ballet teachers in Oakland because of her loving way with children, and Larry, whom she married, heads the stage crew at Oakland's beautiful art deco theater, the Paramount, and also designs television and movie sets.

My friend Shay Stephen was a dancer with the infamous Mitchell Brothers Adult Theatre in San Francisco, but she was also a devoted ballet student. My mother adored Shay for her kindness. I'll never forget Shay's comment as she left our annual holiday dinner. "Someone has to dance naked on Christmas," she purred as she swept out to her exotic Christmas night performance. She was sweet to everyone and wrote an autobiography, *The Naked Eye: A True Account of a Stripper's Journey*, published in 1997 that even sold really well at feminist bookstores (considering the content). A lot of people were curious about her days performing in the exotic dance field. She appeared in Professor Irwin Corey's comic R-rated film, *Can I do It Till I Need Glasses?*

***

All was going well. Jeff was teaching now at an old school building across from Mission Dolores in San Francisco. Remember the beautiful garden where Kim Novak walked through the flowers possessed by the mysterious spirit of Carlotta Valdez in the movie *Vertigo*? Even Hitchcock would have liked the view from the long rectangular windows in the quaint room where students gathered for their weekly ballet class, now used by Jeff and his own students.

One day, right in the middle of the class, the floors of the old building began to shake and pieces of wood fell from the rafters. Never having experienced an earthquake before, Jeff panicked but still kept his wits about him.

He cried out, "Come to me boys and girls! Quickly! Grab hold of my belt!"

And so, 20 children took hold of some part of Jeff as they made their way down the shaking stairwell. They dodged falling planks that began to drop down from the rafted third-floor ceiling, crashing through the building, until they reached the parking lot. The parents, some of them near panic, began to arrive at the base of the stairs to see Jeff's bruised and pale face. He waited until all of the mothers and fathers arrived. They expressed their gratitude that none of their children had been injured.

As the earthquake subsided, the air began to fill with smoke and the sky darkened, except in the Marina District. An unearthly glow emanated from across the sky created by broken and fallen buildings that had been thrown this way and that, and store owners were already standing guard outside their businesses to ward off looters.

Shattered glass spilled out onto the sidewalks and street, dangerous and shining in the unnatural light. Jeff heard on the radio that five blocks away three people were killed as a brick wall fell on their cars while they attempted to drive away.

Jeff started up his own car and edged toward the Oakland Bay Bridge ramp. As he drove onto the huge structure held up by tremendous cement columns and pilings from Yerba Buena Island, he glanced back toward the dark city. While others had sung of leaving "their hearts in San Francisco," his heart was now in his throat. All was pitch black except for the huge flames, which leapt up all around, moving in the direction of Fisherman's Wharf and the Marina.

It was then that Jeff told one of the biggest lies of his life. He was on the bridge caught in the long lines of escaping cars when everyone came to an abrupt halt.

A man jumped out of his car, and dramatically started shouting and waving at the cars. He screamed, "Go back! Go back! The bridge is collapsing!"

Jeff got out of his car, and holding the steering wheel with one hand, began to turn his vehicle around but the long line of departing cars wouldn't let him into the exit lane. He was filled with fear and dread as he thought about the fate of me and my mother across the bay. He had to get to us. He thought we might be injured, in trouble, or caught under debris.

A sudden inspiration came to him. He yelled out loudly at the slowly moving exiting cars, "I've got to pick up my children! Please, please let me in!" The words did the job and the drivers let him in line.

We learned later that part of the bridge did collapse. As the earthquake started, I had been in the living room of my mother's house. The shaking moved from minor to violent motion. I suddenly became Clint Eastwood and picked my mother up and stumbled toward the front door of the house. I tripped and we fell onto the floor, laughing and suddenly unafraid. All the electricity was out. I turned on the portable radio and that was when we heard about the freeway collapsing three miles from where we were, killing 30 people. We stopped the laughing. Stories came in from all over the Bay Area, including the one about the Bay Bridge. We began to worry about Jeff.

Eight hours later there was a knock at the front door. When I ran to open it, a dust-covered Jeff staggered in and dropped limply onto the couch.

He said, "Are you sure you want to stay here? I was really scared! Maybe we should leave California, George!"

Chapter 28
Scorcher

On Sunday mornings in Oakland things seemed more quiet than usual, and to entertain ourselves, we would often go aimlessly to Capwell Emporium, the nearby department store. It started as an ordinary Sunday; tables of shirts had been marked down by 75 percent. I had never cared much for clothes before because I never could afford them, and, a lot of my wardrobe was comprised of gifts or hand-me-downs, so I had only a casual interest in the sale.

As we stepped into the store, I commented to Jeff that the sun seemed an odd shade of orange as it came up over the Oakland Hills. After browsing the sales tables and hunting for the best bargains, we stepped back into the sunlight and noticed with some surprise that it had changed from orange to an ominous dark red.

Surprised and a little alarmed at this sudden change, I said, "Something's not right." Jeff agreed and, as we walked toward our car parked in the Paramount Theatre lot, we began feeling a little uneasy. As we drove up Broadway, our vision became obscured by a light rain of ashes. Then a smoky grey color began invading the ordinary blue of the Sunday morning sky until the blue disappeared altogether.

I was still not distressed or too worried. After all, I had grown up in this neighborhood, and it was as familiar to me as my own backyard. Nothing could happen to me here or to my neighborhood, I thought. That is, until we rounded a curve and I saw houses that had stood as monuments to my childhood engulfed in enormous, raging red and orange flames.

Jeff and I gasped at the frightening sight. As we got to the top of the big hill, a wind, seemingly fueled by a supernatural force, rushed towards us, carrying sparks of burning debris. Our car was pushed to the side of the road and Jeff slowed down to a crawl.

As we drew near my mother's house and our own, we were greeted by a bear of a police officer who roughly told us to turn around and leave the area.

I was stunned and cried out, "But my mother and my dog are just ahead about a mile up the road. I can't leave them there!" My voice rose to an excited shout.

"I have my orders," choked the policeman trying not to inhale the deadly smoke. "You have to turn around and go back!"

Jeff cared about my mother almost as much as I did, especially after losing his own mother a few months earlier. With sudden and unexpected force, he slammed down on the gas pedal. The car surged forward and headed straight through the barricade. I remember thinking, "Clint Eastwood would have been proud!"

The confused policeman stood helplessly by as our car whizzed past and on into the darkness ahead. By the time I reached my mother's house, the sun, obscured by smoking houses and the constant rain of ashes, had turned to a blood red color. I jumped from the car and rushed into the house and just as I expected, my dog was cowering in the corner, yet my mother seemed totally unaware of the complete chaos outside her walls.

Jeff and I rushed around the yard, watering down the walls of the house and then, always thinking ahead and that this was a temporary situation, I slapped together some ham and cheese sandwiches to take with us to eat later. I helped my mother across the street to the house Jeff and I were renting. At that point she couldn't walk without help and relied on Jeff or myself completely. Setting up a folding chair in the driveway, I put my mother down in it and we just stood there looking at the chaotic activities of escaping residents. I just couldn't believe that the fire would eventually make its way to my street. I stayed by my mother's chair, reluctant to enter our house. I was mesmerized by the frenzied escaping people and vehicles and the constant racing back and forth of police cars, screeching out their warnings for all residents to leave the area. The choking smoke and ash and the continuous wail of fire engines rushing to nearby disaster areas to try to stop the advancing flames was nerve shattering.

I didn't want to go indoors. Marsha and Brian Johnson, our neighbors and owners of Café Rouge in Berkeley, were frantically packing their van with many of their treasured possessions, along with survival equipment. I thought they were overreacting. I looked up through the gray falling ash and saw an elderly woman racing her car down the hillside on the wrong side of the street, almost hitting a backpacker who came rushing wildly downward along the side of the road, away from the advancing flames.

I could not believe what was happening. "Why is everyone acting so crazy?" I asked Jeff.

Ellis Weisker, my German neighbor who had a huge collection of clocks in his house, was standing up on his roof watering down his house. I remembered he had told my mother once that he was going to live to be 100.

He called down to us, "I can see the fire coming!" He shouted. "You better leave now and take Sue (my mother) with you!"

We couldn't see the sun at all now. Certainly, the Oakland Fire Department would stop the fire dead in its tracks, I thought hopelessly. I stood there, feeling myself moving into some sort of disorientated state of lassitude, watching as Jeff drove the car over to the end of our driveway.

Jumping out, he yelled to me, "Put what you really need in the car. I'll get Sue in. And hurry!" I walked into our beautiful Spanish-Moorish-style house and stared around in a state of shock. My thoughts were becoming totally incoherent. What would I take with us? In retrospect, I know now that I should have grabbed up all of our important documents, family pictures, and art - those things one can never replace. But in a daze, I said to myself, "If I can't take it all, I'll take nothing." It was getting so hot that I could hardly think, and I began to worry in earnest about whether we were going to get out of this mess alive. A piece of information filtered into my confused mind: lack of oxygen causes heart attacks.

The police on loudspeakers were still ordering us to evacuate. I could hear the PG&E power plants half a mile away crackle and then explode. The tips of palm trees ignited and blew up like bombs. Memories of movies I had seen took over my stalled conscious mind. Yes, I had seen a scene like this twice before. I remembered Hollywood's scenes of hell in *Day of the Locust* and *Apocalypse Now*. Against this memory of hell-like visions on film, I felt real fear for the first time. This was going to happen. It was actually happening now! My past was being destroyed. As we drove off with Jeff at the wheel, my mother sitting in the back, and me sitting in the front seat with our dog Greta in my lap, I panicked. I couldn't breathe, couldn't think. Nothing in my body was responding to my mind except fear. It paralyzed me. The only pictures of my father were in my mother's house. I might never see his image again! My entire past - memories, and physical reminders of all my growing up years - was disintegrating before my eyes.

As our car neared the freeway, we could see that the super highway was jammed with escaping motorists and gawking onlookers. The traffic out of Oakland had come to a complete stop. Somewhere, out of my distant childhood memory, I remembered a back road that I had sometimes used. Maybe this road could be our escape route! A few others also remembered this way out of the hills, and they joined us in our race against the advancing flames.

In just 10 minutes we were registered at the Thunderbird Motel just outside Jack London Square, a million light-years away from the inferno which we had just left behind. The motel didn't allow dogs, so Jeff wrapped Greta up in a blanket and pretended she was a baby. The ploy was pretty convincing until her tail began wagging. Evidently no one saw the wagging tail as we walked by the desk and past the restaurant. All three of us piled into a bed on the second floor with my mother in the other one and watched TV in horror as the flames worked their way through 3,300 homes, burning and destroying them all. Dogs, cats, and other wild animals were running in all directions to escape the fast-moving fire, and the cameras had caught herds of deer stampeding out, moving away from the burning hills.

The television coverage was truly frightening and mind blowing. The rapidity of the spreading flames and the complete inability of the police and fire departments to even make a dent in the advancing fire held us in a nightmarish grip. At that time, only 32 people had been listed as dead, but later that figure would grow. Some residents saved themselves by getting into their swimming pools or a neighbor's. One police officer, caught in the fire, took charge and ordered residents into a pool, and then covered it with the pool covering. It was reported that the water almost reached the boiling point during the ordeal, but in the end, the tactic saved lives that might have been lost. Many died because the 80-foot wall of flames traveled so fast that a city block was destroyed in 45 seconds.

Authorities learned later that 911 unintentionally gave the wrong advice to several young people trapped in their houses high up in the hills. They were told not to move, that help was on the way. But they were eventually cut off and some died, never making it out.

Sare was due in for a visit and we thought about telling her not to come out to California to see us. The devastation was overwhelming to us, but perhaps a friend's presence just might be comforting. Busloads of gawking tourists made driving out of the hills difficult. Up until then, I didn't realize how much Asians love their cameras. They even came around and asked us to pose in front of the ashes of our own house. The level of the heat had even disintegrated the marble table in our living room. Our house, across from my mother's, later was featured on the cover of a book published by *The Oakland Tribune* on the 1991 Oakland fire, the largest urban fire in American history.

The police barricaded the fire area to protect expensive properties from looters, but I imagine there were some families who were never really wealthy, yet found the value of their property escalating over the years, as my own family had.

During the three days of not knowing whether our houses were burned to the ground or still standing, we began visiting the police-guarded area daily. It was then that Jeff noticed some people hiding in the Temescal creek bed about a mile from where we had lived. It ran just behind my mother's house.

The creek had partially dried up during the heat wave preceding the fire and during the fire itself. Jeff found fighting his way up the creek bed to my mother's house to be a grueling experience due to debris from the fire and other live growth, rocks, and gravel, but he was determined to learn the condition of the houses. During these days, helicopters flew low over the area, searching for looters, and hiding from them was risky. Jeff joined other fire fugitives who also were hiding from the helicopters. Had any of them been caught, the whole group would have been hauled off to jail for questioning.

Jeff knew that the creek on the border of my mother's house and the house we had rented across the street would be dry by now. He left the others and made his way up the creek until he reached the area behind my mother's house.

The trip took about an hour with Jeff crouching as police cars went by and then running ahead toward another sheltered area. Most of the houses in that general vicinity were burned to the ground, but mother's house was still standing. Oddly enough, the tomato plants and roses were in fine shape, too. Probably feeling the heat of the fire as the beginning of summer, they actually flourished under the heat and ash-covered soil as the days advanced.

Jeff had just enough time to glance across the street to our home. He had to look twice to believe his eyes. Our house was gone! Knowing all of our belongings, especially the antiques that had belonged to his grandmother, some dating back to the Civil War era, were destroyed, he began to cry.

When he told me later, I couldn't cry, although I wanted to. As usual, I repressed emotion too quickly, something that would change one day.

Sare did come to visit and she walked by herself right up the twisted streets of ashes. In some places entire automobiles had melted into splotches of rubber and metal right on the side of the street. She told me she felt the presence of spirits wandering among the ruins. This sense of grief and sadness was overwhelming so she decided that she didn't want to walk that way again. We later discovered that two teenagers had chosen to stay and watch the flames and had died of smoke inhalation just where Sare had been walking.

There were many heroes connected with the Oakland fire. There was the miraculous story of a fireman who saved a baby by lying on top of it during the inferno. Poor Ellis, my mother's German next-door neighbor and friend, the owner of all those clocks, was seen by all as he walked continuously back and forth by the pile of debris where his house had been. He seemed disoriented and lost. My poor neighbor seemed out of his mind. He didn't live to be 100 as he had promised us. Instead, the emotional shock and other complications took their toll within a month, and he became another casualty of the great fire.

I felt a large part of my past had been lost when the fire took our house. All my memorabilia from my early years was gone. One day out of the blue I received an unexpected package in the mail. It was an envelope postmarked San Jose. It contained many seared photographs of the Memphis Ballet scene. By a twist of fate these photos had blown south and had ended up in the backyard of a man who was kind enough to save them and send them back to me.

How did he find my address?

Chapter 29
In the Amber Light

Looking back, the happiest times of my life were when I was being an artistic and social rebel - one reason the Memphis years meant so much to me. But now I was facing the most spiritual challenge of my life.

With the shadow of the great fire behind us, one evening Jeff, my mother, and I were laughing, watching television, and finishing a take-out meal from a restaurant about a mile away. My mother was 86 years old now, and I thought I would have her for at least a few more years. We had already started the remodeling of the house in the Oakland Hills so that we could live in the back part of the building. My mother was feeling a little insecure alone in the house, even though Jeff and I had rented the house next to hers, and I was always right there for her. I was strong enough to give my mother baths and change her sheets or nightgown at any hour whenever she summoned me. She wore a necklace with a chain that held an emergency locket. If she pressed the button, my phone would ring, even at three in the morning. My brother couldn't believe I was capable of doing this job.

The phone didn't ring that night and later when I went next door to wake my mother, she couldn't speak. I told her not to worry and I called 911. My brother and sister flew in to Oakland and were there within hours.

She knew we were all there before she slipped into a deep coma. The doctors predicted she would never regain consciousness. She had requested in her living trust to have no life support.

I didn't realize how possessive I had become. I was shocked by this revelation because in the past I had always been able to share and even in my own way, control conditions around people, money, and even the limelight. Now I felt a little guilty when I encouraged my brother and sister to return home. Deep inside, I really felt that this would be for the best. I wanted my mother to myself. I talked to her every day when she was in this frustrating state of unconsciousness. As time passed, I began to notice that the room filled with an odd amber light, reminding me of the ballet stage lights.

We had to decide whether or not to put my mother on a feeding tube. I didn't want her to starve to death. Doctor Sternback was head of Neurology at Kaiser Hospital and he and his wife Debbie were good friends of ours and mother's. Coincidentally, at the time Jeff and I decided we would take my mother home and provide a feeding tube for her, Dr. Sternback was writing a pamphlet on this deeply troubling moral dilemma.

Dr. Krause, her physician, gave us a knowing look and said, "Your mother asked for no artificial assistance." Two days later, the morphine drip Dr. Krause had ordered was stopped. I had made my decision, and it was to honor my mother's request, which now took her deeper and deeper toward the other side.

Later, sitting at my mother's bedside, I tearfully told her, "I want you to live, but if you feel better leaving, it's all right."

On that last morning, I left her room for a few minutes to go to the drinking fountain and when I came back into that amber-lit room, my mother had passed on. I finally went out into the gray street in front of the hospital. Berkeley had never looked so bleak and dark. Nothing can ever really prepare us for the death of a parent, and I was in a state of shock.

Chapter 30
Cavalia Magic

There have been many beautiful women in my life. One warm August day several of them had gathered at my house to fill paper shopping bags with hundreds of red apples from the trees in my backyard. The fruit from the heavily laden apple trees was crisp and solid, just ripe enough to be eaten.

I had been studying a little Chinese with my friend Amy Chung, and she was there, along with Patti Hunter, who was practicing her whirling, yet often languid dance steps from tree to tree, as she made the apple gathering more fun.

Patti's dad had always called her Tricia LaRue – the Doll-face Girl, as though referring to a vaudeville act. But, as she matured, she lost the doll-faced look and her beauty attracted the attention of Julio Iglesias. They dated for months.

And then Shay with her turquoise eyes and dark red hair appeared. She had come, as usual, to gather apples for her homeless horses.

We were all fascinated by Shay. She was a dancer, but unlike Amy, Patti, and I, who had struggled all our lives to remain limber and flexible - both required elements for a dancer at any age. Shay had been born with that flexibility. When she took my ballet classes, all I had to do was help her maintain her balance as she stretched out her supple body and let me show her how to build up muscle strength and control.

Shay, with her charming child-like behavior, was a true innocent. One might be surprised to find that she danced in the most infamous exotic shows on the entire West Coast. Her fascinating book is a factual tale about her life with the daring Mitchell Brothers. The movie, featuring Charlie Sheen and Emilio Estevez as the brothers, revealed seamy yet sometimes dramatic or funny vignettes about backstage life at the world-renowned Mitchell Brothers Theater in San Francisco. No one else had written such truths without the words seeming sordid or salacious, but Shay's book had hit just the right note for reader shock and amusement. I once questioned Shay about her background, and she replied, "Read my book! In my book, I was raised by wolves!"

I wanted to believe her. I could see her leaping about with snarling, yelping four- footed creatures swirling and dancing around her feet, her long henna hair creating a mane. Even today I realize Shay still remains a woman of mystery, managing to be youthful, beautiful, and childlike in a Marilyn Monroe kind of way. Her book is still available at Amazon.com.

That particular day I found it difficult to keep my mind on apple picking with mesmerizing Shay around. At last, the apples were divided up and Amy and Patti each took two large bags home with them.

"My family will love these beauties," Amy announced. "You know, it's very Chinese to want everything natural and fresh and, of course, very California!"

Patti helped us load up her car. Shay sighed happily, "These are for my friends, the horses! I'll take you to see my secret ones next Tuesday afternoon."

That evening Patti, Gwen Austin, and Caroline de Vreeze decided to go to a huge tent show set up near Golden Gate Fields. Patti had bought tickets for all of us to see the show *Cavalia* because she dearly loved horses as much as Shay.

Cavalia was a gigantic touring production of trained horses featuring elegant riders, dancers, and musicians. The production was spectacular and spiritual and Patti was moved to the point of tears. To this day, I look for anything that involves horses, even sea horses, hoping to rekindle that spiritual bond.

Tuesday, Shay arrived fashionably late. Jim, one of my night students who had a brilliant mind and appreciated horses and unusual little women with long flowing red hair, arrived earlier. We had spent our time picking more apples for Shay's equine friends.

Shay apologized for being late. I grinned at Jim and shrugged. "How could we ever be angry with her?" Jim nodded his enthusiastic agreement.

Jim said, "She really casts a spell. Sort of like a benign Circe who lured the sailors to the rocks in Greek Mythology."

I joked, "But Shay's a redhead. She wouldn't turn men into swine!"

We drove beyond the Oakland and Berkeley Hills to a place I didn't know existed. The car climbed up a hillside road until the pavement came to a dead end. Daylight was still strong as Shay led us up along a pathway through a forest glowing with, yes, another amber light, turning everything into a burnt orange color.

In the light, Shay's silhouette was amazing. Slim, yet voluptuously sensual, she stood on her toes, and drawing in her breath, uttered a long, loud primitive call reminiscent of a Tarzan yodel. Immediately, we heard the pounding of horse hooves as Shay began to spin around and around in a wide ritualistic circle. She called out again. In my imagination, Shay was the reincarnation of Rima the Bird Girl in Hudson's masterpiece *Green Mansions*.

To spend a day with Shay was like being in a fantastic movie. Her sense of reality was always glamorous, never mundane. Her perceptions seemed to be accompanied by a majestic symphonic score that only she could hear and eventually I knew that I would hear it, too.

I was a little nervous with all those wild horses milling around, and I could barely see Shay or Jim through the rising dust. Then, there they were, Shay, Jim, and the horses outlined in the bright orange-gold beams of the setting sun. The horses stomped their hooves, blew and snorted, and moved in a friendly fashion around Shay. They smelled the apples and nosed and pushed at all of us. Several came over to me and nuzzled at my arm with their soft, velvet mouths. Where the horses in *Cavalia* were slick and well fed, these horses had long ago been deserted and now were almost starving.

"There's more of them out there," Shay called out.

I was surrounded by a little-known Bay Area secret. I was seeing a band of wild horses who had once been owned, well fed, valued, and many, even loved. How could this have happened?

"My friends and I keep them alive," Shay said. "There's a movement to have them exterminated. I won't let it happen," Shay stated, face grim, words filled with strong resolve.

I continued to be nudged by these incredible creatures and deeply moved by their gentleness and natural curiosity. As we mingled among the horses, the smell of sagebrush and half-eaten apples became like an intoxicating perfume mixing well with the salty Pacific Ocean breeze. Shay and the prancing, dancing horses intertwined in a sphere apart from the frantic energy of the hard-driving humanity that was just a few miles away.

Chapter 31

On Meeting Sister Sin Di Vine

I was never attracted to organized religion but have felt more at home as a free- thinking, spiritual person who needs no interception between my own soul and the creative energy of the universe, which most of us call God. I like to think of myself as a spiritual entity. Nuns, I realize, hold a special kind of fascination for me. They represent the "feminine earth and spiritual being." The constantly shifting energy between the earth-feminine and divine virginal spirit found in all women appears like a puzzle taunting the psyche of all males.

The stark symbolism in the book and later the movie, *The Nun's Story*, starring Audrey Hepburn, remained with me for years. So, to me, nuns can represent a special and sacred place for the feminine spirit here on earth.

The religious practice of avoiding one's reflection in the mirror, featured in *The Nun's Story*, seemed a real but difficult way to develop selflessness and to play down one's ego. That practice and many others like it made the lead character's dramatic entry into the harsher outer world at the end of the story painfully traumatic. Perhaps the movie's theme signaled that, in our three-dimensional world, the soul can find better ways to uplift humanity than in the strict codes of religion found in the movie.

My special feeling about nuns received a resounding jolt one day when Jeff and I were out walking, enjoying the sun, in San Francisco's Dolores Park. As we strolled along, I noticed a large gathering of nuns on one of the nearby park slopes.

On that windy day, the nuns' habits seemed more flowing, more like a Ginger Rogers ballroom costumes than habits. The nuns had gathered in a huge circle and their faces could not be seen clearly. At first their movement appeared to be exaggerated as they stood in place. Some of them suddenly began to leap and play - more like Loretta Young and Celeste Holm in *Come to the Stable*. I was fixated on the nuns' actions, especially after having seen these films.

I remember that I was eight years old when my parents took me to the Orinda Theater to see the film *Black Narcissus*. Even to an eight-year-old child the emotional conflict between sexuality and spirituality was obvious. In my sexual pre-consciousness I wondered if this really needed to be a conflict.

Watching the nuns, I thought that they, in their black and white habits, were somehow resolving that ancient conflict this day. While their robes stressed their spiritual awareness, their carefree enjoyment of their "earthy sensuality in the sun and wind" was not wrong.

That day in the park as we drew closer and I began to really study the nuns, I turned to Jeff and asked, "Don't you think it's strange that some of the nuns have long, false eyelashes?"

Jeff nodded in agreement.

As we moved in closer, one of the nuns separated from the group and came up to me, asking, with a wide grin, "Don't you know who I am?"

I replied, "No. Do I know you?"

The nun replied, "It's me! Tommy, your hairdresser! But here in this group, I'm known as Sister Sin Di Vine." He laid a hand reassuringly on my arm, "But you can call me Sister Cindy!"

I almost fell over. Tommy had been cutting my hair for six months and although I discovered we had many old friends in common from early San Francisco theater days, I would never had guessed he was a member of the "Sisters of Perpetual Indulgence," as I found they called themselves.

As we talked, he explained to me that he had been working with this group for years, raising money for gay teens, AIDS research, and Project Open Hand (it feeds the sick and poor in San Francisco).

It made sense. Tommy's work was such a wonderful example of spirit and earth-grounded energy working together to help humanity. He had created a truly feminine balance to the raw warrior energy of the male ego. What Tommy had never told me nor would he tell me during our forthcoming visits, was that for many years he himself had been HIV positive.

Some time after my discovery of Tommy in the park with the nuns, he called me to postpone our hair appointment. Doctors had found that lung cancer was rapidly taking hold because Tommy's immune system was so compromised.

His co-workers, Sharon, Angelo, Kitty, and others were horrified at the idea of losing Tommy, but Tommy managed to keep working until he began to need blood transfusions.

"I hope it is the blood of virgins!" He jokingly laughed in his great Bela Lugosi movie star imitation. "That's the best kind of blood for me!"

How Tommy managed to keep in such good spirits while suffering such unbearable pain endeared him even more to all of us. We could hardly bear to see him suffer.

One day Tommy was put on an oxygen tank because, something went unnoticed by friends until he fainted. He died of a heart attack while receiving oxygen, not from cancer or AIDS, but because his heart had been oxygen deprived due to his unusual condition.

His wake was the largest tribute of its kind I have ever attended. About 200 people turned out. All of them loved Tommy for his generous acts of kindness and his good humor.

The wake was held in the Kennedy Grove. I had never been to the Grove, a cathedral-like circle of huge redwood trees near San Pablo Dam Road. A row of mountainous green hills blocked our view of the San Francisco Bay but the golden rays of sunshine shimmering down through the great redwoods played across our faces as some smiled and others wept, remembering Tommy's positive life force.

I wandered around, uneasy yet at ease. I found many faces there that I recognized. I noticed, too, that there was enough food for at least 500 people.

Just as the ceremonies began, a busload of people pulled up and out jumped about 50 people costumed as nuns.

"We're here for our Tommy!" They all cried. "We want to show our love and respect!" they shouted, and came rushing forward.

Sharon and several of Tommy's other co-workers became teary eyed. A conservative client of Tommy's exclaimed in amazement, "This is the same group that made a political statement by staging a kiss-in at Sun Valley Mall in Concord!" He paused, catching people's attention, "They are a brave bunch," he chuckled approvingly and added, "a wild bunch, too!"

The wake went on for hours and I wandered around in a saddened but euphoric state which could only be described as spiritual. As the sun went down, I wandered back toward the trees to say my last good-bye to Tommy. The trees seemed to be flooded with golden sunrays that soon, to my amazement, turned to soft amber light. Was the amber light following me? Was it talking to me? Showing me something that was beyond normal comprehension? As I pondered the question, a meaning beyond words was coming towards me from that comforting light.

I stood there as the evening gathered shadows about me and I peered into the dusk, my eyes widening. Was that Tommy's elfin-like image peeking at me from behind the huge ferns and tall trees? Was he smiling as he watched all those who loved him enjoying the wine and food in memory of his warm friendship?

I blinked my eyes and looked again, and he seemed to be there. Yes. He was. Tommy was there before me, dancing in the amber light!

Chapter 32

A Potent Situation

While performing, the most idealistic and spiritual sides of my life became evident. But the opposite side of my existence would also be present.

A friend I'll call Patrick and I once drove across the country together, from Memphis to California. We were blown away by the isolation of the people we met in mountainous regions of New Mexico. When we stopped at a restaurant on top of one of the longest mesas, we witnessed people living in some sort of time warp. It was still the 1950s in this place.

The smell of natural gas filled the air. Suddenly we saw the most vivid and gigantic lightening storm cracking through the enormous sky. Oddly, no one had seemed concerned that lightening could cause an oil well to ignite and explode.

Patrick seemed totally heterosexual. But he was never ashamed of the nonsexual intimacy we shared on this long journey, and we became emotionally very close. We arrived in California a week later, taking every unusual back road instead of the main highways. He revealed that one of the main reasons he was traveling to California was to visit a San Francisco doctor we had both heard about who had become notorious for his ability to remove fat from one part of the body and inject it into a man's penis. A person of ordinary size could now become this year's Harry Reems or John Holmes.

The procedure didn't sound safe to me, but my friend was determined to follow his dream of being well hung. He said that relationships had mostly failed for him, and he blamed his size. He was still a young man, and I discouraged him from proceeding.

That's when I began to think most men's egos were, in fact, between their legs.

When we returned to Memphis a week later, my friend had already been to the clinic on Market Street in San Francisco. He was glowing with a new self confidence. I was glad to occasionally perform on stage. I always received a huge feeling of gratification from not being earthbound. I didn't need a doctor to help me feel godlike. I could still be like Apollo, leaping across the sky.

A few months later I read that the penis doctor was being sued by many of his clients. Apparently, the results of his work were only temporary. What once looked long and streamlined eventually collapsed into a misshapen, ugly, inexplicable mess. Women who had once pursued Patrick now fled.

The last I heard, Patrick was headed to Europe for yet another attempt to become perfect. He was also running from his depression.

Chapter 33
Who's that Bad Boy, Anyway?

My emotional growth has always been a core issue bringing me throughout my life to a sequence of therapists who might help me. In Memphis, I saw a therapist at Family Services and, when I moved back to California, I went to see Margaret Fleming, a therapist at the Oak Bay Clinic in Oakland.

With or without therapy, I would continue to mature. My fondest hope was to acquire skills for growing that would make life less painful for me. As a result of all of the help I received from others I gained personal integrity and lost a lot of my fear.

When my mother died I realized I wasn't handling the grief process in a healthy way. Many of my buried emotions were still unresolved. This was unlike my dad's death, which had somehow brought clarity to our father-son relationship. We had no conflict between us, and I truly knew that my father loved me.

I asked my friend Kent Jones to recommend a therapist, preferably a woman this time. That's how I met Gardenia Sarazin. She must have thought of me as a bottomless pit, the way I had once appeared to my first ballet teacher, Carol O'Brien. Carol's ears must have burned as I emotionally recounted events that occurred during much of my childhood and teen-age years in California.

In Memphis, I had talked almost daily to my astrologer, Sare Van Orsdell. I was fascinated by the Jungian and Greek archetypes in astrology that were found in the timeless ancient symbols of the 360-degree birth chart. I was able to understand my own life through the interpretations of my chart as it represented a person's conflicts and victories throughout a lifetime. It still continues to be a consistent source of mental stimulation to me. My *emotional* grief and pain remained, though, and that's why I was so grateful for Gardenia.

A small graceful person - ageless, in fact - Gardenia's energy was commanding. True beauty has nothing to do with age. As I worked with her I still could not seem to find what triggered my frightening feelings of unending emptiness. Life seemed to be perceived in brilliant colors for others, yet my worldview was grey and worse than that, I was feeling grey and still grieving.

Gardenia said, "The quickest way to work through pain is to face your feelings directly. Let yourself *feel* the emotions once and for all. Running away only sustains suffering."

That night I went alone to the hot tub in the garden at my parent's house. Regardless of any anger or passion I had felt toward my mother, the end result of her death was a tremendous feeling of loss. I sat in the rushing hot water, surrounded by the warm heat and the plants and flowers she had always loved.

"I'm bathing in my grief. Literally bathing in my grief," I thought sadly. I became absorbed in my emotions, letting the grief heighten. After a while I was flooded with another emotion which filled with gratitude. "I am lucky to have so much!" I thought. Actually, I realized I just need a different perspective to appreciate all the good things that have happened in my life.

Gardenia was the most incisive therapist I had met. She was also the bluntest and the warmest. Although each therapist's personality was appropriate for me at the time I saw them, all my therapists helped in some way. I realized that talk was no longer necessary. Sometimes I would just walk in and know that Gardenia's healthy glow was nurturing me.

"Life is far more rewarding when you let yourself feel with full intensity whether you're experiencing sorrow or joy," she said.

When I mentioned someone, Gardenia would often ask me about the sun, moon and rising signs in their charts. Amazingly, months later she would remember the person and their astrological data. I told her about my friend, Sare, and how I felt no real spirituality until I knew her and discovered astrology. Up until then my spiritual muses had been music and ballet.

Gardenia had lived in Vietnam during the war and had the horrible experience of finding herself next to a monk who set himself on fire during a protest. His haunting picture is etched in many memories, as he was on the cover of *Time Magazine* the week after his self-immolation.

One day I told Gardenia, "I'm not sure why I believe in the symbolism of astrology."

"Perhaps your belief is an intuition stronger than reason, "she replied.

I decided Gardenia was right. Above all, I believed in free will but I had to concede that not all power is in our own hands. I believe that fate still plays a major role in our lives. She agreed, but said the important thing to remember is to live life with few regrets.

Gardenia demonstrated often that reason was not what governed my life. "I want you to try something that's a form of hypnosis," she said one day. She spoke the usual relaxing, hypnotic words using well-known techniques to help me shut out the world and to go into myself.

Finally, she said, "I want you to imagine yourself as a young child who is sitting next to you on the couch."

I did so, and a moment later she asked, "Now, how do you feel about this child?"

In slow meditative words, I replied, "I don't want to pick the child up and hold it."

I was stunned at myself. So that's how I really felt about me! All of my feelings of exaggerated self worth were only a facade, as deep inside I carried a real sense of shame and disappointment. That's when I asked myself, is this what the "bad boy" is really all about?

Chapter 34
In Recovery

Jeff and I continued to settle into Oakland and the Oakland Ballet community. Through my students I was making many new friends, and that made me happy. One day I was taking a ballet class at our school when I lost control in my left arm, and I stumbled. It was an odd sensation to lose control like that. My friend Verona Levine watched me drop my belongings three times in a row. I felt clumsy and decided that I must have a virus. I went home and cooked dinner for my housemate.

"I'm having a minor stroke," I thought to myself. "I'll see Dr. Krause in the morning. My first thought was to take aspirin, which I did. In the morning when I tried to get out of bed, I couldn't walk. It was difficult, but Jeff and Gerald, an old friend of ours, helped me down to the car. I went to my doctor's office immediately. His stern face said it all.

"You shouldn't be here George. Go to the emergency room" Dr. Krause admonished.

We went immediately to the hospital. I was admitted, given a bed, and put on an intravenous blood thinner. I was scared and crying. I didn't know what was going to happen to me. I told Jeff how lucky we were to have had our long friendship. I knew any stroke was dangerous, and I felt really stupid for not going to the hospital the night before. I was angry at myself for not taking immediate action. Maybe I wouldn't be paralyzed if I had acted quickly instead of going into denial. It was just as well I didn't know the hospital medical staff had been monitoring me closely for a possible artery collapse which could cause even more damage or even kill me.

As the news went out, all my friends began gathering at my hospital room. Sometimes it was standing room only.

Ronit and Lore, two of my devoted students, held my hands for hours. Jeff bravely went ahead with preparations to put on the school's annual recital without me. Gardenia came to see me, bringing love, a Scrabble game, crossword puzzles, and hope.

I got a brain scan. Then a speech therapist, a physical therapist, my neurologist's assistants, and my family doctor came to see me.

I gathered I didn't have a blood clot or a broken artery. I did learn that my blood was too thick to travel to the right side of my brain. I had been drinking almost no water for the last seven days, surviving on Diet Cokes, before the cardiovascular accident. Most strokes, I understood, were the result of blood clots and broken veins in the brain. After all the medical tests were concluded I was urged by my therapists to get up and attempt to walk as soon as possible.

I did have one embarrassing incident in front of some of my friends. I wasn't able to get to the toilet on time, and my own version of Noah's flood came on like a tidal wave. Moments later, Amy arrived with baskets of fresh flowers and lots of cheery conversation, breaking the startled silence that had descended on the three of us.

She took everything in stride and said, "You *will* be well soon, George!"

Learning to walk again wasn't easy. I developed a crush on my physical therapist and found myself in tears when she and I had to part. One morning, holding onto the therapy bar and doing my daily exercises with 10 other men of various ages, I quipped, "You fellows don't know it, but you're taking ballet!" They glared at me. There was definitely a lack of appreciation for my informative comment. If only they knew how rigorous ballet training really was, that there was nothing sissy about it. The exercises we were doing for physical therapy were almost exactly the same as the ones ballet students use to strengthen their own muscles.

I was at the rehab hospital for six weeks. I developed great camaraderie with many of the other patients and became the informal entertainment chairman, something I was good at. I screened campy classic films for them. Their favorites were *She (Who Must Be Obeyed)* and *The Invasion of the Body Snatchers*. After all, hadn't some alien force invaded our own bodies, causing us to change radically? In turn I learned to like basketball and to appreciate Kobe Bryant.

There was the unforgettable African American lady who hated me at first, but later cried when I left to go home. Then there was the young man who stole the best wheelchair in the hospital because he just wanted to get out. He had 32 metal plates in his paralyzed body. There was a BART station three miles downhill. The wheelchair brakes gave out and miraculously he zoomed through several crowded intersections and was finally rescued by the police. We called him Evel Knievel because his original injuries were caused by attempting to jump his motorcycle over a pile of cars.

Then there was the handsome brother, paralyzed from the neck down, who kept us awake with his delusions of angels flying in a circle over his head, with Oprah Winfrey leading them in an airborne chorus.

An elderly Chinese lady, who couldn't speak English, was visited every day by her son, a Chinese movie star. Tall and athletic, he was the most handsome cat-like person I had ever seen. He brought her egg rolls and pot stickers which she shared with me, knowing intuitively that I loved Chinese food.

The entire staff was baffled by why I had so many beautiful women coming to visit me on a regular basis. They also became concerned when I started fainting. No one could understand what was causing the problem except the African doctor who regularly had seen symptoms of dehydration in his homeland.

Every day, Lore, my German student, massaged my paralyzed arm. Gwen Austin collected money for me at the Redwood Center. I'll never forget her kindness. Her friend Alice brought me 40 dollars in quarters for the food machines.

I rarely get embarrassed. But, when the hospital shower broke and I was wheeled naked with a strategically placed washcloth across my lap, this side of my personality was severely tested.

"What doesn't kill us makes us strong," I thought.

During the six weeks I was there I managed to make friends with everyone at the hospital. On my final day, the entire staff of physical therapists took me to a large shower to make sure I could shower by myself.

"Are you re-filming *George Does Dallas*? I quipped, adding, "Could you get anyone else in here?"

At this point, six people were crammed into the shower room. I know they thought this was for my own good. Part of me wondered if this was the erotic highlight of their week.

"Don't worry. Our interest is purely therapeutic," Queenie, a jovial African American nurse, said.

I realized how lucky I was to have a house to go home to. Most of those I left behind had no one. A bonding had taken place and part of me wanted to stay with my new hospital family.

***

Almost a year had passed, and with help from lots of my friends, I began to regain my muscular coordination skills. It was during this time that I got to know two of my neighbors. Kathy Flynn, a longtime resident of Montclair, and a local realtor, and Dave Hyde, who lived just down the street. We started walking together every day, which was good exercise for all three of us. We were there to encourage each other. I think we walked in tune with the music from every movie we had ever seen in our lives. We would free associate as we walked, which made our jaunts around the neighborhood fun to do. We got to know each other, got to keep growing as friends and as people, and of course, we improved our bodies.

As we rounded the bend at Lake Temescal, I talked about the childhood I had spent playing there. Kathy and Dave had parents who were still alive, and their memories together were still being made. With both of my parents gone, I tried to hold onto what I remembered so well. We shared our family histories and the impact our upbringing had left on all of us. We also talked about the importance of the imprint genetics has on our lives.

Good friendships allow us to reveal ourselves to others, and this is what we did by sharing our family stories. The sharing of our true selves can be great therapy. So, those walks helped us become close friends forever while helping me recover from my stroke.

While I was away, Kenny, my gardener, had taken care of my garden, and for a while after I came home, Jeff, along with our friend Gerald, took over that chore. Of course, Gardenia, with her inner and outer beauty, continued to tend my mental garden. She encouraged me to go to a men's support group led by Vince Morgante, the father of two adopted children, someone I knew at the ballet school.

At the group I felt like a cliché from every psychiatrist movie I had ever seen. "Hi, my name is George," I said. "I'm here because I'm recovering from a stroke. And above all, I want to recover from my own homophobia!"

Chapter 35

When Every Day is New

I was angry when I received a copy of *Memphis Magazine*. In one article, the author trivialized my Memphis accomplishments by ignoring many of my career achievements. Of course I had my failures and successes, but to say I had a talent for producing the "wrong ballet at the wrong time" and little more, seemed like an inept tribute to me after a quarter century of hard work. What hurt the most? The fact that no one came to my defense – there was no letter to the editors contradicting that writer's opinion. I guess people were relieved the "Ballet Wars" were finally over.

In retrospect, back in California, I began to realize that my life meant a lot more than a triumph over personal shame. I had many friends in Memphis and in California, and I was now relating to them more honestly. I acquired a new feeling of shared growth and family. I also find lasting reward in knowing that, along with my devoted staff in Memphis, we have been able to enhance the talents of many people of all ages. We succeeded in integrating the great art of dance so that all could participate, even if only temporarily.

I have always loved music, which I always found both sensual and spiritual. The pioneer in me loved children of all races and I had thrilled to the challenge of developing them into fine dancers. In Memphis, I had learned to use the creative process, one of life's greatest satisfactions. No one could take that accomplishment away from me.

Later that year, Jeff and I, along with our friend Patti Hunter, went on a cruise to the Caribbean and Costa Rica. Having earlier been amazed by the beauty and mystery of Panama, we now found the same wonderful tropical atmosphere in Costa Rica.

One day Patti and I left Jeff aboard the ship and set out on our own adventure. We rented a pontoon boat owned by a local

Costa Rican named Hon, a devoted animal lover who spoke little English. We floated down the Tortuga River on this shaky boat. We also walked along a riverside trail, awed by 80-foot high vine-covered trees inhabited by sloths and monkeys dwarfing our presence. Once more, I was amazed at how well people can communicate non-verbally.

The locals in Costa Rica called this river of water the Crocodile River. We would soon see why. We didn't feel safe, but something had led us there, so on we went. From time to time, Patti would lean over the edge of the boat, exclaiming over the beauty of the wildly colored orchids and hibiscus along the mossy banks. Whenever she did that, I worried because our tour guide would quickly rush to move our 30-gallon gas tank to the opposite side of the boat to balance all of our weight. I also noticed a little breathlessly that a lit cigarette dangled from his lips, dangerously close to the greasy gasoline tank. Catching my eye, he smiled his toothless grin and pointed up towards the blissfully sleeping monkeys and the Jesus Christ lizard that literally walked on water. Patti had doubted that the crocodiles were real until one of them opened his sleepy eyes and caught her in a radar stare.

This was an ancient, eternal world. The primordial beauty was timeless and, for that matter, time appeared to stand still in the most beautiful place I had ever seen. Suddenly I was overwhelmed by the experience of just being there, in that moment, and I realized that this is the way most of life has been for me. We were bathed in yet another amber light, now an oddly familiar experience. Everything in my life just seemed to blend together right then and there.

Our guide then asked, *"Todo es nuevo para ustedes?"* Then, he nodded and added softly, *"Todos los dias son nuevos."* (Translation: "Is everything new for you? All days are new.")

Chapter 36
Secrets of the Cayman Islands

Jeff, in many ways, was an ideal traveling companion. He hadn't changed much in 35 years. He still retained his amazing strength, the flexibility of a cat, and his long lean trademark looks. Our Asian friends remarked that they thought he came from a gene pool like their own.

His hair was still a mixture of brown and blonde, cut fairly short. His gaze was very direct. The green-blue-yellow eyes over high cheekbones gave him a bearing part royalty, part mad scientist, and part Native American, something which he had taken with him onto the ballet stage. I think his look has always been part ethereal and part spiritual, with a quality of animal sensuality. Taken together, these components denote power. Then at times, he could be so high strung and difficult to be around. But usually, Jeff was bright, quick, funny, and empathetic.

In the years after my mother's death, we decided to travel, and went to Mexico, Hawaii, Costa Rica, and the Cayman Islands. In the Caymans, we were guided to an area where the locals had a long history of signaling passing ships looking for a port. The signals they gave would trick the ships' captains into believing they had reached a safe harbor. But the islanders knew the ships would sink soon after they hit the hidden Coral Reef surrounding the islands. This practice actually continued until 1960 when English law put in place protections for the visitors. After that, the native population had to find a new way to survive.

In 2004 Hurricane Ivan practically destroyed all the plantations whose crops made up the island economy. Now, tourism became the only means of survival.

Our guide on the islands was a government biologist who taught school children ecology towards the proposition of a better future. Once again Patti and I went ashore and our guide took us to an ancient graveyard from the 1800s. The ocean was just off shore, about 100 feet from the graveyard. Another 100 feet out was the ancient coral reef which we could see at low tide when the water subsided.

One of the graves haunted me from the minute I saw it. I asked Patti to photograph the strange but beautiful words written on the tombstone:

The dead cast no shadows. Rest in Peace.

The locals believed the dead exist in spirit forever, and that the sun can pass through their bodies. Therefore, no shadows are cast.

Chapter 37
"Walk into the light, June."

The psychic in the blockbuster movie *Poltergeist* directed by Tobe Hooper and produced by Steven Spielberg was played by the diminutive actress Zelda Rubenstein. It turned out that she and Irene Adams, my best friend in high school, and Irene's sister, Sally, were close friends.

Irene, whom I had not seen in years, was having a birthday party and Jeff and I decided to go. We knew Zelda would be there. As an old friend, I was excited to see Irene and Sally and as a diehard movie buff, I was looking forward to meeting Zelda for the first time. Irene worked hard to make us all feel comfortable with each other.

Another character in *Poltergeist* was Carol Ann, the young girl and heroine of the movie, who traveled to the "other side" via the television set, leaving her desperate parents to seriously consider whether or not the paranormal existed. The character that Zelda portrayed became her persona throughout the film series and was exemplified by her classic line, "Walk into the light, Carol Ann." Along with Carol Ann's spine-tingling line: "They're here…" the two actresses had made movie history.

Irene also became well-known in Bela Horizante, Brazil, for her work with AIDS- and cancer-afflicted children, and Sally now headed a family, was patron of the arts, and owned property. These two were awesome.

Because of her tiny size, Zelda reminded me of my mother's Shirley Temple doll. She was so tiny that when she sat in a large rocking chair, her feet hung just over the edge of her seat, not even close to touching the floor. During the outdoor party, I realized that, despite her short stature, her spirit and intelligence were enormous.

Zelda confidentially shared, "I didn't make as much money from the Spielberg films as you would think. It was the Skittles and the Apple Computers commercials that made my life the most secure."

I had seen the commercials and most of her movies. I gave her a VHS video of a movie she had made in Spain, *Anguish,* which she had never seen. Tiny as she was, Zelda brought a sense of great command to her movie roles. She could have played Lady Macbeth.

In *Anguish,* she portrays a domineering mother who sends her son on murderous errands. She demands that he present her with the severed eyeballs of his victims as proof that he has done her bidding. Horrors!

My friend's mother, June, and Monte, their brother, were also at the party. Even though they looked many years younger than their actual ages, I was reminded of the passage of time. The last time I had seen my high-school friends, they were in their teens. I had lived with them for a while when I was 18 when their home was on Lawton Street in Oakland. At the time, June and I were both questioning life and would often talk until two in the morning. There were, oh, so many memories.

Jeff had come with me to the party and Zelda had aroused his curiosity as he listened intently as she entertained us with great stories about her movie career. He had the nerve to ask her about her personal life. She replied unabashedly, "I have my young man." Her eyes rolled upward coyly and she grinned with obvious pleasure. He was amazed at her frankness.

A few years later, I was shaken and saddened when Sally called me. "My mother died today. I walked clear around Lake Temescal in the dark and when I came near your house, I thought you wouldn't mind me coming over there."

I immediately assured her that I was there for her.

June's funeral was to be at Mountain View Cemetery, a few miles from my home. (Later I found out that Amelia and William George Latimer, my great-grandparents, were buried there, too. Amelia, the daughter of a Mormon icon, was buried here instead of Salt Lake City.)

June's haunting funeral was held on a foggy, overcast day. I remember those low clouds were like giant sculptures hanging over the elaborate old cemetery as my friend Kathie Long and I remained silent.

Zelda was there, too, and I met her escort, a man in his 20s, her ardent and loving friend. Handsome, with dark hair and a brilliant congenial smile, his gentleness contrasted with Zelda's more dominating nature.

The cemetery was located in an exquisite place with its mossy green hills dotted with traditional and unusual tombstones. Flowers brought by loved ones added color and life to this final resting place. Then we saw shafts of sunlight as they broke through clouds near the Golden Gate Bridge.

We had visited this same cemetery a few months earlier for the funeral of Kathie Long's husband, Dan. The sun, which had crept from behind ominous dark clouds for a few minutes, sent down an amber light illuminating the mist around the many graves as it fell lightly across the graveyard. Could this amazing amber light be emanating from the gravestones, I wondered?

Irene, knowing my passion for film and wanting to be close to me, smiled and suggested, "Doesn't this remind you of Ava Gardner's funeral in *The Barefoot Contessa*?

I couldn't have agreed more.

I studied some of the unusual gothic statues that had been placed around the graves: an angel with wide-spread wings, crypts with large Roman columns, statues of people long gone. The scene was strangely peaceful. I could hear Zelda's voice saying, "Walk into the light, June. Walk into the light!"

Chapter 38
Psychics and the X Factor

My enchantment with mystery partly explains my relationship to Sare Van Orsdell with whom I wrote this book. For me, the mysteries of life are, to a great extent, clarified through the symbolism of astrology, as I have mentioned before. Yet there is something more - an X Factor.

My sister and I wondered about our neighbor who was the chief suspect in a 1940 murder case. The idea of murder had never been part of my reality until I came to live in Memphis. The first was a casual associate, Gayland, who was murdered in Overton Park. I assumed the killer's motive evolved from his homophobia.

There was also the famous Montesi case, which happened just before I got to the South. Due to the participation of Melvin Belli, the famous San Francisco lawyer, it gained national attention. He came to Memphis to work with a local attorney, Frank Glanker, the husband of my ballet volunteer, Teena Glanker.

So, these two lawyers became the defense team in the famous Montesi murder case. A few years after the trial, Teena introduced me to a woman named Betty who had married Montesi after he was acquitted. Following a violent argument, Betty confessed to all of us that she wanted a divorce because she suddenly began to doubt her new husband's innocence.

Here in California in May 2005, a new trial in the Gwen Araju Case was starting. One of my close friends was on the jury. Again the motive was homophobia because the killers, all young men, weren't consciously able to allow themselves to comprehend that Gwen was really male. This famous transgender murder case is being tried again due to a hung jury which ended the first trial. The jury was torn between sympathy for the angry homophobic murderer and outrage over the brutality of the crime. They couldn't decide which it was - a premeditated murder or a crime of passion called Murder Two.

I was glad I was no longer in Memphis. I had no idea that someone like Emily Klyce Fischer would be murdered. Everyone who knew us assumed we were terrible enemies. In reality, I always sort of admired Emily for her gutsy intelligence. The strange irony of the murder brought Carol Klyce into my life. She was the Memphis murder victim's sister-in-law and continues to be one of my best friends. It is the water aerobics classes that she teachers along with our friend Merle that has allowed me to gain my strength back after my stroke.

In an effort to reunite my family of friends, I invited Sare for a 10-day visit to Oakland over the 2003 holiday season. Rebecca Fischer, the late Emily Klyce's daughter, was also invited, along with many of my other friends, including Carol. In recent years Rebecca has become a writer and an electrifying actress with a wide range of performance skills.

Although Sare's work is usually accomplished by phone, she was doing some astrological therapy sessions in person with some of the guests. In a session with Carol Klyce, she identified Emily's murderer as being "someone who lived in the house but was not a family member."

Sare describes the service she provides as both astrologer and therapist. As an astrologer she uses the language, craft, and intuition of astrology and archetype-based psychology.

Later, the Memphis police described DNA evidence possibly connecting a friend of Emily's son to the killing. He lived in Emily's house, just as Sare had indicated. He was one of several suspects, but she pinpointed him as the main perpetrator of the crime. After another trial, the son's friend was incarcerated.

"Sare should be working for the Memphis police!" gasped Carol.

I reminded Carol that psychics have solved many crimes throughout history all over the country. These include our local Sylvia Brown who has written many books on psychic phenomena and appeared regularly on the Montel Williams television show.

But, Sare never ceases to amaze me with her intuitive knowledge and wisdom. She says, "If the client is emotionally open to me and not trying to test me out, the energy between us flows smoothly and my intuition can bring up information from the astrology chart that otherwise would not surface."

Sare and I continue to be friends and she now lives in Oregon. She is a practicing astrologer and works with many clients in their quest to understand themselves using astrology as a tool and guide.

Chapter 39
Our *Quingming*

The practice of *quingming* was a new experience for me, one of many Chinese customs that my close friend, Amy Chung, shared. She was the daughter of poor Chinese immigrants who had come to San Francisco many years ago, worked hard, and became the owners of the largest ginseng import-export company in the United States.

"First, we'll go by the herb shop and get you the herbs necessary to prevent another stroke," Amy said deliberately. "Then we will go to a specialty shop. You will be amazed at what we can buy. Then you will learn about *quingming*!"

Amy led me to a glittery store on Grant Avenue in San Francisco's Chinatown. Together we bought cardboard Cadillacs, bags of fake gold, and brilliant paper flowers. We got delicious variety cartons of dim sum, and other exotic food in paper bags. Loading them into the trunk of her colorful blue Mercedes, we rode over to pick up her grown children, Allison and Adrian. We traveled along, going up the steepest hillside in San Francisco. I couldn't help but stare at her children.

Allison looked like a younger version of my friend. Amy appeared to be too young to be Allison's mother. Her skin was flawless and her dark hair flowed down to her shoulders, glistening in the sunlight as it beamed through a drifting fog and mist against the darkly muted green hills. Like some people of Chinese descent, Amy was firm, muscular, and subtly voluptuous.

"It's your ballet classes that do the trick," she murmured when I complimented her. Adrian, her son, was a Bay Area phenomenon. He was truly androgynous, handsome, yet beautiful.

"Adrian can be anyone he wants to be," said Amy. "Andy, his father, my former husband, and I decided that his integrity was the most important quality for him to have."

As my friend Jim, a dance enthusiast, once said, "Basically, I'm drawn only to women, but Adrian seems to be the exception. I didn't know this was possible." Maybe he wasn't kidding, but I never found out.

We hiked up a rocky path to a hidden sea of gravestones. The fog lifted as the sunlight grew stronger. The dim sum lunch Amy had bought was incredible. Mixtures of seafood, beef, pork, and pastries, all light as air. After we ate, we found a pyre made of all the gifts left there, soon to be sent to the ancestors so they would not be forgotten. There were other families there doing the same ritual. Some seemed to be from much older generations than the Chung family. Amy's voice changed and she began to speak in a Chinese dialect.

Words uttered in different tones when speaking Mandarin or Cantonese take on entirely different meanings. As other families had done before us, we lit the symbolic gifts and watched the fire and smoke carry the presents to the revered ancestors. I was enthralled by this loving traditional ceremony of remembrance. It was exquisitely beautiful, symbolic, and very touching.

Later that afternoon, as the sun appeared to slip into the Pacific Ocean, Amy and I left the children. We went back to my house in Oakland and sat in my hot tub. We removed our clothing carefully, entering the hot water. I realized that nudity meant nothing to Amy, and I tried to adopt her attitude. I guess my therapy with Gardenia was not only opening my mind, it was actually opening my heart. Amy, in her own way, was as attractive and luminous as anyone I had ever seen naked, male or female. Part of me was falling in love.

As Gardenia, my therapist, had pointed out about our bodies, paraphrasing Edgar Cayce, the famous psychic healer of the 1920s,

"In my kingdom there are many mansions." She had opened so many doors for me, and I feel the possibilities are endless as we face life's great adventures.

My stroke had damaged the part of my brain that governed emotional control. The combination of Gardenia's warmth and my brain damage presented a new world to me. That world seemed to radiate a shining and welcoming future. Unable to repress my emotions, now feelings I did not know I had would arise in me. I always knew that there was an emotion reality available to all of us. Now I am experiencing a whole new set of emotions that can sometimes be overwhelming.

Can you believe I even cried when I went to see the movie *Superman?*

Chapter 40
The Watsu Song

It was my birthday and our longtime Memphis friend, Judy Freeman, was visiting. Judy wanted to have a Watsu water massage and Amy Chung, in a gesture of friendship to Judy, offered to take us up to Harbin Hot Springs in the heart of the California wine country, where it could happen.

Judy showed no signs of culture shock. She fit into the world of California experimentation and that old southern charm with equal adaptability. So Amy, our friend Jim Zeigler, Judy, and I set off on our journey, which would also include a visit to the California Culinary Academy near the Christian Brothers Winery. Television watchers might remember the rooftop of the famous winery shown in the credits of the *Falcon Crest* series with Jane Wyman.

As we drove through the beautiful wine country, my imagination went wild as I began to compose *The Watsu Song*.

"We sing the song of the Watsu, of the Watsu! We sing this song. Wiggly and wet, swiggly with sweat, we keep things floating along!" Thinking back, maybe my song was a nervous response to coming events.

No one else appreciated my joking song. Jim appeared oddly self confident and no one seemed to have any agitated anticipation about disrobing in front of hundreds of strangers.

After driving uphill on a winding road that was only rivaled by hundreds of tangling grape vines, we pulled up at a toll booth at the entrance to the springs. Just ahead of us, a family of four who had obviously been shopping at a nearby Safeway grocery store, strolled up the road. Mother, father, and two children were carrying bags of groceries and hiking along before us, totally nude.

The ranger-like person in the booth informed us that no drugs or alcohol were allowed near or in the pools. Also no sexual activity was to take place near the steaming water which rose from natural underground hot springs.

"I guess that means sex is okay everywhere else!" I quipped.

No one laughed. I had a *déjà vu* moment, remembering what it was like to be the only white person at an African American cultural event years earlier. There were 400 or 500 families on picnic blankets lounging around totally nude, and here we were, dressed in street clothes. At that point, I felt more naked than the naked and decided to disrobe.

The pools were luxurious and inviting. Enormous fig leaves, each large enough to cover several Adams and Eves, lay atop a gigantic hot tub in a tent-like structure. From within the hot pool, I noticed that a number of men were looking at me with lascivious envy because Amy, who was beside me, was incredibly beautiful in the steaming water. Judy had disappeared. People assumed I was Amy's love interest. Jim was the next person to take off his clothes. Now I know why Jim was so nonchalant and self confident. He compared really well to all the other nude Adonis types strutting around. It would have taken more than one fig leaf to cover his hidden talent. I was not in my best physical shape so there was no strutting for me. I remained discretely under the water.

Harbin Hot Springs has the reputation for being a spiritual retreat, but there was something else definitely going on. Or was there?

Amy had bought me a massage for my birthday. The massage cabins were about a half mile up a nearby hill. All along the slope of the hill, naked families were picnicking. I had no choice but to trudge uphill wearing nothing but tennis shoes, and this felt worse than being nude. With my backside to all the picnicking families, I passed everyone anticipating my sensual but therapeutic massage.

My masseuse was Dolores, a muscular Australian girl with a touch like a goddess in her, maybe someone whose spiritual practice entailed reading from Masters and Johnson every day.

Coming down the hill wasn't so bad. A hundred feet ahead of me, I saw Geoffrey Keezer and Myrissa, world-class musicians, there with their parents, to whom I had never been introduced. Somehow, I didn't want to meet them without my clothes on. Later, at a party, I was introduced to Geoffrey. I didn't want to say I knew them all quite well already.

As I walked back to Amy, I saw a Grecian deity floating in a pool. Her hair was spread out in the water like a giant frond or a golden lily pad.

"Who is that exquisite creature?" I asked Amy.

She replied, "Oh, that's Judy."

I had never seen Judy looking so otherworldly. She looked like an ethereal water nymph floating by in a sea of peaceful tranquility, and luscious to behold.

Amy added, "She's having her Watsu water massage."

I couldn't help myself. I broke into song, "We sing the song of the Watsu! Of the Watsu! We sing the song!"

Later, I saw a woman as big as an elephant. She wore a delicate necklace of wildflowers around her neck. She went over to a pool where a small man was enjoying the water and when she stepped in and sat down, he disappeared into the waves.

At Harbin Hot Springs one can study yoga, philosophy, or eat in the health-food restaurant. When nude, people seem more alike than not. Our differences seem to disappear when we're naked. I picture us as a tranquil herd of cattle, socializing in a manner more peaceful than I had ever thought possible. With a little more nudity perhaps there would be less war in the world.

Chapter 41
My Fellini Life

As I write one of the final chapters of this book, I seem to be experiencing several symbolic occurrences at once.

My Memphis friend, Bill Kendall, came to Oakland for a visit and we decided to go to San Francisco's Castro District. Many gay people were picketing Les Natoli's Badlands bar accusing them of racial discrimination. Badlands was accused of being selective about who entered the bar when the crush of partygoers at the door became too hard to control. That fact seemed bizarre to me because according to *Time* magazine, gays were the most hated group in the United States. So, how could anyone gay discriminate on a racial basis?

Natoli had hung huge posters all over the Castro to counteract the negative publicity. They showed couples of same gender, mixed gender, mixed race, and mixed ages, all drinking together at the Badlands. His point was to let people know that he did not, in fact, discriminate. I was surprised, and it was hard to hide my astonishment and disappointment. I thought of the "Sweet Willie Wine" story. This was contemporary California, not the Mobile, Alabama of 1960 or Arkansas in 1969.

When I called Les Natoli on the phone, he cordially invited me to visit the club and meet him in person. The *San Francisco Chronicle* had run a story that indicated Natoli was suing his slanderers. The case was pending and how it has been resolved was unclear.

Later that same day Bill Kendall called my friend Chris Ellis in Los Angeles. He said he was interested in touring the classic old Art Deco movie theaters. Chris made it possible for him to see some of the old movie palaces from the 20s and 30s.

Bill loved old decorative theatres and he wanted to see the Paramount Theatre in Oakland. Patti and Larry Hunter arranged for a special tour. As many times as I had been to the Paramount for films or ballet, I had never seen the great artwork in full light adorning the ceiling, walls, and lobby. After a heavy, thought provoking day in the San Francisco Castro, I was ready to be completely enthralled by this visual artistic treat. I looked at Bill and saw tears in his eyes as he took in the huge painted scenes in the classic Art Deco style.

There was a giant gold leaf replica of the Goddess Isis holding the world in her arms. A golden chariot pulled by glittering horses flew over the proscenium arch. Neptune, in all of his muscular definition as the God of the Oceans, was depicted diving into a sea of stars. This is how the arts had always served me. I realized that I could never sink into the more sordid aspects of life for the eternal inspiration of the artist's concept, as now, had always lifted me to another level. France might have the Louvre, the magnificent national museum in Paris, but my hometown, Oakland, has that gigantic explosion of the imagination - the Paramount Theatre.

***

As I recount my life so far it seems to resemble the wild, free characters that fill the fantasy scenes of a Fellini movie. I consider myself fortunate to know so many wonderful people who have played out these scenes with me.

I visualize a giant banquet table with all of my loving friends - the many who have influenced me over the years - in attendance.

I see Verona Levine. She gives me a huge embrace. She has never been bitter about the racism she has experienced as an African American flight attendant onboard United Airlines flights. It is hard to believe that people would actually refuse service from a flight attendant based on her race. As usual, she holds her head high and smiles warmly.

Marilyn Payton, another African American friend and a teacher at our Piedmont Ballet Academy, recalls her days with Mae West. In the movie *Sextet*, that Marilyn was in, Mae's last film, a back brace was constructed with a built-in glittering corset to keep the 86-year-old actress upright. When Mae turned sideways, while delivering her lines, her artificial chest stayed facing forward. They had to reshoot the scenes many times.

Marilyn wasn't bothered that all of Mae's maids were African American. After all, Mae was from a different era. I thought of "Sweet Willie Wine" Watson and the suffering he and his girlfriend, Vi had been subject to over the years.

Marilyn's friend, one of Disney's main choreographers who had early championed her dance talents, once apologized to her for the slowly changing attitudes which held back her career. But it didn't bother Marilyn that there were delays in casting the roles back in 1971 for racial reasons. Things do advance slowly in this country.

As I look back though, my thoughts inevitably turn to that great dancer, my personal inspiration. On March 17, 1938, as Neptune, ruler of ballet, shined his mysterious wonders upon the earth, Rudolph Nureyev was born on a Siberian train near Irkutsk. He was from a Tartar family, which accounted for his lusty, fiery temperament. He learned to sing and dance the cultural folk songs of his people at an early age, beginning his dance career in 1955 in Leningrad's Vaganova Institute attached to the Kirov Ballet. He was recognized immediately for his talent.

As I wrote earlier, Nurevey's defection to the West while touring in France in 1961 had made global headlines. His escape at 23 was not only for artistic freedom. It was rumored that he was being investigated by the KGB for his homosexual lifestyle. In order to save his life, Nureyev had no choice but to defect. His doing so changed my life forever, as it did for thousands of other dancers. He was arrogant, yet kind, and became a role model for those who had a passion for dance. The stamp of his genius influenced all dancers, male and female, across all borders. His sex drive was legendary, but spoken of only in whispers. He was a loyal friend and continued to support many new dancers coming up through the ranks even after he was diagnosed with a fatal illness.

January 6, 1993: as my friends Freesia, Liz, Kathie, Jeff, and Claire, and I were participating in a ballet class that left us breathless, Freesia leapt higher than any of us. We had been laughing with joy when we heard that Nureyev had died of AIDS at 55.

We all froze in place, looking at each other like orphaned children. A huge cloud of sadness settled around us and the room was still. In unison we observed a moment of silence in honor of this great dancer. The loss was an incredibly heavy one for me, like a light going out. My life may never feel the same. He left an indelible legacy.

As with any loss, there is also hope for the future. I think of the twinkling eyes and toothless smile of the best boat driver in Costa Rica as he uttered those unforgettable words, *"Todos los dias son nuevos!"* All days are new.

Spiritual message on gravesite in Grand Cayman Islands
(Photo by Patti Hunter)

Devastating loss of Latimer home in Oakland Hills Fire (1991)
(Photo by Oakland Tribune)

Latimer and Stuart in Hawaii. (1996)

Epilogue
A Life Beyond Reason

It was a typical summer morning in the San Francisco Bay Area, warm but foggy and everyone awaited the first rays of sunshine to brighten the day. Carol Klyce heard a knock on the door and was greeted by a Federal Express delivery man who carried a huge mysterious box. It was addressed to her children, the grandchildren of Mary Byrd Klyce, Carol's deceased mother-in- law.

When Carol opened the box, she was startled to find a huge reptile inside. The preserved skin of the gigantic snake was still intact. The eyes gleamed up at her, but seemed less menacing now that when it had hung from the wall of the Klyce family home on McLean Street in Memphis.

She laughed quietly to herself, but tears came to her eyes as she remembered a time and culture not so long ago.

***

I guess my life is in semi-retiré by now. Time passes quickly these days and I have random musings about friends from the past. I wonder if Diane Keaton still flies to Memphis to eat at Charlie's Vergos Rendezvous. Does William Huettle's company, United Paint, still continue to supply paint for struggling arts groups with creative scenery designs?

I give thanks to Bill Barlow, my brilliant and witty friend who got us involved with the Oakland Ballet. Ronn Guidi still contributes choreography even though he retired as Artistic Director. Jeff's ballet school, the Piedmont Ballet Academy, started out so small and now has 250 students and is one of the most successful ballet schools in the San Francisco Bay Area. We're still in the dance world.

Bill Romanowski, the Oakland Raiders football player famed for his tough-guy image, brings his daughter to our ballet classes. He treats his daughter with such gentleness that he reminds us of the gentle giant in children's stories. Frank Shawl, the dancer, is still performing in his 70s. He doesn't age. He is an inspiration to all of us to exercise and take vitamins. John Ryckman, the hero of my 20s, is still happily married to his wife Mary. Marina Baden, the fiery flamenco teacher, now lives in New Mexico and is a magnetic catalyst for bringing people together for dance. Ruth Bossieux, Sandy Hollister of Berkeley, and I are once again united as friends. Marina forgives me for only halfway succeeding as a flamenco dancer.

I wonder if dancers Laura Simmons, Rebecca Bowden, Charles Abrahams and others still take ballet, even though they have flown to the far corners of the country. I read Lowell Smith and Joe Dowdy are extremely successful in the dance world. One is teaching in New York and the other is in Los Angeles.

We are all trying to recover from the untimely death of Carlton Johnson. At the Ballet South reunion in Memphis so many dancers and friends were present, except for Carlton. We decided, as a large group, to visit him at his hospital bed.

My own family has evolved, too. My brother Bill, now retired, has become a political activist. His children Diane and Cheryl have successful careers, and my brother and his wife, Gail, are very proud of them.

With each passing month as a widow my sister Colleen becomes a stronger and more independent person. She and her family live in the Seattle area and her children have successful careers. Her son Mathew has built his home in front of an 80-foot tall waterfall. He and his wife, Carrie, have two young sons. Maggie lives in Portland, Oregon, a true free spirit, and Amanda is a psychologist who works with the American Indians at the Canadian border. She specializes in drug and alcohol withdrawal treatment. Amanda also owns a Llama farm and has built several houses nearby. Independence has remained a theme in my family, and now we all communicate as often as possible.

The last time my family was together we had dinner at the Lake Merritt Hotel. I had been there recently to see Debbie Sternbach's great recreation of Hollywood production numbers. We laughed as we remembered that once, as children in the 1940s, we had witnessed the time a huge stag deer that had gotten disoriented jumped through the glass façade and into the dining room during the elegant dinner hour, shocking the customers.

A few months earlier we all discovered that we were the great-great-grandchildren of Edward Hunter, one of the founders of the Mormon Church in Salt Lake City. A history of polygamy had been part of our family and we had all met kindly and generous Mormons in our recent history. But the discriminatory ways in which African Americans were treated by the Mormon Church did not sit well with us. The fact that Proposition 8, the California law that is still in dispute because it denies equal rights in marriage to gays and lesbians was largely supported by Mormons, was disappointing.

How could my liberal family have come from such narrow-minded relatives? We shook our heads in amazement.

What will tomorrow bring?

Carlton Johnson in The Nutcracker (1982)

George Latimer

George Latimer hails from the San Francisco Bay Area where his early experiences as a dancer placed him in the realm of great ballet artists and musicians. Influenced early by the fantasy world of Hollywood movies and an unusual family background, he had colorful adventures in 1960s San Francisco, then moved to Memphis, Tennessee to become an entrepreneur. He brought the likes of Nureyev, Baryshnikov, and stars of the New York City Ballet and the American Ballet Theater to the South. He won a Martin Luther King Award for his contribution to racial integration in the arts as director of his Memphis ballet company, Ballet South.

In this funny, moving, and nostalgic trip through time and the American dance scene, Latimer candidly recounts his entertaining adventures with talented artists, gives his take on newsworthy events of the day, and tells of living through the Loma Prieta earthquake and surviving the devastating Oakland fire of 1991.

Sare Van Orsdell

Sare Van Orsdell is an editor, writer, and a practicing astrologer. She has written for many newspapers during a long journalism career. Sare was editor and staff writer for the Marietta Journal's 49 weekly newspapers in the greater Atlanta, Georgia counties. Her book, *Thunder Below*, is an adventure novel about the eruption of the New Madrid fault line across the United States.

Follow Sare's work at sarevanorsdell.com.

Made in the USA
Columbia, SC
18 December 2021

52017395R00165